EDUCATION

SWIMMING III

International Series on Sport Sciences

Series Editors: **Richard C. Nelson and Chauncey A. Morehouse**

The principal focus of this series is on reference works derived primarily from international congress and symposium proceedings. These should be of particular interest to researchers, clinicians, students, physical educators, and coaches involved in the growing field of sport science. The Series Editors are Professors Richard C. Nelson and Chauncey A. Morehouse of The Pennsylvania State University. The series includes the eight major divisions of sport science: biomechanics, history, medicine, pedagogy, philosophy, physiology, psychology, and sociology.

Each volume in the series is published in English but is written by authors of several countries. The series, therefore, is truly international in scope and, because many of the authors normally publish their work in languages other than English, the series volumes are a resource for information that is often difficult if not impossible to obtain elsewhere. Organizers of international congresses in the sport sciences desiring detailed information concerning the use of this series for publication and distribution of official proceedings are requested to contact the Series Editors. Manuscripts prepared by several authors from various countries consisting of information of international interest will also be considered for publication.

The *International Series on Sport Sciences* serves not only as a valuable source of authoritative, up-to-date information but also helps to foster better understanding among sport scientists on an international level. It provides an effective medium through which researchers, teachers, and coaches may develop better communications with individuals in countries throughout the world who have similar professional interests.

International Series
on Sport Sciences, Volume 8

SWIMMING III

Proceedings of the Third International Symposium
of Biomechanics in Swimming, University of
Alberta, Edmonton, Canada

Edited by:
Juris Terauds, Ph.D.
and
E. Wendy Bedingfield, Ph.D.
Dept. of Physical Education
University of Alberta
Edmonton, Alberta, Canada
Series Editors:
Richard C. Nelson, Ph.D.
and
Chauncey A. Morehouse, Ph.D.
The Pennsylvania State University

University Park Press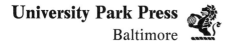
Baltimore

39591

UNIVERSITY PARK PRESS
International Publishers in Science, Medicine, and Education
233 East Redwood Street
Baltimore, Maryland 21202

Typeset by Action Comp Co., Inc.
Manufactured in the United States of America by The Maple Press Company.

Proceedings of the Third International Symposium
of Biomechanics in Swimming, held in July, 1978,
University of Alberta, Edmonton, Canada.

Library of Congress Cataloging in Publication Data

International Symposium of Biomechanics in Swimming,
3d, University of Alberta, 1978.
Swimming III: Proceedings of the Third International
Symposium of Biomechanics in Swimming, University of
Alberta, Edmonton, Canada.

(International series on sport sciences; v. 8)
Includes bibliographical references.
1. Swimming—Congresses. 2. Human mechanics—
Congresses. I. Terauds, Juris. II. Bedingfield,
E. Wendy. III. Title. IV. Series.
QP310.S95156 1978   612'.76   79-4170
ISBN 0-8391-1352-8

Contents

Contributors
Conference Organization
Sponsors
Preface

SWIMMING STARTS AND TURNS

TRAINING METHODS

SOMATOTYPE AND MORPHOLOGY

Contributors

M. Adrian Department of Physical Education, Washington State University, Pullman, Washington 99163 USA *(110)*

J. Alloway Department of Human Movement Studies, University of Old Brisbane, Q4067, Australia *(275)*

C. G. S. Araújo Physical Fitness Lab, LAFISCS-Estadio Lauro Gomes, São Caetauo do Sol, Brazil *(329)*

K. M. Barthels Department of Physical Education, California Polytechnic State University, San Luis Obispo, California 93407 USA *(45)*

J. A. Bloom Health and Physical Education Department, University of Houston, Houston, Texas 77004 USA *(215)*

W. L. Boomer Division of Sports and Recreation, University of Rochester, Rochester, New York 14642 USA *(265)*

N. Zh. Bulgakova Chair of Swimming, Central Institute of Physical Culture, Sirenevij, Bulv. 4, Moscow, USSR *(199)*

N. M. Chaplinsky Chair of Biomechanics, Central Institute of Physical Culture, Sirenevij, Bulv. 4, Moscow, USSR *(199)*

J. P. Clarys Instituut voor Morfologie, Faculty of Medicine, Vrije Universiteit Brussel, Campus Jette, Laarbeeklaan 103, 1090 Brussel, Belgium *(3, 153, 307)*

A. B. Craig, Jr. Box 642, Department of Physiology, University of Rochester, School of Medicine and Dentistry, Rochester, New York 14642 USA *(235, 265)*

B. Czabański Academy of Physical Education, Al. Olimpijska, 51-612 Wroclaw, Poland *(148)*

H.-O. Daehne Department of Physical Education, University of Pretoria, Pretoria, South Africa *(240)*

A. M. Dahl Pacific Lutheran University, Tacoma, Washington 98400 USA *(298)*

D. A. Dainty Department of Kinanthropology, University of Ottawa, Ottawa, Ontario K1N 6N5, Canada *(338)*

D. J. Daly Instituut voor Lichamelijke Opleiding, Tervuursevest 101, 3030 Heverlee, Belgium *(182)*

J. G. Disch Health and Physical Education Department, Rice University, Houston, Texas 77001 USA *(215)*

R. Dupuis Department of Physical Education, Washington State University, Pullman, Washington 99163 USA *(110)*

J. F. Gibbons Division of Sports and Recreation, University of Rochester, Rochester, New York 14642 USA *(265)*

P. S. Gomes Laboratory of Human Performance, Universidade Gama Filho, Rua Manuel Vitorino 625, ZC-13 Rio de Janiero, Brazil *(329)*

Numbers in parentheses refer to page(s) where contributor's chapter(s) begin.

R. G. C. Hoeven Instituut voor Lichamelijke Opleiding, Tervuursevest 101, 3030 Heverlee, Belgium *(182)*

I. Holmér Work Physiology Unit, National Board of Occupational Safety and Health, S-17184 Solna, Sweden *(118)*

W. W. Hosler General Dynamics, Human Factors Engineering, Fort Worth, Texas 76101 USA *(215)*

M. Jack Department of Physical Education, Washington State University, Pullman, Washington 99163 USA *(110)*

R. K. Jensen School of Physical and Health Education, Laurentian University, Sudbury, Ontario, Canada *(137)*

J. Jull Department of Physics, Queensland Institute of Technology, P.O. Box 246, North Quay Q 4000, Australia *(275)*

T. Koszczyc Academy of Physical Education, Al. Olimpijska, 51-612 Wroclaw, Poland *(148)*

F. Krüger Institut für Sport und Sportwissenschaften, Ginnheimer Landstrasse, 39, 6000 Frankfurt 50, West Germany *(222)*

M. Kumamoto Kyoto University, Sakyo-ku, Kyoto, 606, Japan *(167)*

W. H. Laverty Department of Mathematics, University of Saskatchewan, Saskatoon, Saskatchewan, S7N 0W0, Canada *(250)*

E. R. Lewis Hofstra University, Hempstead, New York 11550 USA *(289)*

D. Lorch The Stony Brook School, Stony Brook, New York 11790 USA *(289)*

D. L. Luedtke Division of Physical Education, University of Minnesota, Minneapolis, Minnesota 55455 USA *(281)*

J. D. McClements College of Physical Education, University of Saskatchewan, Saskatoon, Saskatchewan, S7N 0W0, Canada *(250)*

J. McIlwain School of Physical and Health Education, Laurentian University, Sudbury, Ontario, Canada *(137)*

J. McMillan Medizinische Abteilung Bad Ragaz, H-7310 Bad Ragaz, Switzerland *(173)*

D. I. Miller Hutchinson Hall DX-10, University of Washington, Seattle, Washington 98195 USA *(298)*

C. A. Morehouse Sports Research Institute, The Pennsylvania State University, University Park, Pennsylvania 16802 USA *(207)*

K. Nicol Institut für Sport und Sportwissenschaften, Ginnheimer Landstr. 39, 6000 Frankfurt 50, West Germany *(173, 222)*

H. Oka Osaka Kyoiku University High School, Midorigaoka, Ikeda, 563, Osaka, Japan *(167)*

T. Okamoto Kansai Medical School, Uyama Higashi-machi, Kirakata, 573, Japan *(160, 167)*

R. C. Pavel School of Physical Education, Universidade Gama Filho, Rua Manual Vitorino 625, ZC-13 Rio de Janeiro, Brazil *(329)*

U. J. J. Persyn Katholieke Universiteit te Leuven, Instituut voor Lichamelijke Opleiding, Tervuursevest 101, 3030 Heverlee, Belgium *(182, 320)*

G. Piette Institut voor Morfologie, Vrije Universiteit Brussel, Bosstraat, 1090 Brussel, Belgium *(153)*

D. E. Pittuck Canadian Amateur Swimming Association, 333 River Road, Ottawa, Ontario, Canada *(338)*

K. Reischle Institut für Sport und Sportwissenschaft der Universität Heidelberg, Im Neuenheimer Feld 700, 6900 Heidelberg, Federal Republic of Germany *(127)*

R. E. Schleihauf, Jr. New Rochelle Aquatic Club, 82 Brambach Road, Scarsdale, New York 10583 USA *(70)*

M. Schmidt-Hansberg Institut für Sport und Sportwissenschaften, Ginnheimer Landstr. 39, 6000 Frankfurt 50, West Germany *(173)*

P. J. Smit Department of Physical Education, University of Pretoria, Pretoria, South Africa *(240)*

J. R. Stevenson Biomechanics Laboratory, School of Health, Physical Education, and Recreation, Indiana University, Bloomington, Indiana 47401 USA *(207)*

E. S. Steyn Department of Physical Education, University of Pretoria, Pretoria, South Africa *(240)*

L. J. Stoner Biomechanics Laboratory, Division of Physical Education, University of Minnesota, Minneapolis, Minnesota 55455 USA *(281)*

H. Tokuyama Osaka Kyoiku University, Jyonan-cho, Ikeda, 563, Japan *(167)*

R. Treffene Department of Physics, Queensland Institute of Technology, P.O. Box 246, North Quay, Q 4000, Australia *(275)*

B. Ungerechts Arbeitsgrüppe Funktionelle Morphologie, Ruhr-Universität-Bochum, 4630 Bochum, West Germany *(55)*

G. Van Wyk Department of Physical Education, University of Pretoria, Pretoria, South Africa *(240)*

L. Vertommen Instituut voor Morfologie, Faculty of Medicine, Vrije Universiteit Brussel, Campus Jette, 1090 Brussel, Belgium *(307)*

H. U. B. Vervaecke Katholieke Universiteit te Leuven, Instituut voor Lichamelijke Opleiding, Tervuursevest 101, 3030 Heverlee, Belgium *(320)*

E. W. Welch Instituut voor Morfologie, Faculty of Medicine, Vrije Universiteit Brussel, Campus Jette, 1090 Brussel, Belgium *(307)*

S. L. Wolf Center for Rehabilitation Medicine, 1441 Clifton Road, N.E., Atlanta, Georgia 30322 USA *(160)*

T. C. Wood Chelsea School of Physical Education, Brighton Polytechnic, Eastbourne, East Sussex, BN20 7SR England *(62)*

Y. Yoneda Aichi University of Education, Aichi, Japan *(110)*

M. Yoshizawa Fukui University, Bunkyo 3-chome, Fukui, 910, Japan *(167)*

V. M. Zatsiorsky Chair of Biomechanics, Central Institute of Physical Culture, Sirenevij, Bulv. 4, Moscow, USSR *(199)*

Third International Symposium of Biomechanics in Swimming

Conference Organization

ORGANIZING COMMITTEE

Juris Terauds . . . . Chairman
E. Wendy Bedingfield . . . . Budget, Abstracts
Mohan Singh . . . . Registration
Elaine Coachman . . . . Housing
Shirley J. Terauds . . . . Special events
Pierre Baudin . . . . Instrument exhibits
Andre Dorion . . . . Text exhibits
Alison Griffiths . . . . Public relations
Hans Gros . . . . Computer communications
Ray Manz . . . . Sports medicine
Dieter Schumann . . . . Customs
Doreen Brown . . . . Local tours
John Hogg . . . . Swimming clinic
Jan P. Clarys . . . . Honorary Director
Leon Lewillie . . . . Honorary Director
Barry A. Kerr . . . . Member

EXECUTIVE COMMITTEE

Juris Terauds . . . . Chairman
E. Wendy Bedingfield . . . . Executive Treasurer
Mohan Singh . . . . Executive Director
Jan P. Clarys . . . . Honorary Director
Leon Lewillie . . . . Honorary Director
John Hogg . . . . Clinic Director

SCIENTIFIC COMMITTEE

Dr. M. Adrian
Dr. E. Asmussen
Dr. Per-Olof Astrand
Dr. E. Banister
Dr. K. M. Barthels
Dr. W. Bedingfield
Dr. J. P. Clarys
Dr. J. M. Cooper
Dr. J. Counsilman
Dr. A. Craig
Dr. T. K. Cureton
Dr. J. Dessureault
Dr. D. Donskoi

Dr. K. Fidelus
Dr. I. Holmer
Dr. R. K. Jensen
Dr. E. Kreighbaum
Dr. L. Lewillie
Dr. M. Miyashita
Dr. C. A. Morehouse
Dr. R. Nelson
Dr. M. Singh
Dr. J. Terauds
Dr. B. Thompson
Dr. V. M. Zatsiorsky

Sponsors

Adidas
Adidas Canada Limited
550 Oakdale Road
Downsview, Ontario M3N 1W6

Air Canada
Edmonton District Office
10024 Jasper Avenue
Edmonton, Alberta T5J 1R9

**Alberta Recreation, Parks and
  Wildlife**
107 Legislative Building
Edmonton, Alberta T5K 2B6

Canadian Office of Tourism
Ottawa, Canada K1A 0H6

CP Air
Convention Travel Service
Vancouver International Airport
Central Vancouver V7B 1V1

Crosstown "Motor City"
104 Avenue at 120 Street
Edmonton, Alberta

Faculty of Physical Education
University of Alberta
Edmonton, Alberta

**Instrumentation Marketing
  Corporation**
820 South Mariposa Street
Burbank, California 91506

NAC Incorporated
17 Kowa Building
Nashi-Azubo 1-Chome
Tokyo, Japan

Photo-Sonics Inc.
820 South Mariposa Street
Burbank, California 91506

Research Center for Sports
Box 9131
Station E
Edmonton, Alberta Canada
T5R 2Y7

Travel Alberta
10065 Jasper Avenue
Edmonton, Alberta T5J 0H4

University of Alberta
Edmonton, Alberta

Preface

Swimming III contains papers presented at the Third International Symposium of Biomechanics in Swimming held at the University of Alberta in Edmonton, Canada, July 25-29, 1978. The high quality of papers presented during the proceedings of the Symposium gives the organizing committee great pleasure in presenting this volume.

Sports researchers and practitioners came together in open forum at the University of Alberta to learn from each other and so begin to "BRIDGE THE GAP." This theme is reflected very favorably in the quality of papers presented in Swimming III. In line with the theme and as a part of the Symposium, clinics were organized by the outstanding Canadian swimming coach John Hogg. The interest and enthusiasm in the scientific approach to sports was exemplified throughout the conference, and contributions came from all parts of the world. Coverage was most complete in the area of hydrodynamics and propulsion of swimming, as evidenced in the following pages. We can only hope that the spirit of the theme to BRIDGE THE GAP between researcher and practitioner will spread and become emphasized whenever sports research is being conducted.

The editors wish to thank the authors for an excellent response in following the format outlined for writing their papers and to Richard C. Nelson and Chauncey A. Morehouse for their part as editors of the International Series on Sports Sciences. Both spent many hours before and after the conference checking technical details. The editors and the organizing committee wish to thank all other persons who contributed long hours of work and gave of themselves to the success of the conference. We also wish to thank all members of the Scientific Committee who evaluated papers for presentation and publication. The organizations that made contributions to make the Symposium a success are acknowledged elsewhere in this volume.

At this time we can only hope that this volume will provide the reader with new knowledge and further stimulate research that can be applied to swimming in competition, swimming for pleasure and recreation, and swimming for rehabilitation purposes. Let us continue to BRIDGE THE GAP.

Juris Terauds
E. Wendy Bedingfield

Keynote
Address

Human Morphology and Hydrodynamics

J. P. Clarys

GENERAL HYDRODYNAMIC ASPECTS OF A BODY IN LOCOMOTION

The propulsion of a body in a liquid requires energy, which must either be provided by an outside towing force or be developed by an inside propulsive force. In the simplest case, i.e., a uniform movement in the horizontal plane, neither the potential energy nor the kinetic energy of the body changes, so all energy being developed must be absorbed by the liquid. Therefore, the kinetic energy of the liquid particles should increase.

The force (per unit of time) corresponding to this change in quantity of movement (change in impulse) of liquid mass is the drag that the body encounters in the liquid and that must be overcome by the towing or propulsive force. However, the human body, like the shape of a ship, presents an additional difficulty, in the sense that it moves in the boundary plane between two media: water and air, whereby changes in flow also cause changes in the level of the boundary plane (waves). In other words, the problems are much more complex than those of a body moving in a single medium. If one adds to these problems the uneven and poorly streamlined shape of the human body plus its possibility for "self-propulsion," the problems seem endless. One purpose of this study was to clarify some of these points through systematic and fundamental investigations.

WAVE MAKING, VISCOSITY, BOUNDARY
LAYER THEORY, AND DRAG PHENOMENA

A body cutting through the water surface causes a disturbance in potential flow, and the boundary layer between water and air is subsequently curved. This motion is referred to as wave making. The body, with its

3

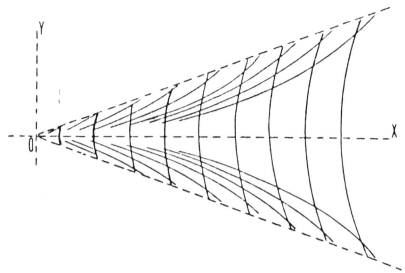

Figure 1. Wave system of a moving pressure point (Lap, 1954).

various pressure points (head-shoulders, gluteal region, feet), thus causes changes in pressure. Because each pressure point creates its own wave system (Figure 1) with equal propagation speed, one can say that the resulting wave is characterized by sudden large increases in pressure (i.e., formation of waves) at the level of head and shoulders (bow wave), the gluteal region (middle wave), and the feet (stern wave). Between the waves one always finds a decrease in pressure or a wave hollow. Direct observation confirms this general description (Figure 2). Wave making, therefore, is the result of variations in pressure caused by a disturbance of the water's surface. In still water, the propagation speed of the waves is equal to that of the body that is cleaving through the water surface (primary wave forming). Primary waves can be considered as a collection of oscillating pressure points, each of which originates a new system (secondary wave making) (Van Lammeren, Troost, and Koning, 1948; Lap, 1954).

Thus far consideration has been given to an ideal liquid, and the "paradox" of hydrodynamics has been accepted. In reality, however, resistance phenomena are always being recorded, i.e., each liquid (or gas) is characterized by a certain viscosity. This characteristic implies that liquid particles in contact with a moving body are being carried along and thus have a relative speed equal to zero. It is known that at a distance x from the body a relative speed exists, but this speed drops to zero in the layer of liquid immediately adjoining the body (Rouse, 1946; Van Lammeren, Troost, and Koning, 1948; Lap, 1954; Schlichting,

Figure 2. Wave formation at a towing velocity of 2.0 m/sec.

1960). This layer is referred to as the boundary layer (Prandtl, 1904, 1952; Kramer, 1960; 1962).

The velocity transition from "V" to "O" occurs in the boundary layer, whose thickness decreases as the friction becomes smaller. The layer theory is based on the fact that the flow at the level of the body wall causes a separation from the eddy flow originating behind the separation point (Figure 3). These boundary layer separations occur mainly around the body where the flow is either greatly slowed (pressure increase) or accelerated (pressure decrease). These changes in flow occur

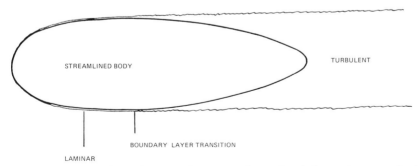

STREAMLINED BODY

TURBULENT

BOUNDARY LAYER TRANSITION

LAMINAR

Figure 3. Boundary layer, boundary layer separation and turbulence of a streamlined body (laminar profile).

where the body suddenly changes shape, such as the shoulders, the hips, the knees, etc.—i.e., where most pressure points can be found.

Concerning the drag phenomena, frictional resistance results from the viscosity characteristics and the flow phenomena of a liquid. In the boundary layer of technical liquids (those with very low internal friction), such as water and air, the velocity of the actual potential flow around the body of those liquid particles immediately adjoining the wall (skin) is reduced to a relative velocity of zero. This velocity gradation exerts a tangential shearing pressure on each surface of the body. Integrating these frictional forces over the entire (wet) body surface gives the frictional resistance.

Similarly, the eddy resistance results from the viscosity characteristics of the liquid and would be nonexistent in an ideal liquid. Because of the separation of the body's boundary layer, the disturbance in the potential flow counteracts the conversion of velocity into pressure. This implies that the same pressure that develops at the bow (head-shoulders) cannot develop behind the body contrary to what was stated in connection with an ideal liquid (hydrodynamic paradox). The result of this disturbance is a resistance force that is perpendicular to the body surface elements. This is called eddy resistance because eddy flow formation always occurs near the boundary layer separation.

Finally, the wave-making resistance component is an immediate result of wavemaking; contrary to frictional and eddy resistance, it can occur in an ideal liquid. We know that a body (a collection of pressure points) moving in the surface layer of water will create a certain wave system because of a disturbance in potential flow. This wave system is characterized by a certain amount of energy, derived from the moving body, that determines the height of the waves and their persistence. The wave theory of a moving body is considered to be complex (Lap, 1954).

According to Froude (1872) the total resistance is subdivided into frictional resistance and residual or rest resistance. The latter therefore includes both the wave-making resistance and the eddy resistance. It is also referred to as form resistance because it is the result of the three-dimensional form of a body that causes the eddy and wave-making resistance.

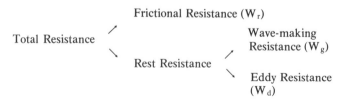

From Froude, 1872

In the study of the hydrodynamic resistance of a moving human body, additional problems must be faced. For instance, the resistance (D) can originate both from the passive movement of a body caused by an external towing force or from the active propulsion caused by the body itself. In the former case, there is theoretically no energy consumption by the individual or active participation in its propulsion, or, in principle, any change in body shape. This is called the passive resistance of a towed position (D_p). During active participation in propulsion, however, energy is being spent while changes in body shape take place. This problem does not have to be dealt with either in general hydrodynamics or in shipbuilding research. This phenomenon is called active resistance or towed movement resistance (D_s).

SURVEY OF PUBLISHED MATERIAL

Resistance and propulsive forces that the human body either undergoes and/or originates can be measured directly: the resistance can be derived from the propulsive force and vice versa and is always a function of the velocity. One must distinguish, however, between force recordings of "active" body movements and those of "passive" body positions. Most publications refer to the former as propulsive force recordings; only in exceptional cases do they deal with resistance. The latter situation always refers to resistance recordings of a towed body.

The forces of man's hydrodynamic locomotion can also be described in terms of mathematical analyses of the body's shape and movement (Seireg and Baz, 1971; Miyashita, 1974; Francis and Dean, 1975; Jensen and Blanksby, 1975). The complicated procedures of these studies deviate, however, from the direct hydrodynamic considerations of this discussion. Also, their results are still hypothetical and have not been tested against the actual hydrodynamic forces.

Propulsive Force Research

Studies to determine the propulsive force of a moving body in water can be classified according to four different approaches as described below. The first approach is propulsive force recording of a body moving in one spot (at zero velocity), also referred to as tethered swimming. Houssay (1912) studied the propulsive force of five untrained subjects, whom he connected to increasing amounts of weight via a rope-and-pulley system. Subjects had to swim until the added weights prevented them from moving forward. At that moment, maximum propulsive force had been reached. The principle of this method corresponds to the maximum force recording of a body moving at zero velocity and has been

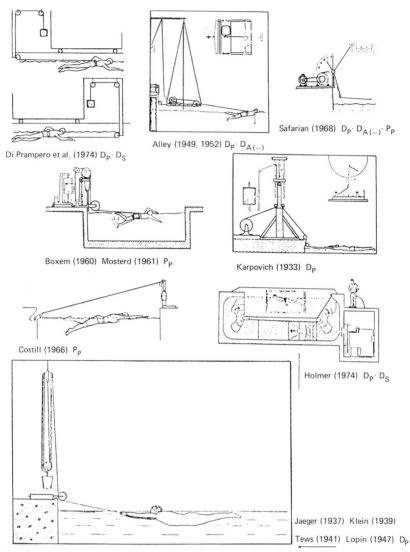

Figure 4. Some devices for measuring forces in water.

used subsequently to measure the force of arm and leg movements separately, together with the maximum propulsive force.

The weight system, however, was replaced by a spring dynamometer system, whereas a kymograph and more recently a series of potentiometers were used for the recording (Figure 4). (Cureton, 1930; Karpovich and Pestrecov, 1939; Tews, 1941; Campbell, 1948; Allen, 1948; Poulos, 1949; Boxem, 1958, 1960; Mosterd, 1960, 1961; Martinez,

1960; Onoprienko, 1961; Mosterd and Jongbloed, 1964; Absaljamov, 1964; Belokovsky, 1968; Safarian, 1968; Gordon, 1969; Goldfuss and Nelson, 1971; Zaciorsky and Safarian, 1972; Malzahn and Stafenk, 1973). To establish the average propulsive force, similar techniques were used, but the experiments included a time factor (Boxem, 1958, 1960; Mosterd, 1960, 1961; Mosterd and Jongbloed, 1964).

This writer agrees with Onoprienko (1961) that the maximum propulsive force does not correspond to the real situation because it can be maintained only for 3-5 sec. In this writer's opinion, this is the reason why the average propulsive force as a function of a certain period of time (Boxem, 1958; Mosterd and Jongbloed, 1962) provides a better picture of the propulsion of bodies swimming in the same place. A variation of this approach is the ergometric recording technique of Costill (1966), Faulkner (1966), Magel and Faulkner (1967), and Magel (1970, 1971), in which subjects were swimming in the same place against a time limited increased resistance.

The second approach is the propulsive force recording of a body moving at velocity greater than zero (surplus propulsive force). When measuring the propulsive force at zero velocity, it is also possible to establish the resistance because both forces are equal at constant (including zero) velocity. In other words, at constant velocity, the propulsive force being developed is sufficient to overcome the hydrodynamically counteracting resistance. Therefore, the propulsive force measured at zero velocity is the force necessary to overcome the resistance at (theoretically) maximum velocity.

According to Alley (1949, 1952) however, different forces are being recorded for a body moving in the same place than the actual propulsive forces of locomotion (i.e., at velocity greater than zero). Subsequently, Counsilman (1951, 1955), Kruchoski (1954), Thrall (1960), Safarian (1968), Zaciorsky and Safarian (1972), and Malzahn and Stafenk (1973) verified the same principle, although its final interpretation sometimes varied. Except for a few technical details, all these researchers used similar recording instruments: a cable or nylon rope attached to the subject via a pulley system and rotation drum to an electric motor and a force recorder (spring dynamometer or strain gauge). Force recording was achieved either mechanically on a kymograph or electrically by potentiometers and galvanometer recorders. In most studies, velocity recordings were fairly accurate while the instruments could be adapted to subjects swimming by virtue of their own efforts (propulsive force recording) or being towed (resistance recording) (Figure 4). The propulsive force recorded in this manner has been described as the additional propulsive force that a subject is able to develop at a given velocity after overcoming the resistance at that velocity. The total propulsive force is then calculated by adding the additional propulsive force to the passive resistance at that particular velocity.

Thrall (1960), who was only interested in the propulsive force of the legs, dealt with the problem in the reverse manner. Subjects were towed at a velocity greater than that they could develop by themselves. In this way, however, he measured a resistance from which the propulsive force of the leg movements was deducted. The resistance without leg movements minus the resistance with leg movements gave the total propulsive force component of the legs at the velocity under consideration. Although this interpretation is correct, it seems that the choice of velocity does not correspond to the real situation. Malzahn and Stafenk (1973) proceeded like Alley (1949, 1952) and others but considered the supplementary propulsive force as the total propulsion; therefore, their final results cannot be used.

The third approach to assess the amount of propulsive force developed is the measurement of energy consumption during locomotion (swimming). This technique can be either combined with one of the previously mentioned propulsive force recordings or simply examined as a function of time and distance (without propulsive force recordings) (Liljestrand and Stenström, 1919; Greene, 1930; Schmelkes, 1935, 1936; Egolinskii, 1940; Karpovich and Lemaistre, 1940; Karpovich and Milmann, 1944; Van Huss and Cureton, 1954; Andersen, 1960; Åstrand et al., 1963; Adrian, Singh, and Karpovich, 1966; Costill, 1966; Magel and Faulkner, 1967; Miyashita, Hayashi and Furuhaski, 1970; Magel and McArdle, 1970; Holmér, 1971, 1972, 1974a, b, 1975; Magel, 1971; McArdle, Glaser and Magel, 1971; Holmér and Åstrand, 1972; Rennie et al., 1973, Shepperd, Godin, and Campbell, 1974; di Prampero et al., 1974; Lipke, 1974; Holmer, Lundin and Eriksson, 1974; Eriksson, Holmér, and Lundin, 1974; Rennie, Pendergast, and di Prampero, 1975; Secher and Odderschede, 1975; Magel et al., 1975; Kemper et al., 1976).

Finally, propulsive force can be measured by dynamometer registrations on dry land (Schramm 1958, 1959).

Resistance or Drag

The direct recording of a body's hydrodynamic resistance as a function of velocity involves an experimental setup that allows subjects to be towed both in a selected position, and while moving. The prone horizontal position, with the arms stretched forward, has been studied frequently. (Liljestrand and Stenström, 1919; Karpovich, 1933; Jaeger, 1937; Klein, 1939; Tews, 1941; Lopin, 1947; Alley, 1949, 1952; Counsilman, 1951, 1955; Schramm, 1958-1959, 1960-1961; Thrall, 1960; Hairabedian, 1965, 1966; Onoprienko, 1967; Safarian, 1968; Kent and Atha, 1971; Zaciorsky and Safarian, 1972; Malzahn and Stafenk, 1973; Clarys,

Jiskoot, and Lewillie, 1973; di Prampero et al., 1974; Clarys et al., 1974; Holmer, 1974 a, b, c, 1975; Rennie, Pendergast, and di Prampero, 1975; Klauck and Daniel, 1975; Jiskoot and Clarys, 1975; Clarys and Jiskoot, 1975; Clarys, 1976; Miyashita and Tsunoda, 1978). On the other hand, the stretched-back position has only been tested by Du Bois-Reymond (1927), Liljestrand and Stenström (1919), Karpovich (1933), Kruchoski (1954), and Schramm (1958-1959). Certain researchers examined the influence on hydrodynamic resistance of the head position and the body inclination (Karpovich, 1933; Schramm, 1958-1959; Hairabedian, 1965, 1966; Onoprienko, 1967; Kent and Atha, 1971; De Goede, Jiskoot, and Van der Sluis, 1971; Jurina 1972-1974; Clarys, Jiskoot and Lewillie, 1973; Clarys, 1976). This inclination, defined as the angle between the stretched body and the water surface, results from the sinking of the legs at low towing speeds. With increasing velocity there is less tendency of the legs to sink, so that at a particular point the body (without support from the feet) will be in a totally horizontal plane. This is called "hydrodynamic lift," and at even greater velocities it is called "hydroplaning" (Karpovich, 1933; Jaeger, 1937; Tews, 1941; Lopin, 1947; Alley, 1949, 1952; Counsilman, 1955; Schramm, 1958-1959; Hairabedian, 1965; Onoprienko, 1967; Jurina, 1972-1974; Clarys, Jiskoot, and Lewillie, 1973; di Prampero et al., 1974; Holmér, 1974a, b; Clarys et al., 1974; Clarys, 1976). Again, only a few authors have studied the hydrodynamic resistance of various positions (Counsilman, 1951, 1955; Schramm, 1958-1959; Hairabedian, 1965, 1966; Kent and Atha, 1971; Malzahn and Stafenk, 1973; Jiskoot and Clarys, 1975; Clarys and Jiskoot, 1975; Clarys, 1976).

Some researchers emphasized the importance of body shape and dimensions in the assessment of hydrodynamic resistance (Liljestrand and Stenström, 1919; Amar, 1920; Karpovich, 1933; Jaeger, 1937; Alley, 1949; Counsilman, 1951; Schramm, 1960-1961; Gadd, 1963; Safarian, 1968; Jurina, 1972-1974). They based their research on existing hydrodynamic principles and on empirical reasoning. However, the influence of the body surface, maximum transverse surface, length, weight, and other anthropometric data have been studied experimentally only by Klein (1939), Tews (1941), Lopin (1947), Onoprienko (1967), Zaciorsky and Safarian (1972), Clarys et al. (1974), Clarys (1976), and Miyashita and Tsunoda (1978).

Holmér (1974a, b, 1975) studied the hydrodynamic resistance of the prone position in an "aquatic swim mill" (or swimming flume), an instrument designed according to the wind tunnel principle (Åstrand and Engelsson, 1971; Björkman, 1972; Wilkinson, 1973). The subject moves opposite the water flow with the velocity of the water accurately controlled. The water flow, however, is laminar, contrary to the assumed

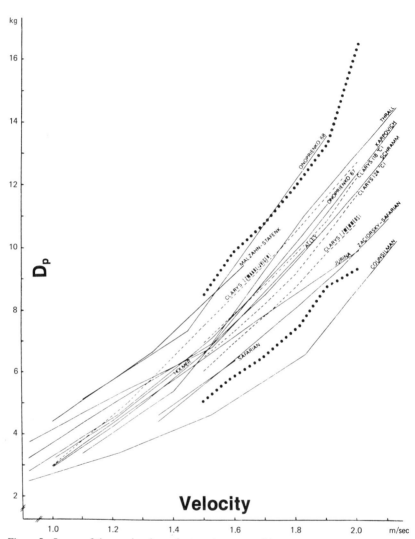

Figure 5. Survey of the passive drag of a towed prone position.

turbulence around a passive body normally moving through water (Gadd, 1963; Taggart, 1966; Francis and Dean, 1975; Clarys, 1976). A survey of the passive drag results of the prone position is shown in Figure 5.

In contrast with the abovementioned research of passive (towed) drag, the towed movement (of arms and legs together), i.e., the active drag, has never been measured directly. The passive towing position had always been considered the nearest approach to the hydrodynamic resistance that a swimming body would encounter, until Alley (1949,

1952) stated that they were quite dissimilar: the active drag is not only a function of velocity but also of each moving part of the body. According to Safarian (1968), it is extremely difficult to measure the body's total active drag even with accurate recording instruments.

Di Prampero et al. (1974) were the first to describe the total active drag of a crawl stroke swimmer. They determined the drag at a constant velocity as a function of oxygen consumption. They extrapolated the linear regression between VO_2 net and the added propulsion and added drag to VO_2 net $= 0$. At constant velocity, propulsive force $=$ resistance. This method was applied in a flume by Holmér (1974a, b, c, 1975), by Rennie, Pendergast, and di Prampero (1975), and by Pendergast et al. (1978). This procedure, however, is not straightforward but complicated and must be repeated in its entirety for each velocity recording point.

MORPHOLOGICAL DATA FOR HYDRODYNAMIC INVESTIGATIONS

Experiments with water mammals have shown a relationship between the morphological characteristics of the body and its propulsive efficiency in water. From ship design research and fundamental hydrodynamics it is known that drag is determined partly by the viscous characteristics of the fluid and partly by body form.

The form of the human body is obviously an essential element in the study of its resistance in water. There are, however, only a few hydrodynamic studies that use a form parameter, and those that do have not been involved with body movement. An exact formulation of the relationship between hydrodynamic drag and the propulsion of the human body is not possible because sufficient data concerning drag caused by bodies of arbitrary shape are not available. Hence, what is needed is an interdisciplinary approach that combines hydrodynamic principles with anthropometric and morphologic knowledge to generate sufficient information to permit the study of drag created by the body.

To reduce the number of variables, our studies have been restricted to a sample population consisting of 63 students from the Academy of Physical Education of Amsterdam and nine Dutch competitive swimmers (Olympic level). Data for all subjects are given and include their age, body, height, weight, and a series of measurements consisting of diameters, lengths, and circumferences. The body build is expressed by a length factor, a breadth factor, and a muscle factor. The fat factor, measured by a series of subcutaneous skin folds, was measured but has been omitted because there are doubts about the value of fat measurements when applied to hydrodynamic research (Clarys, 1976). The anthropometric measurements were taken according to the techniques

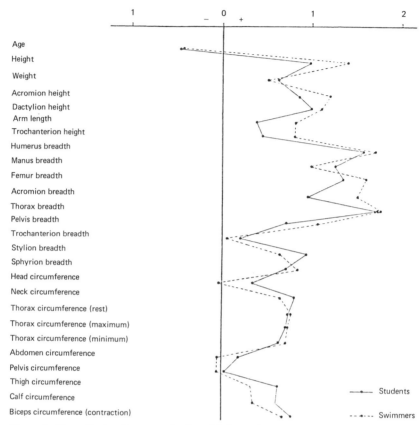

Figure 6. Normalized anthropometric data (Molison diagram) of PE students and swimmers versus a reference group of 572 military men (*vertical line*).

of Twiesselman (1952), Martin-Saller (1957), and Tanner (1964). Data from our sample were plotted against the corresponding values of Belgian military men (Figure 6). The graphical representation of these normalized values indicates analogous body development of both the physical education (PE) students and the swimmers. Figure 7 is a graph of the mean height and weight of various PE student samples taken from the literature. On the basis of the quetelet index it seems that our subjects are similar to the PE students of Dunedin, Overveen, New York, Prague, Camarilla, and Brussels.

Figure 8 describes a series of depth and breadth values of our subjects, compared with a series of similar populations. In general the agreement is best with the data of Wilmore and Behnke (1969) and Hayez and Delatte (1967), although several separate diameters show similarities. Figures 9 and 10 list circumferences, which most clearly

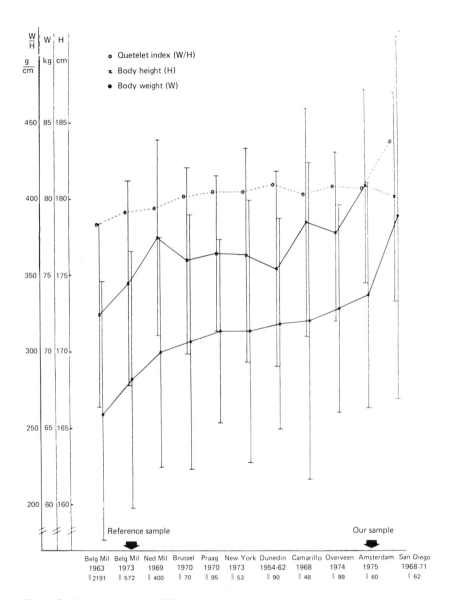

Figure 7. Height and weight of PE students and military men.

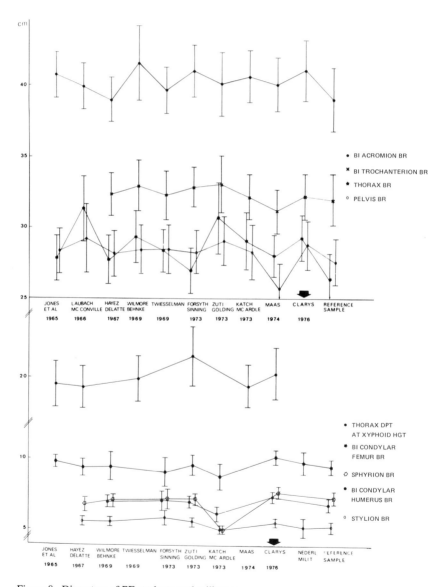

Figure 8. Diameters of PE students and military men.

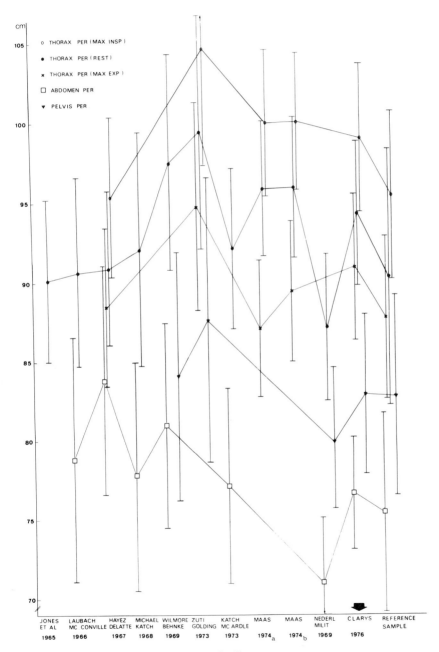

Figure 9. Circumferences of PE students and military men.

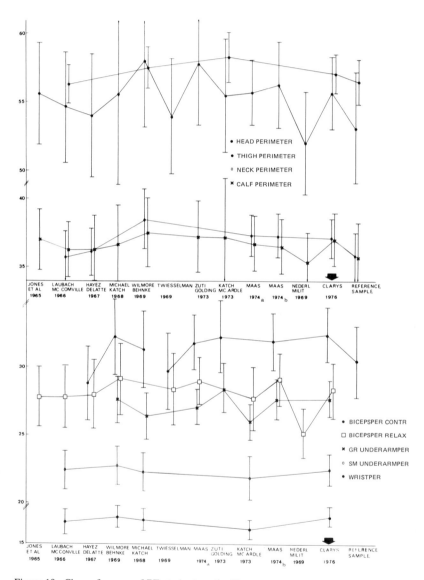

Figure 10. Circumferences of PE students and military men.

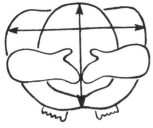 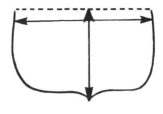

Figure 11. Maximum body cross-section and midship section.

correspond to the findings of Michael and Katch (1968) and Maas (1974).

During swimming, the human body is situated at the interface of two fluid media, air and water. Thus, streamlining is interrupted and energy is dissipated in the form of surface waves and turbulence. The theoretical hydrodynamic formulation becomes mathematically unmanageable if, in addition, we consider the irregular human body form and its continuing change in shape caused by swimming movement. Our sample has been described as a series of anthropometric measurements, but this description must be extended with body composition data that correspond to the hydrodynamic variables, such as body surface, the maximum body cross-section, the hydrostatic weight, and density.

The body surface was chosen because of the fundamental importance of the "wet" surface as used in hydrodynamics and in ship model research, as well as because of previous findings that human body surface influences drag (Karpovich, 1933; Tews, 1941; Faulkner, 1966; Onoprienko, 1967). The body surface is measured according to the semidirect measuring technique of Weinbach (1938), based on a series of circumferences that were plotted against height. The actual surface value is measured with a planimeter. A multiple stepwise regression analysis indicated that for our sample the body height and weight were the best predictors of surface area (R = 0.94).

Surface = 0.0112 weight + 0.0051 height − 0.0718   (Clarys, 1976)

The maximum body cross-sectional diameter ($\otimes$) corresponds to the midship section in ship model research (Figure 11). The specific surface measurement indicates the quantity of water displaced in a lateral direction and thus determines the degree of wave-making resistance. This parameter was measured according to a simple photographic technique and was planimetered on a scaled photograph. Again, the multiple stepwise regression analysis indicated that body weight and height were the best predictors of the maximum body cross-sectional diameter (R = 0.71).

$$\otimes = 6.9256 \text{ weight} + 3.5043 \text{ height} - 377.156 \qquad \text{(Clarys, 1976)}$$

where $\otimes$ = maximum body cross-sectional diameter.

The hydrostatic weight, body volume, and body density were chosen as representative measurements for buoyancy. The hydrostatic weight was measured according to the method described by Katch, Michael, and Horvalth (1967). The volume was calculated by applying Archimedes' principle. Because of the specific hydrodynamic use of these parameters they were measured in expiration and corrected for residual lung volume and gastrointestinal gas, and *also* in inspiration without any correction because the latter corresponds to the real hydrodynamically needed volume and hydrostatic weight.

The body density (d) was calculated according to the equation:

$$d = \frac{\text{weight}}{\text{weight} - \text{hydrostatic weight} - \text{residual volume}}$$

The mean observations of these body composition data are summarized in Table 1. In addition, hydrodynamic science uses a series of nondimensional relationships for which adequate "human" alternatives must be found. These nondimensional relationships indicate, respectively, the extent of the frictional, wave-making, and eddy resistances.

It is known that the length/thickness ratio is a measure used for determining the eddy resistance, the length/surface ratio is used as a measure for the frictional resistance, and the slenderness relation gives

Table 1.   Means and standard deviations of body composition data

Parameter	Students		Swimmers	
	$\overline{X}$	SD	$\overline{X}$	SD
Body surface (m^2)	1.6669	0.118	1.677	0.1584
Greatest body cross-section (cm^2)	767.33	92.51	766.66	123.887
Hydrostatic weight[a] (expiration) (kg)	3.936	0.633	3.539	0.756
Hydrostatic weight (inspiration) (kg)	−1.098	0.846	−1.677	0.575
Volume (expiration) (liters)[a]	68.409	7.329	67.001	8.476
Volume (inspiration) (liters)	74.883	7.786	74.534	9.108
Density (g/ml)[a]	1.0760	0.0090	1.0709	0.0066

[a] Corrected for the residual volume.

Table 2. Nondimensional form relationships for hydrodynamic research

Length/breadth ratio	H/B	body height/biacromial breadth
Length/depth ratio	H/T	body height/thorax depth (xyphoid level)
Length/thickness ratio	$H^2/\otimes$	body height^2/greatest body cross-section
Length/surface ratio	H^2/S	body height^2/body surface
Slenderness degree	$H/\Delta^{1/3}$	body height/body volume$^{1/3}$
Breadth/depth ratio	B/T	biacromial breadth/thorax depth (xyphoid level)

an indication of the degree of wave-making resistance. The length/depth and length/breadth ratios give information about the streamline of the body.

The human morphology equivalents are illustrated in Table 2. Complementary to these nondimensional form ratios and in the context of the hydrodynamic drag determination, both form and drag can be studied for all subjects if the data are used with laws of similarity (Van Lammeren, Troost, and Koning, 1948). Because the mathematical description of the problems of the human body moving in water is so complex, the hydrodynamic problems of the human body cannot be treated mathematically. Quantitative results have to be obtained entirely by empirical methods. Even though measurements are made on full-scale subjects, the absolute hydrodynamic data are impracticable and too inaccurate for comparison between subjects. Therefore, one must use a series of nondimensional comparison indexes, such as the Reynolds number and drag coefficient, for the laminar and turbulent flow determination, and the Froude number and drag indexes for the nondimensional resistance/velocity relationship (Table 3).

Table 3. Comparison indexes for hydrodynamic research

Reynolds number	$v \cdot H/\nu$	velocity and body height/H_2O viscosity
Froude number	$v/\sqrt{g \cdot H}$	velocity/$\sqrt{9.81 \times \text{body height}}$
Drag force index (i)	D/W	drag/body weight
Drag force index (ii)	D/Δ	drag/body volume
Drag coefficient	$D/0.5 \cdot d \cdot \otimes \cdot V^2$	drag/0.5 × density × cross-section × velocity^2

PROCEDURES FOR MEASURING HYDRODYNAMIC FORCES

We have measured the drag force of a towed individual in the horizontal prone position, referred to as passive drag (D_p); of a towed horizontal but $45°$ longitudinally inclined position, referred to as $D_{P45°}$; of a towed prone position, 60 cm under the water surface, referred to as D_{PH_2O}; and the effective propulsion has been measured as well as the effective drag of the towed swimming movement, referred to as the added propulsion ($D_{A(-)}$) and added resistance ($D_{A(+)}$). For this purpose the equipment of the Dutch ship model basin was used, which consisted of a water tank 200 m long, a towing carriage driven on rails by an electric motor with precisely controlled speed, and a recording device for automatic recording of drag and velocity data in kg/m/sec. This test setup has been described (Clarys et al., 1974; Clarys and Jiskoot, 1974, 1975).

The forces being measured by a telescopic rod system (Figure 12) were converted into electrical signals by strain gauges and were amplified. Together with the towing velocity, they were recorded on ultraviolet (self-developing photographic) paper. This graphic recording takes on various shapes, depending on the position or movement being measured and the velocity selected. The recordings of different towing positions showed smaller differences in amplitude (oscillations) than those of a movement (Figure 13). The average force for each velocity was derived from direct recording. Each average resistance was then plotted as a function of its corresponding velocity (Figure 14). In this way, the average force for each velocity was graphically displayed for each subject and the relationship between resistance and velocity could be seen. The recorded forces could be either positive or negative. A positive force referred to a towing force, i.e., a force developed by the towing carriage that towed the body through the water. A negative force implied a pushing force, that is, the body pushes against the towing mechanism. The force recordings for the various "towing positions," therefore, were always positive; this corresponded to the passive resistance (D_P, D_{PH_2O}, $D_{P45°}$).

Force recordings of the crawl movement were negative if the velocity of the swimming subjects was higher than that of the towing carriage. In fact, the subject was able to exert a pressure force on the rod system since the constant velocity of the towing carriage remained below that of the subject to which it was connected. The force recording of the crawl movement became positive as soon as the subject was unable to keep up with the towing carriage. Therefore, despite his propulsion movements, the swimmer was being towed by the carriage which moved faster than he did. In other words:

positive recording = towing force = resistance
negative recording = push force = propulsion

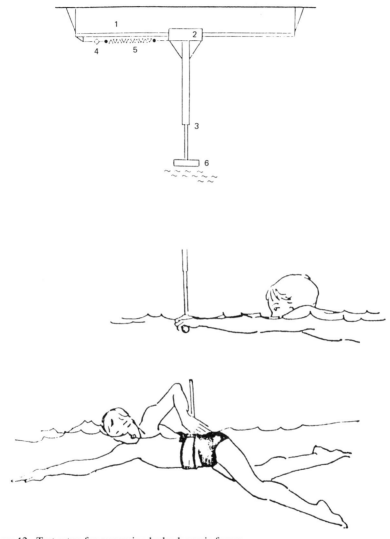

Figure 12. Test setup for measuring hydrodynamic forces.

These forces and their graphic representation as a function of velocity are shown in Figures 14 and 15. Thus, positive forces indicated passive resistance (D_P, D_{PH_2O}, or $D_{P45°}$) on the one hand, and "an" active resistance, on the other. This active resistance, however, corresponded to a towing force which was in addition to the propulsive force developed by the subjects. That is why it was referred to as added resistance ($D_{A(+)}$).

Negative forces always reflected a propulsive force that was developed after subjects had overcome water resistance. In other words,

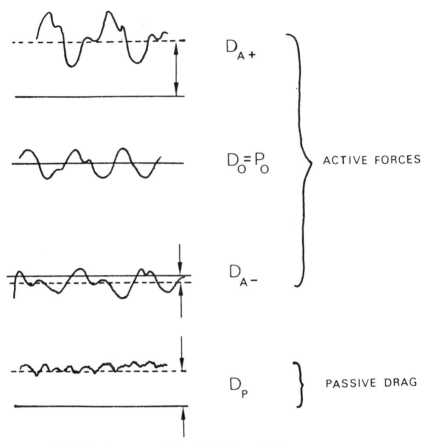

D_{A+}

$D_O = P_O$ } ACTIVE FORCES

D_{A-}

D_P } PASSIVE DRAG

Figure 13. Registration patterns of the electrical force signals.

at certain velocities a subject developed a force that was larger than his resistance. This was called the "surplus" propulsive force or added propulsion ($D_{A(-)}$).

Neither the added propulsion nor the added resistance corresponded to the real total forces involved in the front crawl movement. At a certain velocity point on the graph (Figure 14) $D_{A(-)}$ changed to $D_{A(+)}$. At that point propulsion equals resistance, and no force was registered because the subject progressed at the same speed as the carriage. The real force exerted at that point was needed to calculate the total drag.

We have mentioned that the absolute propulsive force can be measured directly with tethered recording of the swimmer at zero velocity. Indirect evaluation of the absolute propulsion and resistance forces also is possible by extrapolating the added force curve ($D_{A(-)}$ and $D_{A(+)}$) of the towed movement to zero velocity. The relationship between absolute

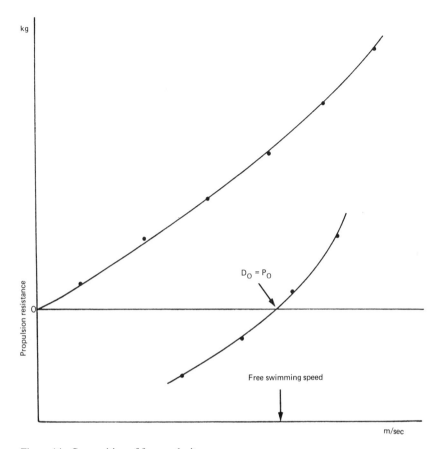

Figure 14. Composition of force-velocity curves.

and added forces has been simplified and is illustrated in Figure 15. The extrapolated force at zero velocity has been added to the $D_{A(-)}$ and $D_{A(+)}$ values to obtain the total drag. Extrapolation of the force curve ($D_{A(-)}$ and $D_{A(+)}$) was, therefore, merely the displacement of force recordings from the original zero line to a new zero line.

CHOICE OF VELOCITY POINTS
IN THE DETERMINATION OF ACTIVE DRAG

We know the hydrodynamic relationship between resistance, propulsion, and velocity. However, there is no proof of a similar situation regarding the human body. As a matter of fact, Jaeger (1937), Tews (1941), and Lopin (1947) reported that the relationship between resistance and velocity was not significant, whereas the relationship between propulsion

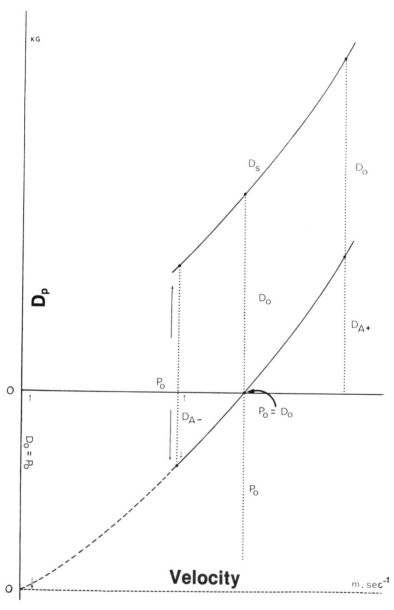

Figure 15. Simplified extrapolation of added propulsion ($D_{A(-)}$) and added drag ($D_{A(+)}$) at zero velocity.

and velocity was statistically significant. That is why it was desirable to avoid arbitrary, empirically selected velocity criteria, which might be redundant. The velocities for each subject were selected separately on the basis of his individual "free swimming speed." For each subject, six to 10 velocity points were selected, which were $\pm$ 0.5 m/sec below and $\pm$ 0.3 m/sec above his individual free velocity. For the entire experiment, free velocities ranged from 1.10 to 1.85 m/sec. The free velocity thus became a reference, indicated on the graphs by an arrow on the abscissa (Figure 14).

PASSIVE DRAG (D_P, D_{PH_2O}, $D_{P45°}$)
DATA (FUNDAMENTAL HYDRODYNAMICS)

According to the theories on laminated and turbulent flow and as a function of the drag coefficients (C_D) and Reynolds number (R), a turbulent flow occurs around the human body. This is illustrated in Figure 16. For all values beyond the "laminated turbulence" transition line, a turbulent flow is assumed. The C_D values as a function of R for our sample obviously lie in the range of turbulent flow. According to hydrodynamic principles, turbulent flows around the body are accompanied by an increase in pressure resistance. This confirms Gadd's hypothesis (1963). According to him, the boundary layer around a human body moving in water is totally turbulent and originates, as seen in Figure 2, at the head, neck, shoulders, lumbar region, hips, thighs, knees, and feet.

There is no indication whatsoever that this turbulence (and therefore the total drag) can be reduced. However, Onoprienko (1967) stated that the resistance of the female body is less than that of the male body; this can be explained, among other things, by the fact that a woman's skin is softer than a man's; the consequent increase in elasticity would contribute to a laminated flow at the body surface. According to Onoprienko, the flows occurring around a female body might be compared with those of a dolphin, who, thanks to a specific skin structure, can oppress the turbulent flow and therefore avoid boundary layer separations. On the basis of the results obtained and the C_D/R ratio, such a statement was impossible to confirm. The only statement that can be accepted from Onoprienko (1967) is that the female body is less angular, and therefore the boundary layer separation occurs less suddenly. Probably, a better horizontal position in water resulting from better floating abilities (Rork and Hellebrandt, 1937; Cureton, 1943; Highmore, 1955; Howell, Moncrieff, and Morford, 1962; Lane and Mitchum, 1963; Whiting, 1963; Duffield, 1969; Guilbert, 1970; Broer, 1973; De Raeve, 1974) could explain lower drag values for the female body. It may be stated that

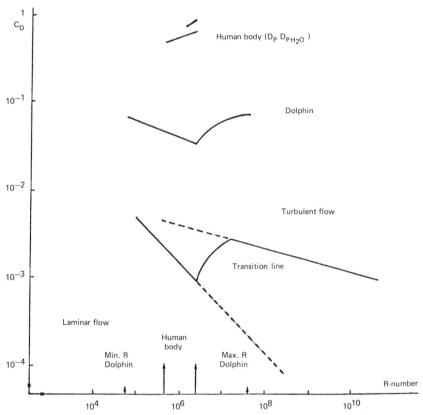

Figure 16. Laminar and turbulent flow regions as a function of the drag coefficient (C_D) Reynolds number (R) ratio.

the flow around a (human) body is and remains turbulent in all circumstances. According to hydrodynamic standards, eddy resistance and therefore total drag as a function of the small velocity range remain high.

In the towing experiments, 60 cm under the water surface, the Reynolds (R) numbers and resistance coefficients were calculated for $V = 1.5\text{--}2.0$ m/sec. The evolution of C_D for equal R numbers, however, was significantly higher ($\alpha \leq 0.001$) than the C_D evolution of the prone position during towing at the water surface. This implies that an even greater turbulence occurs, i.e., an increase in eddy resistance (Figure 16).

Under the given circumstances and as a result of the irregular shape of the human body, there is doubt about whether the eddy resistance will be reduced, or even influenced, by a favorable length/breadth ratio. On the basis of the individual range of drag results (as a function of a limited velocity range) the favorable hydrodynamic influence that should be expected by a hydrodynamically "good" range of Reynolds numbers ($2.10^5 < R < 2.10^6$) is also questioned. In other words, the small resistance variation that should accompany the R numbers in question does not apply to human shapes.

In cold water, heat loss and the energy consumption of a resting body are higher than in warmer water (Molnar, 1946; Pugh and Edholm, 1955; Carlson et al., 1958; Beckman et al., 1961; Cannon, 1963; Keatinge, 1939, 1978; Arborelius et al., 1972; Holmér, 1974a; Nielsen, 1978). However, the original hypothesis was that physiological variations within the body do not affect the recording of a purely physical dimension—namely, hydrodynamic, passive drag. Nevertheless, it was found that the water temperature had a significant influence on the drag recordings, which is shown in Figure 17. Therefore, at higher water temperatures the drag becomes smaller and significantly different ($\alpha \leq 0.001$) from the drag measured at temperatures of 5°-6°C less. Simply stated, one can say that within the limits of the temperatures studied the hydrodynamic drag of the human body diminishes with increasing water temperatures.

To quantify the relationship between passive drag and body shape, all anthropometric and body composition data were combined with the hydrodynamic data in a correlation analysis. This analysis led to the following conclusions:

1. Not all shapes and mass variables of the body that were studied showed a significant relationship with the passive drag data (D_p, D_{PH_2O}, $D_{P45°}$).
2. The relationship between body shape and passive drag usually increases with increasing velocity.
3. Quantitatively, there were fewer shape and mass variables that influenced the passive drag for velocities above 1.70 m/sec.
4. The shape variables that indicate a relationship with the passive drag are usually, *but not always,* the same for towing experiments conducted in water of 18°C and 24°C.

In any case, the correlation analysis provided enough data to indicate that for the poorly harmoniously shaped body (in prone and inclined positions) the drag was proportionally influenced by the circumferential dimensions of those parts, in the upper part of the body.

An important part in the hydrodynamic drag determination was played by the body surface area if one refers to the studies of, for example, Amar (1920), Karpovich (1933), Tews (1941), Onoprienko (1967), Faulkner (1968), Jurina (1972-1974), Blanksby (1973), and Broer (1973), and to fundamental hydrodynamics. An increase in frictional resistance is directly proportional to an increase in body surface area and thus

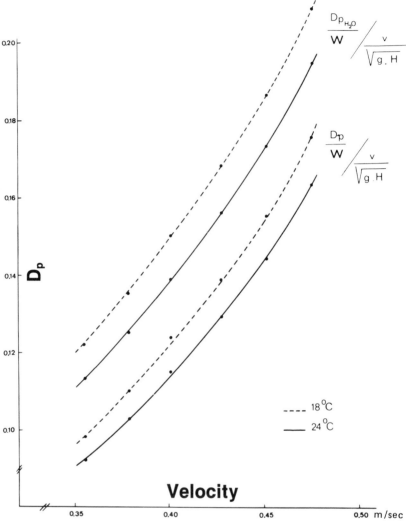

Figure 17. Nondimensional representation of passive drag on and under the water surface at temperatures of 18° and 24°C.

to the total drag. Until now, this principle has been generally accepted, to the extent that certain textbooks on swimming science state it as fact. From a hydrodynamic point of view, the principle is perfectly correct for all geometric, harmonious, and streamlined bodies, and the idea is being used in ship model research (Lap, 1954). Application to our sample, however, requires that: 1) the human body is streamlined, and 2) the frictional resistance is an important part of the total hydrodynamic drag.

The first requirement has been commented upon, whereas the contrary was shown to be true by Gadd (1963). It is also impossible to meet the second requirement for the following reasons:

1. Experiments show no relationship between the hydrodynamic passive drag and the body surface at any velocity, either in water at 18° or 24 °C.
2. No correlation has been observed between the drag and the length/ surface ratio, which is also the case for the nondimensional representation of the passive drag and the same ratio.
3. An important turbulent flow occurs around the body, and the separating boundary layer at various places on the body indicates the existence of an important eddy resistance.

These reasons indicate that for the human body, frictional resistance is proportionally low and becomes unimportant in the sense that the body surface did not influence the hydrodynamic drag of our sample.

Contrary to the body surface, the maximum cross-section plays an important part in the passive drag determination. This hypothesis was supported by the significant relationship between the resistance values and the length/thickness ratio $H^2/\otimes$). Considering that this index indicates eddy and wave-making resistance (Van Lammeren, Troost, and Koning, 1948), it may be stated that the increase in eddy and wave-making resistance, i.e., in the total resistance of the towed body (since the frictional resistance is very low) is proportional to an increase in the maximum body cross-section and to a decrease in length/thickness ratio.

COMMENTS ON THE TOTAL ACTIVE
DRAG DATA (APPLIED HYDRODYNAMICS)

Results of the average active drag for the entire sample and for two different water temperatures (Figure 18) follow a parabolical function: $F = K \cdot v^n$ where K and n are predetermined constants and V is the velocity of swimming. The large range of absolute results as well as the large variety of individual K and n values at different velocities indicate that the active drag (D_s) of the self-propulsion body is determined by different factors. For D_s, $n > 2$ ($1.973 < n < 4.313$). For each subject the specific drag constantly varied from 1.34 to 7.93 with respective velocities and in both experiments, which were significantly higher than the values recorded for passive drag.

Contrary to the experiments of passive drag, it was difficult to check the similarity of all circumstances (physical effort, movement, respiration, etc.) in both series of tests, i.e., in water temperatures of 24° and 26 °C. In spite of this limitation it was noted that the water temperatures influence the different subjects and the same subject within

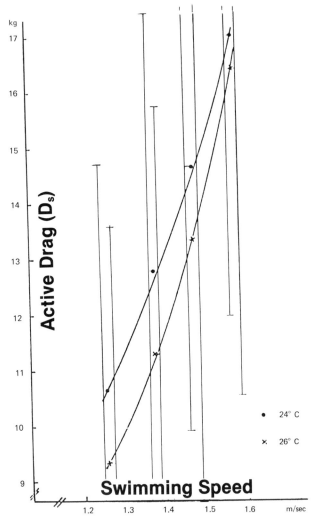

Figure 18. Mean and standard deviation of total active drag (D_s) at 24° and 26°C.

the respective velocity ranges. Therefore: 1) at higher water temperatures the active drag of a swimming body is less than that in water at lower temperatures with the identical velocities, and 2) the influence of the temperature decreases with increasing velocities. In other words, at equal velocities a smaller propulsive force has to be developed to overcome the total active drag than when water temperatures are increased.

Comparison of the D_p data with the D_s data showed (Figure 19) that the active drag (D_s) is ca. 1.5 to 2 times higher than the passive drag (D_p). This means that a hydrodynamically fundamental error is

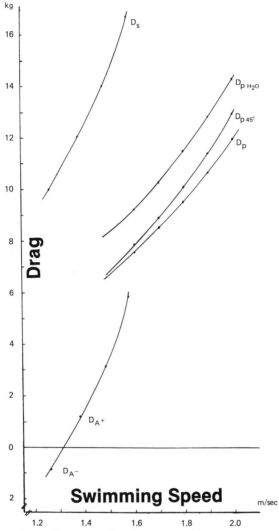

Figure 19. Comparison of mean passive drag results (D_p, D_{PH_2O}, $D_{P45°}$) and active drag data ($D_{A(-)}$, $D_{A(+)}$, D_s).

made when the total propulsive force of a moving body is derived from the resistance data from a passively towed body, which has been done quite often until recently. This also means that the D_s results we obtained approximate those reported by di Prampero et al. (1974), Holmér (1974a, c), Rennie, Pendergast, and di Prampero (1975), and Pendergast et al. (1978).

D$_s$ results recorded so far are shown in Figure 20. Average hydro-

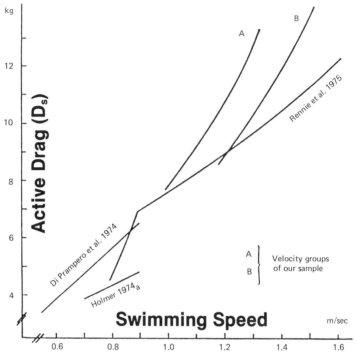

Figure 20. Active drag data from the literature.

dynamic drag forces of different velocity ranges have been added because they correspond closely to the velocities examined by previous authors. Direct comparison, however, remains difficult since di Prampero et al. (1974) and Holmer (1974a, c) made their recordings at only two velocities, whereas Rennie, Pendergast, and di Prampero (1975) used a different sample for each velocity.

Until now, the relationship between the drag and the shape of bodies moving in water has only been derived from an intuitive (faulty) application of generally accepted hydrodynamic principles in ship building research and from unilateral observations of passive drag; therefore its general validity has to be suspect. A correlation analysis was used to determine the relationship between the D_s results as a function of different velocity recordings and of the shape of the body.

The usefulness of correlations is limited; besides, they were very small. Only four body dimensions showed any correlation with the active resistance. Only the width of the thorax and the circumference of the thigh showed a significant correlation at velocities above 1.55 m/sec ($r = 0.441$ and $r = 0.456$, respectively). On the other hand, a correlation between D_s and abdomen and calf circumferences existed at all velocities

$(0.40 < r < 0.463)$. This means that the shape of the human body has hardly any influence on the active drag and that other factors are more important. Thus, shape, composition, and dimensions of the body exert little or no influence on the hydrodynamic resistance (in independent crawl locomotion). There is a reason to believe that the active drag is mainly, if not solely, influenced by the changes in shape (changes in position) and the movement of the body segments. Increases and decreases in resistance, therefore, must be explained through correct or faulty swimming techniques.

REFERENCES

Absaljamov, T. M. 1964. Cited in: V. M. Zaciorsky and I. G. Safarian, 1972. Untersuchung von faktoren zur bestimmung der maximalen geschwindigkeit im freistilschwimmen (Investigation of factors for the determination of maximal speed in freestyle swimming). Theor. Prax. Körperkult. 8:695–709.

Adrian, M. J., Singh, M., and Karpovich, P. V. 1966. Energy cost of leg kick, arm stroke and whole crawl stroke. J. Appl. Physiol. 21:1763–1766.

Allen, T. H. 1948. A study of the leg stroke in swimming the crawl stroke. Masters thesis, State University of Iowa, Iowa City.

Alley, L. E. 1949. An analysis of resistance and propulsion in swimming the crawl stroke. Ph.D. thesis, State University of Iowa, Iowa City.

Alley, L. E. 1952. An analysis of water resistance and propulsion in swimming the crawl stroke. Res. Q. 23:253–270.

Amar, J. 1920. The Human Motor. Routledge and Sons, Ltd., London.

Andersen, K. L. 1960. Energy cost of swimming. Acta Chirur. Scand. (suppl. 253): 169–174.

Arborelius, M., Jr., Balldin, U. I., Lilja, B., and Lundgren, C. E. G. 1972. Hemodynamic changes in man during immersion with the head above water. Aerospace Med. 43:592–598.

Åstrand, P. O., and Engelsson, S. 1971. An aquatic swim-mill. In: L. Lewillie and J. P. Clarys (eds.), Proceedings of the First Internat. Symposium on Biomechanics in Swimming, pp. 197–198. Presse Universitaire de Bruxelles, Brussels.

Åstrand, P. O., and Engelsson, S. 1972. A swimming flume. J. Appl. Physiol. 33:514.

Åstrand, P. O., Engström, L. D. O., Eriksson, R., Karlberg, V., Nylander, I., Saltin, B., and Thoren, C. 1963. Girl swimmers. Acta Paediatr. (suppl. 147).

Beckman, E. L., Coburn, K. R., Chambers, R. M., DeForest, R. E., Augerson, W. S., and Benson, V. G. 1961. Physiologic changes observed in human subjects during zero G simulation by immersion in water up to neck level. Aerospace Med. 32:1031–1041.

Belokovsky, V. 1968. Cited in: V. M. Zaciorsky, and I. G. Safarian, 1972. Untersuchung von faktoren zur bestimmung der maximalen geschwindigkeit im freistilschwimmen (Investigation of factors for the determination of maximal speed in free style swimming). Theor. Prax. Körperkult. 8:695–709.

Björkman, S. 1972. The swimmer's treadmill. Swimming Tech. 8:122–123.

Blanksby, B. A. 1973. Biomechanics of swimming. Int. Swimmer 12:6–8.

Boxem, A. 1958. Meting van stuwkracht bij zwemmers (The measurement of swimming propulsion). Unpublished, Fysiologic laboratory Utrecht.

Boxem, A. 1960. Meting van stuwkracht bij zwemmers (The measurement of swimming propulsion). An arrangement by L. Mosterd of a dissertation by Boxem (1958). Konikl. Ned. Akad. Wetenschap. Proc. C63:664-675.

Broer, M. 1973. *Efficiency of Human Movement*, 3rd Ed. W. B. Saunders Company, Philadelphia.

Campbell, C. R. 1948. A study of the relationship of arm and shoulder strength to speed and endurance in freestyle swimming. Master's thesis, State University of Iowa, Iowa City.

Cannon, P. R. N. 1963. Cold immersion. J. Roy. Naval Med. Sci. 49:88-92.

Carlson, L. D., Hsieh, A. C., Fullington, F., and Elsner, R. W. 1958. Immersion in cold water and body tissue insulation. J. Aviation Med. 29:145-152.

Clarys, J. P. 1976. Onderzoek naar de hydrodynamische en morfologische aspekten van het menselijk lichaam (Investigation of the hydrodynamical and morphological aspects of the human body). Ph.D. thesis, Vrije Universiteit Brussel, Brussels.

Clarys, J. P., and Jiskoot, J. 1974. Aspects de la résistance à l'avancement lors de différentes positions du corps chez le nageur (Aspects of resistance to forward movement due to different positions of the swimmer's body). Travail Humain 37:323-324.

Clarys, J. P., and Jiskoot, J. 1975. Total resistance of selected body positions in the frontcrawl. In: J. P. Clarys and L. Lewillie (eds.), Swimming II, pp. 110-117. University Park Press, Baltimore.

Clarys, J. P., Jiskoot, J., and Lewillie, L. 1973. A kinematographic, electromyographic and resistance study of waterpolo and competition frontcrawl. In: S. Cerguiglini, A. Venerando, and J. Wartenweiler (eds.), Biomechanics III, pp. 446-452. S. Karger Verlag, Basel.

Clarys, J. P., Jiskoot, J., Rijken, H., and Brouwer, P. J. 1974. Total resistance in water and its relation to body form. In: R. C. Nelson and C. A. Morehouse (eds.), Biomechanics IV, pp. 187-196. University Park Press, Baltimore.

Costill, D. L. 1966. Use of a swimming ergometer in physiological research. Res. Q. 37:564-567.

Counsilman, J. E. 1951. An analysis of the application of force in two types of crawl stroke. Ph.D. thesis, State University of Iowa, Iowa City.

Counsilman, J. E. 1955. Forces in swimming two types of crawl stroke. Res. Q. 26, 2:127-139.

Cureton, T. K. 1930. Mechanics and kinesiology of swimming. Res. Q. 1:87-121.

Cureton, T. K. 1943. Warfare Aquatics, Course Syllabus and Activities Manual Styles. Stiles Publishing Company, Champaign Ill.

De Goede, J., Jiskoot, J., and Van der Sluis, A. 1971. Over stuwkracht bij zwemmers (On the propulsion of swimmers). Zwemkroniek 48:77-90.

De Raeve, G. 1974. Studie van het drijfvermogen bij vrouwelijke zwemmers (Study of buoyancy of female swimmers). Master's thesis, Vrije Universiteit Brussel, Brussels.

di Prampero, P. E., Pendergast, D. R., Wilson, D. W., and Rennie, D. W. 1974. Energetics of swimming in man. J. Appl. Physiol. 37:1-5.

Du Bois-Reymond, R. 1927. Der wasserwinderstand des menschlichen körpers (The water resistance of human bodies). Pflügers Arch. 216:770-773.

Duffield, M. H. 1969. Exercise in Water. Bailière, Tindall, and Cussel, London.

Egolinskii, E. A. 1940. Expenditure of energy in competitive swimming. J. Physiol. 28:700-706.

Eriksson, B. D., Holmr, I., and Lundin, A. 1974. Maximal oxygen uptake, maximal ventilation and maximal heart rate during swimming compared to running. Acta Paediatr. Belg. (suppl. 28):68-78.

Faulkner, J. A. 1966. Physiology of swimming. Res. Q. 37:41-54.

Faulkner, J. A. 1968. Physiology of swimming and diving. In: H. B. Falls (ed.), Exercise Physiology, pp. 415-466. Academic Press, Inc., New York.

Forsyth, J. L., and Sinning, W. E. 1973. The anthropometric estimation of body density and lean body weight of male athletes. Med. Sci. Sports 5:174-180.

Francis, P., and Dean, N. 1975. A biomechanical model for swimming performance. In: J. P. Clarys and L. Lewillie (eds.), Swimming II, pp. 118-124. University Park Press, Baltimore.

Froude, W. 1872. Experiments on the surface friction experienced by a plane moving through the water. Report of the British Association for the Advancement of Science.

Gadd, G. F. 1963. The hydrodynamics of swimming. New Sci. 355:483-485.

Goldfuss, A. G., and Nelson, R. C., 1971. A temporal and force analysis of the crawl arm stroke during tethered swimming. In: L. Lewillie and J. P. Clarys (eds.), Proceedings of the First Symposium on Biomechanics in Swimming, pp. 129-142. Presse Universitaire de Bruxelles, Brussels.

Gordon, S. M. 1969. Cited in: V. M. Zaciorsky and I. G. Safarian, 1972. Untersuchung von faktoren zur bestimmung der maximalen geschwindigkeit im freistilschwimmen (Investigation of factor for the determination of maximum speed in free style swimming). Theor. Prax. Körperkult. 8:695-709.

Greene, M. M. 1930. The energy cost of track running and swimming. Master's thesis, University of Springfield, Springfield, Mass.

Guilbert, P. R. 1970. La flottabilite du nageur (The buoyancy of the swimmer). Bull. Liaison E.N.C.E.P.S. 17:21-24.

Hairabedian, A. 1965. Kinetic resistance factors related to body position in swimming. Ph.D. thesis, Stanford University, Stanford.

Hairabedian, A. 1966. Kinetic resistance factors. Swimming Tech. 2:105-106.

Hayez-Delatte, F. 1967. Le dimorphisme sexuel (Sexual demography). Biomet. Hum. II:147-178.

Highmore, G. 1955. An initial investigation into the nature of human flotation. Phys. Educ. 47:148, 5-11.

Holmér, I. 1971. Oxygen uptake during swimming at different speeds in the aquatic swim mill. In: L. Lewillie and J. P. Clarys (eds.), Proceedings of the First International Symposium on Biomechanics in Swimming, pp. 199-205. Presse Universitaire de Bruxelles, Brussels.

Holmér, I. 1972. Oxygen uptake during swimming in man. J. Appl. Physiol. 33:502-509.

Holmér, I. 1974a. Physiology of swimming man. Acta Physiol. Scand. (suppl. 407).

Holmér, I. 1974b. Energy cost of arm stroke, leg kick and the whole stroke in competitive swimming styles. Eur. J. Appl. Physiol. 33:105-118.

Holmér, I. 1974c. Propulsive efficiency of breaststroke and freestyle swimming. Eur. J. Appl. Physiol. 33:95-103.

Holmér, I. 1975. Efficiency of breaststroke and free-style swimming. In: J. P. Clarys and L. Lewillie (eds.), Swimming II, pp. 130-136. University Park Press, Baltimore.

Holmér, I., and Åstrand, P. O. 1972. Swimming training and maximal oxygen uptake. J. Appl. Physiol. 23:510-513.

Holmér, I., Lundin, A., and Eriksson, B. O. 1974. Maximal oxygen uptake during swimming and running by elite swimmers. J. Appl. Physiol. 36:711-714.

Houssay, R. 1912. Forme, Puissance et Stabilité des Poissons (Form, Force and Stability of Fish). Hermann et Fils, Paris.

Howell, M. L., Moncrieff, J., and Morford, W. R. 1962. Relationship between human buoyancy measures, specific gravity and estimated body fat in adult males. Res. Q. 33:400-404.

Jaeger, L. D. 1937. Resistance of water as a limiting factor of speed in swimming. Master's thesis, State University of Iowa, Iowa City.

Jensen, R. K., and Blanksby, B. 1975. A model for upper extremity forces during the underwater phase of the frontcrawl. In: J. P. Clarys and L. Lewillie (eds.), Swimming II, pp. 145-153. University Park Press, Baltimore.

Jiskoot, J., and Clarys, J. P. 1975. Body resistance on and under the water surface. In: J. P. Clarys and L. Lewillie (eds.), Swimming II, pp. 105-109. University Park Press, Baltimore.

Jones, P. R. M., Worth, W. J. C., Stone, P. G., Ellis, M. J., and Jeffrey, A. 1965. The influence of somatotype and anthropometric measures on heart rate during work in students and specialist sporting groups. Loughborough College of Technology, Loughborough.

Jurina, K. 1972-1974. Comparative study of swimming of fish and men. Translated from Russian (Theor. Praxe Telesne Vychovy 20:161-166) and Spanish (Novidades Natacion, Madrid, pp. 19-28).

Karpovich, P. V. 1933. Water resistance in swimming. Res. Q. 4:21-28.

Karpovich, P. V., and Lemaistre, F. H. 1940. Prediction of time in swimming the breaststroke based on oxygen consumption. Res. Q. 11:40-44.

Karpovich, P. V., and Millman, N. 1944. Energy expenditure in swimming. Am. J. Physiol. 142:140-144.

Karpovich, P. V., and Pestrecov, K. 1939. Mechanical work and efficiency in swimming crawl and back strokes. Arbeits. Physiol. 10:504-515.

Katch, F. I., and McArdle, W. D. 1973. Prediction of body density from simple anthropometric measurements in college men and women. Human Biol. 45:445-454.

Katch, F., Michael, E. D., and Horvalth, S. M. 1967. Estimation of body volume by underwater weighing. Description of a method. J. Appl. Physiol. 23:811-813.

Keatinge, W. R. 1939. Survival in Cold Water. Blackwell Scientific Publications, Oxford.

Keatinge, W. R. 1978. Cold immersion: Survival and resuscitation. In: B. Eriksson and B. Furberg (eds.), Swimming Medicine IV, pp. 305-309. University Park Press, Baltimore.

Kemper, H. C. G., Verschuur, R., Clarys, J. P., Jiskoot, J., and Rijken, H. 1976. Efficiency in swimming the front crawl. In: P. Komi (ed.), Biomechanics VB, pp. 243-249. University Park Press, Baltimore.

Kent, M. R., and Atha, J. 1971. Selected critical transient body positions in breast stroke and their influence upon water resistance. In: L. Lewillie and J. P. Clarys (eds.), Proceedings of the First International Symposium on Biomechanics in Swimming, pp. 119-126. Presse Universitaire de Bruxelles, Brussels.

Klauck, J., and Daniel, K. 1976. The determination of man's drag coefficients and effective propelling forces in swimming by means of chronocyclography. In: P. Komi (ed.), Biomechanics VB, pp. 250-257. University Park Press, Baltimore.

Klein, W. C. 1939. Tests for the prediction of body resistance in water. Master's thesis, State University of Iowa, Iowa City.

Kramer, M. D. 1960. Boundary layer stabilization by distributed damping. J. Am. Soc. Naval Eng. 72:25-33.

Kramer, M. D. 1962. Boundary layer stabilization by distributed damping. J. Am. Soc. Naval Eng. 74:341-348.

Kruchoski, E. P. 1954. A performance analysis of drag an propulsion in three selected forms of the back crawl. Ph.D. thesis, State University of Iowa, Iowa City.

Lane, E. C., and Mitchum, J. C. 1963. Buoyancy's predicted by certain anthropometric measurements. Res. Q. 35:21-26.

Lap, A. J. W. 1954. Fundamentals of Ship Resistance and Propulsion. National Shipbuilding Progress (Publ. 129a; N.S.M.B.), Rotterdam.

Laubach, L. L., and McConville, J. T. 1966. Relationship between flexibility anthropometry and the somatotype of college men. Res. Q. 37:241-251.

Liljestrand, G., and Stenström, N. 1919. Studiën über die physiologie des schwimmens (Studies of the physiology of swimmers). Scand. Arch. Physiol. 39:1-63.

Lipke, L. 1974. Differences of the oxygen intake values determined during free swimming and during tests on the bicycle ergometer. Third Medico Scientific Conference of FINA, Barcelona.

Lopin, V. 1947. A diagnostic test for speed in swimming the crawl stroke. Master's thesis, State University of Iowa, Iowa City.

Maas, G. D. 1974. An anthropometric study of Dutch sportsmen. Ph.D. thesis, Universitaire pers, Leiden.

Magel, J. R. 1970. Propelling force measured during tethered swimming in the four competitive swimming styles. Res. Q. 41:68-74.

Magel, J. R. 1971. Comparison of the physiologic response to varying intensities of submaximal work in tethered swimming and treadmill running. J. Sports Med. Phys. Fitness 11:203-312.

Magel, J. R., and McArdle, D. W. 1970. Propelling force and metabolic and circulatory considerations in swimming. Scholastic Coach 40:58-67.

Magel, J. R., and Faulkner, J. A. 1967. Maximum oxygen uptake of college swimmers. J. Appl. Physiol. 22:929-933.

Magel, J. R., Foglia, G. F., McArdle, W. D., Gutin, B., Pechar, G. S., and Katch, F. I. 1975. Specificity of swimming training on maximum oxygen uptake. J. Appl. Physiol. 38:151-155.

Malzahn, K. D., and Stafenk, W. 1973. Zur effektivität verschiedener bewegungsvarianten im burst- und kraul-schwimmen (The effectiveness of different movement variations in breast and crawl stroke swimming). Theor. Prax. Körperkult. 22:724-735.

Martin, R., and Saller, K. 1957. Lehrbuch der Anthropologie (Textbook of Anthropology). Gustav Fisher Verlag, Stuttgart.

Martinez, R. H. 1960. Physiologic effects of swimming 100 yard races in H_2O of 5 temperatures. Ph.D. thesis, State University of Iowa, Iowa City.

McArdle, W. D., Glaser, R. M., and Magel, J. R. 1971. Metabolic and cardiorespiratory response during free swimming and treadmill walking. J. Appl. Physiol. 30:733-738.

Michael, E. D., and Katch, F. I. 1968. Predictions of body density and percent body fat from skin fold and girth measurements of 17-year old boys. J. Appl. Physiol. 25:747-750.

Miyashita, M. 1974. Method of calculating mechanical power in swimming the breast stroke. Res. Q. 45:128-137.

Miyashita, M., and Tsunoda, R. 1978. Water resistance in relation to body size. In: B. Eriksson and B. Furberg (eds.), Swimming Medicine IV, pp. 395-401. University Park Press, Baltimore.

Miyashita, M., Hayashi, Y., and Furuhaski, H. 1970. Maximum oxygen intake of Japanese top swimmers. J. Sports Med. Phys. Fitness 10:211-216.

Molnar, G. W. 1946. Survival of hypothermia by man immersed in the ocean. JAMA 131:1046-1050.

Mosterd, W. L. 1960. Analysis of the propelling force in swimming the breast stroke and the dolphin breast stroke. Konikl. Ned. Akad. Wetenschap. Proc. C63:394-399.

Mosterd, W. L. 1961. Stuwkrachtmeting en slaganalyse bij getrainede zwemmers (The measurement and analyses of the propulsion of trained swimmers). Ph.D. thesis, Universiteit van Utrecht.

Mosterd, W. L., and Jongbloed, J. 1962. Analysis of the stroke of highly trained swimmers. Arbeitsphysiologie 20:288-293.

Nielsen, B. 1978. Physiology of thermoregulation during swimming. In: B. Eriksson and B. Furberg (eds.), Swimming Medicine IV, pp. 297-304. University Park Press, Baltimore.

Onoprienko, B. I. 1961. The force of swimming movement in different swimming technique (translation from Russian). Theor. Pract. Phys. Educ. (U.S.S.R.) 4:842-847.

Onoprienko, B. I. 1967. Influence of hydrodynamic data on the hydrodynamics of the swimmers (translation from Russian). Theor. Pract. Phys. Educ. (U.S.S.R.) 10:47-57.

Pendergast, D. R., di Prampero, P., A., Graig, and Rennie, D. 1978. The influence of selected biomechanical factors on the energy cost of swimming. In: B. Eriksson and B. Furberg (eds.), Swimming Medicine IV, pp. 367-378. University Park Press, Baltimore.

Poulos, G. E. 1949. An analysis of the propulsion factors in the American crawl stroke. Master's thesis, State University of Iowa, Iowa City.

Prandtl, L. 1904. Ueber Flüssigkeitsbewegung (Concerning Speed of Fluid Flow). Handwörterbuch der Naturwissenschaften (Dictionary of Natural Science), part IV. Gustav Fisher, Jena.

Prandtl, L. 1952. Essentials of Fluid Dynamics. Blackie Publications, London.

Pugh, L. G. C., and Edholm, O. G. 1955. The physiology of channel swimmers. Lancet II:761-768.

Rennie, D. W., di Prampero, P., Wilson, D. R. and Pendergast, D. R. 1973. Energetics of swimming the crawl stroke. Fed. Proc. 32(abstr.):1125.

Rennie, D. W., Pendergast, D. R., and di Prampero, P. E. 1975. Energetics of swimming in man. In: J. Clarys and L. Lewillie (eds.), Swimming II, pp. 97-104. University Park Press, Baltimore.

Rork, R., and Hellebrandt, F. A. 1937. The floating ability of women. Res. Q. 8:20-27.

Rouse, H. 1946. Elementary Mechanics of Fluids. John Wiley & Sons, Inc., New York.

Safarian, I. G. 1968. Hydrodynamic characteristics of the crawl (translation from Russian). Theor. Pract. of Phys. Educ. (U.S.S.R.) 11:18-21.

Schlichting, H. 1960. Boundary Layer Theory, 4th Ed. McGraw-Hill Book Company, New York.

Schmelkes, B. 1935-1936. Contribution to research in gaseous exchange in swimming. Przel. Fizjol. Ruchu. 7:201-206.

Schramm, E. 1958-1959. Untersuchungsmethode zur bestimmung des widerstandes der kraft und der ausdauer bei schwimm sportlern. (Research techniques for the determination of drag forces of swimming teachers). Wiss. Z. Deutsch. Hochshule Körperkult. Leipzig. 1:161-180.

Schramm, E. 1960-1961. Die abhängigkeit der leistungen im kraulschwimmen vom kraft widerstand—verhältenus (The independence of performances in crawl swimming from the drag ratio). Wiss. Z. Deutsch. Hochshule. Körperkult. Leipzig. 3:161-180.

Secher, N. H., and Odderschede, I. 1975. Maximal oxygen uptake rate during swimming and bicycling. In: J. P. Clarys and L. Lewillie (eds.), Swimming II, pp. 137-144. University Park Press, Baltimore.

Seireg, A., and Baz, A. 1971. A mathematical model for swimming mechanics. In: L. Lewillie and J. P. Clarys (eds.), Proceedings of the First International Symposium on Biomechanics in Swimming pp. 81-104. Presse Universitaire de Bruxelles, Brussels.

Shepperd, R. J., Godin, G., and Campbell, C. 1974. Characteristics of sprint, medium and long distance swimmers. Eur. J. Appl. Physiol. 32:99-116.

Taggart, R. 1966. Propulsive efficiency of man in the sea. Naval Eng. J. 34:17-24.

Tanner, J. M. 1962. Growth at Adolescence, 2nd Ed. Blackwell Scientific Publications, Oxford.

Tanner, J. M. 1964. The Physique of Olympic Athletes. G. Allen and Unwin, London.

Tews, R. W. J. 1941. The relationship of propulsive force and external resistance to speed in swimming. Master's thesis, State University of Iowa, Iowa City.

Thrall, W. R. 1960. A performance analysis of the propulsion force of the flutter kick. Ph.D. thesis, University of Iowa, Iowa City.

Twiesselman, F. 1952. Aide-mémoire d'Anthropometrie (Guide to Anthropometry). Inst. Royal Colonial Belge, Mémoire, 25 Fasc. 4.

Twiesselman, F. 1969. Développment Biométrique de l'Enfant à l'Adulte (Biometrical Development from Child to Adult). Presse Universitaire de Bruxelles, Brussels.

Van Huss, W. D., and Cureton, T. K. 1954. Relationship of selected tests with energy metabolism and swimming performance. Res. Q. 26:205-221.

Van Lammeren, W. P. A., Troost, L., and Koning, J. G. 1948. Resistance propulsion and steering of a ship. H. Stam Technical Publishing Co., Amsterdam.

Weinbach, A. P. 1938. Contour map, center of gravity, moment of inertia, and surface area of the human body. Human Biol. 10:356-371.

Whiting, H. T. A. 1963. Variations in floating ability with age in the male. Res. Q. 34:84-90.

Wilkinson, E. 1973. The swimmers treadmill. Swim. Times (July):36.

Wilmore, J. H., and Behnke, A. R. 1969. An anthropometric estimation of body density and lean body weight in young men. J. Appl. Physiol. 27:25-31.

Zaciorsky, V. M., and Safarian, I. G. 1972. Untersuchung von factoren zur bestimmung der maximalen geschwindigkeit im freistilschwimmen (Investigation of factors for the determination of maximal speed in free style swimming). Theor. Prax. Körperkult. 8:695-709.

Zuti, W. B., and Golding, L. A. 1973. Equations for estimating percent fat and body density of active adult males. Med. Sci. Sports 5:262-266.

Propulsion, Lift, Drag, and Efficiency

The Mechanism for Body Propulsion in Swimming

K. M. Barthels

In recent years explanations of propulsion in swimming have focused attention on the nature of drag and lift forces, but few have addressed the way in which these forces can provide translation of the total body through the water. Indeed, it is the understanding of that process that is basic to quality teaching and coaching as well as to proper design of research experiments and mathematical models. Those who are involved in developing mathematical models for human swimming need to have a valid conceptual model for propulsion if they are to reflect and to predict quantifiable variations in performance.

Models or analogies that have been put forth to represent human swimming have included such man-made propulsive devices as the paddle wheel and the propeller, as well as the propulsive movements of aquatic mammals, reptiles, birds, and fishes. Human beings have movement and shape characteristics that are different from other segmented animals, which create both disadvantages and advantages in terms of aquatic locomotion. For example, although our bodies and limbs are not ideally suited for underwater locomotion, the degrees of freedom available within the spine, arms, and legs, and the fin-like shapes of our hands and feet, plus the creative intelligence to utilize these assets, permits our adaptation to movement in water, which is unique to human beings.

PURPOSE

This paper offers a qualitative model of the swimming mechanism that is the result of an attempt to piece together, into a meaningful whole, the isolated bits of information currently at our disposal. Within this modest proposal is an attempt to provide a logical rationale for the desirability of generating maximum forward lift force and minimum forward drag force on the body segments as the most efficient combination to be used for propelling the body.

RELATIVE MOTION AND FLUID FORCES

Most descriptions of swimming define limb movements relative to the swimmer's body. The popularity of this viewpoint undoubtedly stems from the perception of what the arms and legs *seem* to be doing in a stroke as well as from what the limbs *appear* to be doing from the point of view of the observer. As a result of such kinesthetic and visual impressions, the true nature of the forces that are operating usually remains obscure. To identify the forces and counterforces that are produced by the swimmer's movements in the water, it is necessary to focus on the nature of the flow of water past the moving part because it is this flow, relative to the *limb*, that is responsible for the forces used for propulsion (Alexander, 1968).

Consider the two types of force that can be produced by a swimmer's hand and arm as it moves through the water: drag force and lift force (Shapiro, 1961). Drag force, commonly thought of as resistance against the swimmer's forward progress, also acts against the moving body segments. The direction of the drag force is always opposite the direction of segment motion. When drag force on the body segments acts in the forward direction, it is called *propulsive drag*. This propulsive drag results from a paddling or pushing motion of the hands through the water and tends to resist the backward hand motion. A high pressure zone is created on the palm, and a low pressure zone is created on the back of the hand. The faster the hand movement and/or the larger the hand, the greater the drag force produced against its motion. Figure 1 shows how a drag force is produced on the hand if it moves through the water so that it creates a flow directed against the palm.

A popular notion is that to move the body directly forward, the swimmer must pull or push his hands, used as paddles, directly backward through the water. It is true that great pressure is felt on the hands and arms when this is done, and this pressure has been interpreted by the performers as being the force responsible for body propulsion. If the hand is pushed backward slowly, less force is perceived. Therefore, the swimmer who wishes to swim fast tends to pull his hands back through the water as fast as he can to feel the most force against them in the forward direction. On face value this reasoning may seem valid. However, it is important to remember that the purpose of the arm movements is to move the swimmer's whole body forward, not merely to feel a great amount of pressure on his hands.

IDEAL AND ACTUAL SWIMMING MECHANISMS

To approach what is proposed as the swimming mechanism responsible for progress through the water, consider the following. The ideal circumstance would be one in which the hand could grip an underwater

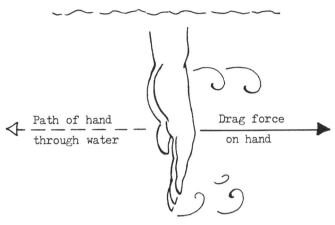

Figure 1. Drag force on the hand caused by its backward motion through water.

handle that would not slip backward as the hand pulled on it. With such a handle, the contraction of the arm and shoulder muscles would then cause the body to be pulled forward toward and past this handle as the arm moved through its range of motion at the joints. However, if this underwater handle were not fixed solidly within a section of water, but slipped backward relative to the water as the hand pulled on it, then by the time the arm had moved through the same joint range of motion as before, the body unit would not have been moved forward through the water as far. Instead, the body unit would be moved forward only a small distance as the hand pushing on the slipping handle moved backward. Figure 2 illustrates the effect on body progress when the hand uses a hypothetical fixed handle and when it uses a slipping handle. Because the purpose of a stroke is to move the body mass forward, any backward hand movement through the water results in less forward motion of the body per arm stroke. Recall now that forward-directed drag force on the hand is produced only when the hand moves backward relative to the water. If drag force on the hand were to form a handle used for propulsion, it would have to be a "slipping handle." Moreover, if a greater drag force were needed to provide a greater counterforce, the hand would have to move backward through the water even faster, thus yielding even less forward body motion by the time the arm reached the end of its underwater stroking movement. Such straight back hand motion is not characteristic of skilled swimmers' movements, even though they may feel as if their hands pull backward through the water (Brown and Counsilman, 1970; Barthels, 1977). The inefficiency of using the hands solely to create a forward-directed drag force by pushing straight back through the water is apparent from the analogy provided.

The other type of force that can be produced by a swimmer's hand

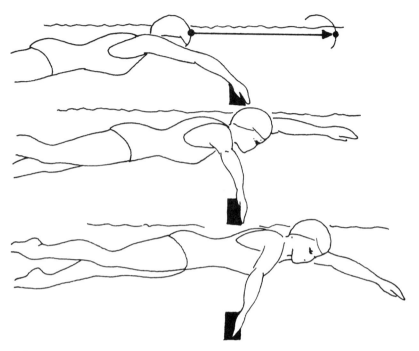

(a) Forward displacement of body if the hand were "fixed"
     in a section of water during the pulling effort

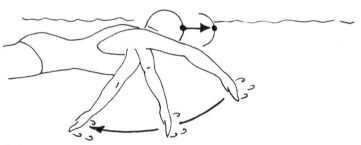

(b) Forward displacement of body if the hand moves back
     through the water during the pulling effort

Figure 2. Comparison of the forward movement of the body as a result of the hands pulling on a "fixed" handle and on a slipping handle.

motion through the water is lift force. Hydrodynamic lift is the type of force that is generated in a direction perpendicular to the flow direction past a foil-shaped object, such as the hand, moving through the water. The hand must be oriented in a certain position relative to the flow direction past it for lift to be generated. Such orientation of the foil is described

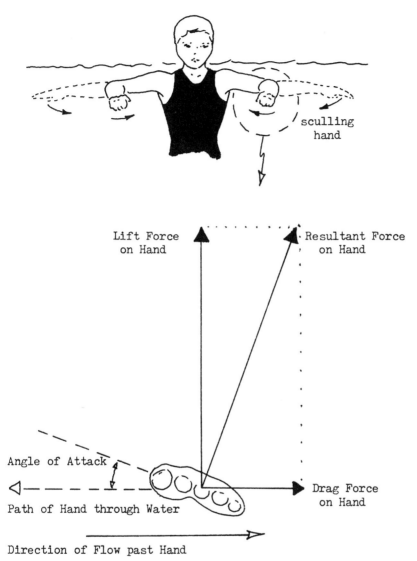

Figure 3. Generation of lift and drag forces on the sculling hand while treading water. The lift force, perpendicular to the path of the hand through the water, is used for support.

by its angle of attack, which is the angle formed between the direction of flow and the chord of the foil. The chord of the foil may be thought of as the major plane of the foil. The lift force is felt as pressure on the palm when the slightly tilted hand slices or blades through the water, as in sculling movements.

Figure 3 shows the hand blading through the water and being subjected to a lift force caused by a low pressure zone across the back side of the hand and a high pressure zone on the palm. This lift-force producing motion of the hands is used for treading water without using the legs. In this example, the hands are used as foils, and the arms move horizontally so that broad blading, or sculling, movements provide a "layer of force" for the hands to use to support the weight of the head above the water's surface. Note that the angle of attack must be small so that the palms are facing primarily toward the feet as they scull. The flow must encounter the palmar surface of the hand as it blades medially and laterally, so the lateral sweep demands more forearm pronation to produce the proper angle of attack for the hand.

Lift force, like drag, is a function of speed, and the faster the foil moves through the water at an effective angle of attack, the greater will be the lift force produced. It is unfortunate that the term "lift" is given to this type of force because the immediate assumption is that it always acts in an upward direction, which, of course, it does not. Note that there is also a drag force acting directly against the hand's motion. The drag is perpendicular to the lift force. If the angle of attack becomes too large, the drag force increases and the flow becomes so turbulent that lift force is lost (stall occurs). For a given foil shape and velocity, it is possible to obtain an angle of attack that will provide maximum lift force. Figure 3 shows the lift, the drag, and the resultant of these two forces acting on the sculling hand treading. Even though the resultant force is not directly upward, it is the upward component of the total force that counteracts the downward pressing of the arms. This upward force generated on the hands serves as a stable handle, and with fixation of the shoulder joint by the adductor muscles, the arm unit will not be abducted further, and the head will be supported above the surface. Note that the hands are not used as pushing paddles i.e., they do not push down toward the feet for upward support. In the treading example, lift force is being used as supportive lift force and is directed vertically up to counter the tendency of the body to sink down.

When the hands are used in a similar fashion within a swimming arm stroke pattern, the palms should be facing primarily back toward the feet, and the resulting lift force on the hand would be directed forward toward the direction of body travel. The lift force would be used then as a force resisting backward hand movement when the shoulder muscles shortened. Consequently, to move the body unit forward through the water, there must be greater forward force on the hand and arm than there is backward force on the body. This forward force on the hand can be generated only if relative motion exists between the water and the hand. When the shoulder extensor and adductor muscles contract and shorten, therefore, the body would be moved forward relative to the hand and the water. If

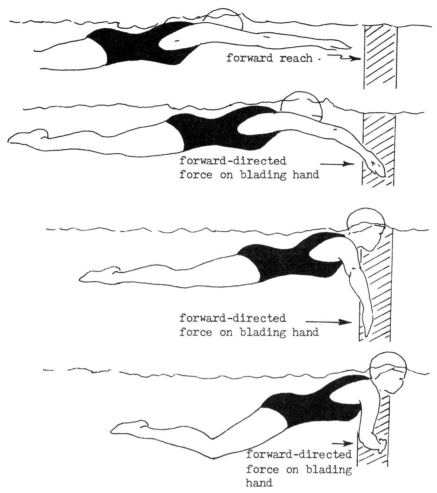

Figure 4. Generation of lift force on the hand as it blades through a vertical section of water with minimal backward motion. As the shoulder muscles shorten, the body unit is pulled forward past the hand, which is prevented from moving backward by the forward-directed lift force.

the hand can be made to blade in a vertical plane in the water, the forward-directed lift force on the hand would provide a fairly stable handle, and the contraction of the muscles would pull the body unit forward. The more effective the sculling hand is in generating forward lift, the greater is the stability of the handle, and the less backward movement, or wasted movement, there is by the hand. Figure 4 illustrates such an ideal case.

Highly skilled swimmers demonstrate just such a "handle" effect whenever their hands are made to scull in planes perpendicular to the

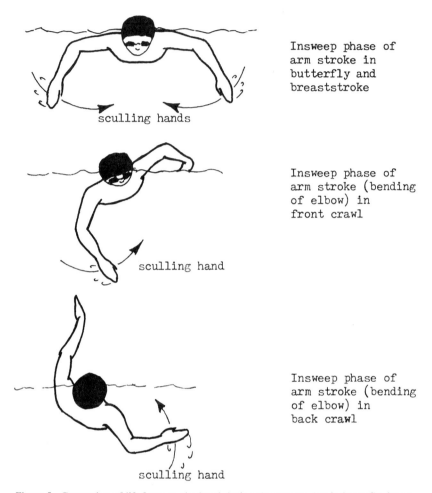

Insweep phase of
arm stroke in
butterfly and
breaststroke

Insweep phase of
arm stroke (bending
of elbow) in
front crawl

Insweep phase of
arm stroke (bending
of elbow) in
back crawl

Figure 5. Generation of lift force on the hand during the arm strokes in butterfly, breaststroke, front crawl, and back crawl. Maximum sculling speed of the hand occurs during
elbow flexion.

direction of body travel. The hands do not move directly backward
through still water, although that is usually the kinesthetic impression of
the swimmer. Figure 5 shows the formation of such propulsive lift force
during elbow flexion in the breaststroke, butterfly, front crawl, and back
crawl. Propulsive lift can be seen to operate in other, noncompetitive,
styles of swimming. If the "bent-elbow stroking" seen in the competitive
styles is examined closely, it will be evident that it is not the *bent* elbow per
se that is the important part of the stroke but the *bending* of the elbow
that gives the hand speed as it sculls for forward lift.

The propulsive mechanism involved in the breaststroke kick is very

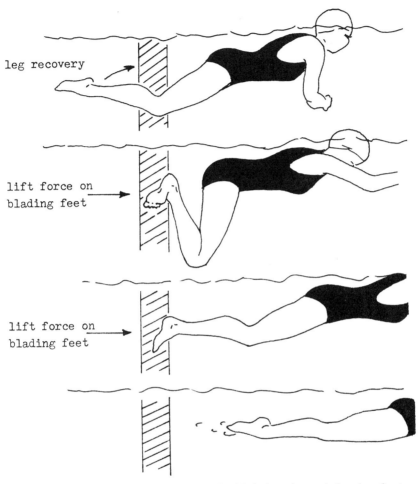

Figure 6. Generation of lift force on the feet as they blade through a vertical section of water to form a "force wall" against which the legs extend to push the body unit forward in the breaststroke kick.

similar to that of the "lift force handles" created in the sculling arm strokes. As the feet are circled in a spiral-like path in a vertical plane behind the swimmer, the flow engages the sole of each foot at an angle of attack, and some lift force is generated on the foot in a forward direction. This lift force provides a "force wall" against which the legs can extend and push the body forward. The swimmer senses that his feet and legs are being thrust backward through the water because in extending the legs pressure is noticeable on the soles of the feet. Actually, the feet are sculling and remain in a vertical section of water while the body moves forward in response to leg extension. Figure 6 illustrates the movement of the body forward relative to the swimmer's feet, which are spiraled through the water to obtain a forward lift force. Just as in the case of the arm strokes, if the feet are moved through the water so that maximum forward lift is obtained, the body will move a greater distance forward per kick. The mechanism of undulatory propulsion as exhibited by fishes and aquatic mammals is analogous to that which occurs in the flutter kicks of the crawl strokes and of the dolphin butterfly. Consideration of this mechanism is beyond the scope of this discussion.

It is hoped that the foregoing presentation has clarified the process by which forward translation of the body occurs. Perhaps future swimming research might be directed to the expansion or modification of this theory. In any case, it is important that those who are engaged in investigating human swimming variables give some attention to how the results of their particular experiments fit into the total picture of the swimming mechanism.

REFERENCES

Alexander, R. M. 1968. Animal Mechanics. University of Washington Press, Seattle.
Barthels, K. M. 1977. Re-evaluation of swimming movements based upon research. In: M. Adrian and J. Brame (eds.), Research Reports, Vol. III, pp. 86–96. AAHPER, Washington, D.C.
Brown, R. M., and Counsilman, J. E. 1970. The role of lift in propelling the swimmer. In: J. M. Cooper (ed.), Selected Topics on Biomechanics, pp. 179–188. The Athletic Institute, Chicago.
Shapiro, A. H. 1961. Shape and Flow. Doubleday and Company, Inc., New York.

Optimizing Propulsion in Swimming by Rotation of the Hands

B. Ungerechts

The coach who is attempting to assist less talented swimmers is forced to increase his knowledge of the biomechanics of swimming because the average swimmer needs explicit instructions to approximate the proficiency of a champion. Biomechanics may be able to determine if the functional properties of the locomotor apparatus might fit the mechanical or the hydrodynamic demands. The hydrodynamic principles of competitive swimming have been recognized and listed (Reischle, 1976). The application of these principles in coaching or teaching, however, is in its early stages.

Normally, it is hoped that swimmers acquire a feeling for the details of highly skilled swimming through trial and error. In the early stages of learning, while obtaining the idea of the gross pattern this may be reasonable and sufficient. However, in the advanced stages this sort of learning will take a long time, perhaps too long for the swimmer to remain competitive. Knowledge of the functional properties of the locomotor system may help the swimmer to improve his performance.

PURPOSE

After the curvilinear stroke pattern made its way into competitive swimming the question arose as to whether the hand should be oriented normal to the flow or should be pitched. Hands, moved in a direction perpendicular to the oncoming flow, as in the paddles of a canoe, produce drag forces. Pitching the hand will create a lift force (Schleihauf, 1974), by which propelling thrust in swimming direction is increased.

The production of lift force is related to an optimal angle of attack (the angle between the axis of the hand and the actual oncoming direction of flow) and also to a correct hand position, with fully extended fingers that

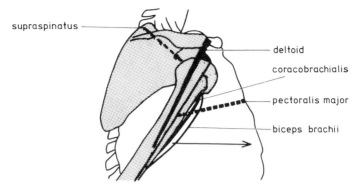

Figure 1. Muscles responsible for flexion of the humerus.

are slightly opened (Löhr and Ungerechts, 1976). This rough explanation of lift force production holds true only when the flow velocity does not
change. Because of the changing velocities of the hand (in magnitude or
direction) during a stroke cycle, the angle of pitch (angle between the surface of the water and the axis of the hand) must be adjusted constantly.
This fact has been derived from the study of twisted propeller blades of
airplanes (Bilo and Nachtigall, 1977).

Therefore, all phases of a stroke cycle must be considered, not only
selected sequences that are oriented toward the "S"-pattern stroke. The
latter fulfills a hydrodynamic law, which says that "efficient propulsion is
obtained by pushing a large mass of water a short distance without much
acceleration" (Counsilman, 1971). However, the "S" pattern itself does
not lead to lift force production per se.

It is also known that fishes control the angle of pitch in each phase of
their stroke, but this seems natural because they are adapted to swimming. This article shows that a backstroke swimmer, although not
adapted specifically to swimming, could do the same.

ACTIVITY OF MUSCLES

Descriptions of the activity of brachial muscles in relation to the various
phases of the stroke cycle are mostly confined to semiempirical data
because EMG studies during swimming are limited. The line of action of
the force developed by an individual muscle follows from its loci of origin
and insertion.

In Figure 1 the line of action of the muscles during flexion of the
shoulder joint is shown. The principle force is supplied by the anterior
fibers of the deltoid, the supraspinatus, and the coracobrachialis. The
pectoralis major with its clavicular fibers and the long head of the biceps
brachii are involved to a lesser extent.

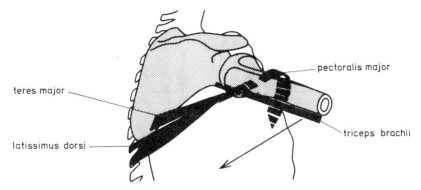

Figure 2. Adductors of the arm.

The adductors, which lower the lifted arm, are shown in Figure 2. The main adductors are the pectoralis major and the latissimus dorsi, which are strongly assisted by the teres major. The long head of the triceps brachii is also a strong adductor, in a lifted arm.

The pectoralis major and the teres major are also involved in medial rotation of the arm. They support the action of the subscapularis, which is the most powerful muscle for this turning motion (Figure 3).

The biceps brachii flexes the shoulder joint as well as the elbow joint. Its distal tendon is attached to the radius. The radius, carrying the hand with it, articulates with the ulna. Movements in the proximal radioulnar joint result in pronation or supination of the hand (Figure 4). Pronation is affected by the pronator quadratus and pronator teres. (In Figure 4 these muscles are prepared to twist the hand.) The radius is carried across the ulna, the thumb is moved toward the body, and the tendon of the biceps brachii is wound around the radius. In supination, the radius is situated lateral to and parallel with the ulna and the thumb is positioned laterally.

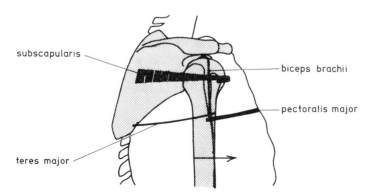

Figure 3. Muscles responsible for medial rotation.

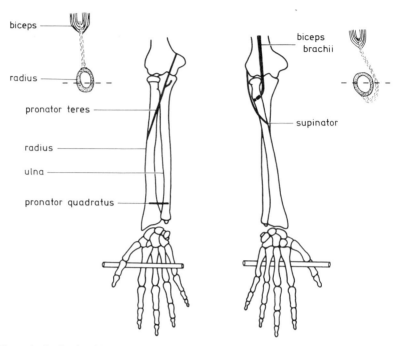

Figure 4. Supination (*left*) and pronation (*right*) with position of the tendons of the biceps brachii.

The most powerful supinator is the biceps brachii, which exerts its greatest flexing moment when the forearm is in supination. The only extensor of the elbow joint is the triceps brachii (Figure 2), which influences two joints. Its long head may assist in pulling a lifted arm backward and adducting it to the thorax.

ANALYSIS OF MUSCLE ACTION
DURING THE ARM CYCLE IN BACKSTROKE

At the beginning of the "transitional phase" the arm is extended, and the palm of the hand points toward the bottom of the swimming pool. The specific muscles contributing to the lifting of the arm out of the water correspond to those of flexion (Figure 1). When the hand is lifted out of the water, it is in a position between supination and pronation. It is then placed in "extreme pronation" by the pronator teres and pronator quadratus, and the tendon of the biceps brachii is wound around the radius. Having passed the "perpendicular position" above the body during the "recovery phase", the arm is under the influence of gravity. The following movement of the arm is controlled mostly by the muscles shown in Figure 1.

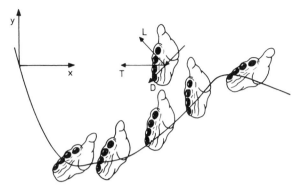

Figure 5.   Proposed hand position during the backstroke ("pull phase") L, lift; D, drag; T, thrust.

During the "introductory phase," in which "essential preliminary movements for the production of propulsion are created," (Wiegand, Wuensch, and Jaehnig, 1975), the arm is lowered deeper into the water. The elbow joint remains extended. The swimmer starts to roll about a longitudinal axis with the hand still in a pronated position.

At the beginning of the "propulsive phase," the hand starts to twist as a result of the action of the biceps brachii and the supinator. The innervation of the biceps brachii causes three effects; it: 1) supinates the forearm, 2) adducts the arm, and 3) flexes the elbow. Having passed its deepest position in the water, the hand, still supinated, is turned back in pronation by the action of the pronator teres. Moreover, the pronator teres flexes the elbow joint, assisting the biceps brachii. The hand should be rotated according to the flow pattern.

Bending of the elbow brings the hand near the surface. In its highest position, the palm is not oriented normal to the flow but is pitched. The elbow joint is flexed to an extent but not to its maximum. The arm is perpendicular to the body. This part of the propulsive phase is known as the "pull-phase" (Figure 5). While adductive motion is maintained, the flexed elbow is extended. The velocity of the hand is increased beyond that of the elbow.

The elbow joint is extended by the contraction of the triceps brachii. The shortening of the adductor muscles (Figure 2), which have been contracted all the time, leads to medial rotation of the arm. Because of their morphology and line of action the adductor muscles create an increasing rotary component when the arm is close to the body. By vectorial addition of the three movements (extension, adduction, and medial rotation), the hand is forced toward the feet on a curved line.

The subscapularis completes the medial rotation of the arm, and initiates the raising of the shoulder out of the water to make the final recovery of the arm much easier. At the end of the "propulsive phase," the palm of the hand is directed toward the bottom of the swimming pool.

CONCLUSION

The analysis of the specific muscles contributing to actual performance in the arm movements of the backstroke shows a useful interplay of the action of the muscles and hydrodynamic demands, especially rotation of the hand. At the beginning of the "propulsive phase" the stretched arm is flexed. The muscle initiating this flexion—the biceps brachii—generates its best mechanical efficiency when the forearm and the hand are in a position of supination. Because the hand is first pronated, it is necessary to place the hand thereafter in supination. This occurs just before the hand reaches its deepest position in the water.

Twisting of the hand facilitates the action of the biceps brachii. Moreover, the pronator teres is tensed and therefore is better prepared to assist in flexion of the elbow. Its contraction pronates the forearm, and the hand assumes a position, wherein lift force may be produced (Figure 4). This hand pattern is different from the popular opinion that the palmar surface should be oriented normal to the flow and should be moved normal to the direction of body motion. In the latter case propulsion is accomplished by drag. As Counsilman (1971) has shown, this is an ineffective way of producing propulsion, and will require more energy to obtain the same swimming speed compared with a pitched hand. The mechanical efficiency of the thrust-producing muscles is increased because the lift forces dominate the drag forces. Therefore, lift production should predominate not only during the "pull phase" but also during the "push phase" of the arm stroke. A swimmer has to alter slightly the coordination of his arm segments because he never experiences constant velocity since there are definite fluctuations in both magnitude and direction in each phase of the stroke. Conditions are also changed at higher swimming speeds.

Assumptions about the magnitude of the angle of attack cannot be made because little evidence is available about hand speed relative to a three-dimensional reference frame.

REFERENCES

Bilo, D., and Nachtigall, W. 1977. Biophysics of bird flight: Question and results. Fortschr. Zool. 24(2/3):217-234.
Counsilman, J. E. 1971. The application of Bernoulli's principle to human propulsion in water. In: L. Lewillie and J. P. Clarys (eds.), First International Symposium on Biomechanics in Swimming, pp. 59-71. Universitie Libre de Bruxelles, Brussels.

Löhr, R., and Ungerechts, B. 1976. Experimentelle Bestimmung der optimalen Fingerstellung beim Kraulschwimmen (Experimental determination of the optimal finger position in crawl swimming). Leistungssport 4:312-314.

Reischle, K. 1976. Das Antriebsproblem beim Schwimmen (The propulsive problem in swimming). Leistungssport 4:302-310.

Schleihauf, R. E. 1974. A biomechanical analysis of freestyle. Swimming Tech. 11:89.

Wiegand, D., Wuensch, D., and Jaehnig, W. 1975. The division of swimming strokes into phases, based upon kinematic parameters. In: L. Lewillie and J. P. Clarys (eds.), Swimming II, pp. 161-166. University Park Press, Baltimore.

A Fluid Dynamic Analysis of the Propulsive Potential of the Hand and Forearm in Swimming

T. C. Wood

For many years a predominant theory in swimming has been than momentum is achieved by the form drag force created by the hand (Counsilman, 1968), and swimmers have been advised to pull in a straight line, horizontally directly backward. Recently, however, observations of skilled swimmers by film analysis (Counsilman, 1969; Barthels and Adrian, 1975) have shown that this does not occur.

Deviating limb tracks in the alternating swimming strokes are clearly associated with movements counteractive to rotational forces generated elsewhere in the body and in the symmetrical strokes with anatomic and physiological considerations (Wood, 1978). It has been suggested that in following such deviating pathways the hand behaves as a fluid foil, creating forces of lift that act perpendicular to the direction of movement of the foil or hand. It has been suggested further that these lift forces, rather than form drag forces that operate in the opposite direction to the line of motion of the hand, are the main propulsive forces generated by the hands in swimming (Counsilman, 1969; Schleihauf, 1974).

This study arose out of this "lift versus drag" controversy and was designed to examine the fluid foil characteristics of the hand and forearm (Wood, 1977) in model form, in a controlled and measurable situation, to determine the nature and magnitude of the forces that the upper limb can generate.

METHOD

The problem was investigated by studying the behavior of hand and forearm models under conditions of air flow in a wind tunnel.

The author wishes to acknowledge the help of L. E. Holt, Ph.D., School of Physical Education, Dalhousie University, Halifax, Nova Scotia.

Independent Variables

One model left hand and forearm shape was taken from each of three swimmers of national caliber, in a shape shown by film observation to be favored by that swimmer in the strokes. Each hand and forearm unit was subjected to wind tunnel tests in two basic positions relative to the direction of flow. In test series I it was positioned laterally in each of 13 conditions, representing incremental changes of 15° through a total range of 180°. Conditions 1-7 provided flow at changing angles across the ulnar border, and conditions 7-13 were similar across the radial border. For test series II the unit was placed longitudinally—i.e., providing flow across the distal border in each of seven conditions, representing a changing angle of incidence of 15° through a total range of 90°. Each hand unit in each condition within each series was subjected to five different flow speeds, ranging from 60 ft/sec to 140 ft/sec. Measures were taken to control proximal end circulation and to prevent direct influence by the flow on anything except the foil.

Dependent Variables

The sting to which the hand shapes were mounted at their centers of gravity, in turn, permitted the measurement of drag and lift strains that were recorded for each wind speed, within each condition and each series. Drag and lift strain, through calibration, was then converted to drag and lift lb/force, drag and lift lb/ft,[2] and finally to drag and lift coefficients, which are nondimensional parameters representing the lift and drag of a body in a specific pattern of flow.

RESULTS

The results for all subjects showed marked similarities in all respects other than in the range and magnitude of forces generated and clearly showed that:

1. The hand has fluid foil characteristics, and under particular conditions of flow, and at certain orientations to the flow line, it is able to generate forces of both lift and drag.
2. With increasing velocities in any specific orientation both lift and drag forces increased in magnitude.
3. At fixed velocities with increasing angles of incidence, drag forces increased to a maximum at an orientation nominally perpendicular to the flow line.
4. At fixed velocities lift forces increased with increasing angles of incidence up to an angle of optimum lift, beyond which lift forces decreased gradually (Table 1).
5. At fixed velocities maximum drag forces exceeded maximum lift

forces, grossly in series I conditions, i.e., flow across the ulnar and radial borders but only very slightly under series II conditions, i.e., flow across the distal border (Table 2).

Table 1.   Averaged maximum lift coefficients at optimum angles of incidence in the different flow orientations for all subjects (flow speeds 100, 115, and 130 ft/sec)[a]

	C_L^{max}	Angle of incidence	$180° - Li°$	Flow
Subject 1, series I	(1-7)	0.4624	35°	ulnar
I	(7-13)	−.5957	125°	(55°) radial
II		1.0723	50°	distal
Subject 2, series I	(1-7)	0.4377	15°	ulnar
I	(7-13)	−.5320	120°+	(60°) radial
II		0.8807	55°	distal
Subject 3, series I	(1-7)	0.5711	35°	ulnar
I	(7-13)	−.6844	125°	(55°) radial
II		1.0127	50°	distal

[a]If the experiment notation for angle of incidence in the series I conditions 7-13 section is subtracted from 180° and the minus sign for the corresponding C_L is omitted, radial and ulnar flows in series I will be separated, and all angles of incidence can be compared more easily.

Table 2.   Maximum recorded values of coefficients of drag and lift with lb force/ft^2 conversions at a fixed velocity (130 ft/sec) for all subjects

Subject	Flow orientation	C_L^{max}	Lift (lb/ft^2)	C_D^{max}	Drag (lb/ft^2)
1	Ulnar	0.4378	8.6583		
	Radial	0.5334	10.5470		
	Distal	1.0706	21.1702	1.1008	21.7669
2	Ulnar	0.4165	9.2372		
	Radial	0.5326	10.5317		
	Distal	0.8921	17.6402	1.0650	21.0591
3	Ulnar	0.5478	10.9333		
	Radial	0.6712	13.2725		
	Distal	1.0166	20.1024	1.0682	21.1233

The notable measurement differences between subjects were considered to be a function of the difference in hand shapes, and the following findings resulted:

1. In the distal flow orientation the open-fingered shape of subject 2 produced markedly less lift than the closed-fingered shapes of subjects 1 and 3 (Table 2).
2. In the radial flow orientation the taper-pitched shape of subject 3, in the fashion of a propeller, sufficiently cancelled end circulation around the fingers to produce greater lift than the hand shapes of subjects 1 and 2 (Table 2).
3. The open-fingered shape of subject 2 produced as much form drag pressure as the closed-fingered shapes of subjects 1 and 3.

STUDY EXTENSION

The logical extension of the study was to use the data of the experiment in conjunction with data obtained from digitized film of one of the swimming strokes to determine:

1. The nature and magnitude of the forces being generated at different stages in the stroke.
2. Whether or not the angles of incidence of the hand and forearm to the flow line shown in the stroke are sufficient to maximize the lift forces available at the hand speeds being used.

The filmed pathway of a swimmer using front crawl was digitized, and relevant data—hand velocities, angles of incidence—were extracted, and flow orientations—distal, radial, ulnar—were identified (Alexander, Holt, and Beer, 1974).

In equating the performance of the foil in the experimental situation in air to the observed swimming situation in water, Reynold's number was used (Equation 1). In the dynamically similar flow conditions of air and water where the Reynold's number has the same value, a direct comparison can be made, and velocity relationships can be established (Equation 2).

Using the equating velocities for the same hand in matching orientations to the flow line the forces being generated in water under these specified conditions utilizing coefficients of lift and drag (Equation 3) were computed:

$$R = \frac{\rho\,VD}{\mu} = \frac{VD}{\nu} \tag{1}$$

$$\text{Air}\,\frac{VD}{\nu} = R = \frac{VD}{\nu}\,\text{Water} \tag{2}$$

$$\text{Air} \frac{L}{1/2\rho V^2} = C_L = \frac{L}{1/2\rho V^2} \text{Water} \qquad (3)$$

where ρ = density of fluid (known for air and water), μ = viscosity of fluid (known for air and water), $\nu = \mu/\rho$ = kinematic viscosity (known for air and water), V = relative flow velocity (known for water from film observation), D = characteristic dimensions of the foil (the same for both situations), and L = lift, lb/ft^2 (known for air; to be calculated for water).

Vector analyses were made of the computed lift and drag forces generated at different stages in the stroke, and the horizontal components of these forces were calculated because it is these components that must be identified in a consideration of propulsion. Figures 1 and 2 show two of these vector analyses; the inserts show the entire pathway of pull, indicating the point of the stroke being analyzed.

Figure 1 shows an analysis from that section of the stroke, A to B, where the hand moves forward as it moves down, creating flow over the distal border, and in which there is an opposition of horizontal forces. Early in this section other analyses indicate that there is no propulsive contribution by the arm because the horizontal drag component acting backward completely negates the forward-acting lift component. As the vector rotates, however, the horizontal component of drag diminishes until eventually there is no horizontal component of drag and no vertical component of lift. At this stage (Figure 2) the propulsive force is entirely that of lift, which is considerable. Note that with an angle of 35° the possible maximum lift force is not being generated. An angle of incidence of 50° at this point, at the same hand velocity, would have produced 18.81 lb/ft^2 more propulsive force.

Early high elbow positions in front crawl have been advocated with the intention of placing the forearm perpendicular to the swim line in an attempt to maximize form drag forces. The main propulsive force, however, at the stage of the stroke shown in Figure 2 is that of lift, and the incidence conditions for maximizing this in a distal flow orientation are clearly indicated by the research data. Whether or not a swimmer can handle the forces generated at this stage by optimizing the angle of incidence is debatable.

As the hand progresses into section B to C (see insert in Figure 1) the horizontal lift and drag components work together, and the propulsive force to the swimmer increases dramatically. As the hand continues to the bottom of the pull path and the lift/drag vector rotates, the horizontal lift component diminishes until it disappears, when the only force acting horizontally is that of drag.

In section C to D (see insert in Figure 1) the hand has entered into a radial flow situation. Here there is little or no horizontal drag component,

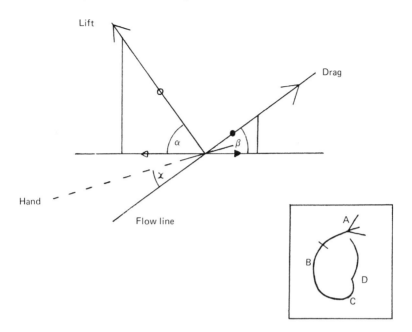

	Lift	Drag
Coefficient	.37	.17
Pressure	O 14.714 lb/ft^2	● 6.760 lb/ft^2
Horizontal component	◁ 8.432 lb/ft^2	▶ 5.570 lb/ft^2
Horizontal resultant		2.862 lb/ft^2

Relative velocity	6.47 ft/sec
Angle of incidence X	20°
α	55°
β	35°

Figure 1.   Vector analysis of front crawl arm stroke at point 1.

and with the appropriate angle of incidence, which was achieved, the lift force generated acts almost entirely horizontally forward and is the main propulsive force.

DISCUSSION OF THE FINDINGS

1. The hand must move through the water to create the pressure differentials necessary for force generation. A condition of flow must ex-

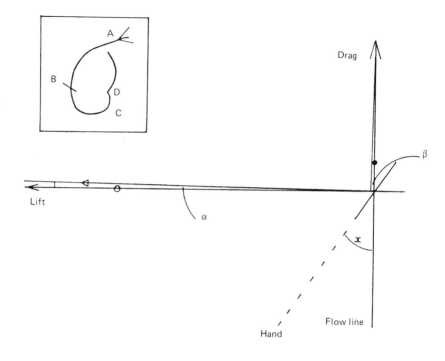

		Lift	Drag
Relative velocity		7.08 ft/sec	
Angle of incidence X		35°	
α		1°	
β		89°	

		Lift	Drag
Coefficient		.68	.29
Pressure	○	32.4 lb/ft^2	● 13.8 lb/ft^2
Horizontal component	◁	32.39 lb/ft^2	▶ .24 lb/ft^2
Horizontal resultant		32.63 lb/ft^2	

Figure 2.   Vector analysis of front crawl arm stroke at point 2.

ist. It is an oversimplification to speak of the hand pushing water backward or searching for still water, or of fixing the hand against the water.

2. The magnitude of the lift and drag forces created is directly related to the speed of the hand and arm through the water.

3. The opportunities that exist for making full propulsive use of the

possible maximum form drag forces, which in certain cases are only marginally greater than the possible lift forces, seem limited within the framework of existing stroke patterns and by anatomical constraints which prevent the hand and forearm from being used perpendicular to the swim line for an extended period within any stroke cycle.

4. To create the best lift force in swimming, optimum angles of incidence of the hand to the pull line must be adopted (Table 1). These angles differ for different flow orientations, i.e., distal, radial, or ulnar.

5. Where possible, to create maximum lift force, distal flow orientations in all strokes should be encouraged in preference to radial and ulnar flow. Where this is not possible, radial flow situations should be encouraged in preference to ulnar flow. The implications of these recommendations for the development of technique are considerable.

6. Swimming propulsion is the result of subtle and changing combinations of lift and drag forces. The opportunities for either one or the other to be solely responsible for swimming propulsion are very limited, and roles are seen to change.

The so-called "lift versus drag" controversy would seem to be ill-founded. Both forces have roles to play.

REFERENCES

Alexander, A. B., Holt, L. E., and Beer, R. 1974. Manual for Cinema-Computer Analysis. Dalhousie University Biomechanics Laboratory, Halifax (mimeographed).

Barthels, K., and Adrian, M. 1975. Three-dimensional spatial hand patterns of skilled butterfly swimmers, In: J. P. Clarys and L. Lewillie (eds.), Swimming II, pp. 154–160. University Park Press, Baltimore.

Counsilman, J. E. 1968. The Science of Swimming. Prentice-Hall Inc., Englewood Cliffs, New Jersey.

Counsilman, J. E. 1969. The role of sculling movements in the arm pull. Swimming World 10:12 (Dec.).

Schleihauf, R. 1974. A biomechanical analysis of freestyle. Swimming Tech. 11:3 (Fall).

Wood, T. 1977. A fluid dynamic analysis of the propulsive potential of the hand and forearm in swimming. Masters thesis, Dalhousie University, Halifax, Nova Scotia.

Wood, T. 1978. Movements of rotation and counter rotation in swimming. In preparation.

A Hydrodynamic Analysis
of Swimming Propulsion

R. E. Schleihauf, Jr.

The laws that govern propulsion in water are well defined by the established theories of hydrodynamics. However, the application of these theories to specific questions of hand propulsion in swimming is difficult because of a lack of background research data. Inspection of fluid mechanics texts reveals that although highly detailed studies of wings, plates, and other miscellaneous shapes in a fluid flow abound, there is virtually nothing specifically on the hand.

To answer the practical questions on hand propulsion in swimming, we must turn to our original background research in biomechanics. Of course, we can fall back on the general theories of hydrodynamics to guide our investigations, and we can use research procedures and conventions consistent with established hydrodynamic theory. However, in the final analysis, this research must be designed to meet the unique requirements of swimming biomechanics.

The initial steps in the investigation of hand propulsion in swimming have already been made. Counsilman (1971) revolutionized current thinking on propulsive techniques. His research originated the idea of looking at hand and airfoil motions in analogous terms. Since then, Barthels and Adrian (1975), Rackham (1975), and Schleihauf (1974, 1976, 1977) have generally confirmed the idea that lift as well as drag forces contribute to propulsion.

The research that remains to be done is the application of general hydrodynamic theories to specific hand force measurements in swimming. In this paper we approach the problem in two stages. First, we investigate forces on hand models in the fluid lab, using procedures pioneered by aerodynamic researchers. These lab studies generate coefficients of lift and drag values for the hand that will enable us to estimate the size of hand forces produced under a wide range of flow conditions. The second stage of research is to apply pure data from the laboratory to realistic swimming motions. Through motion picture studies key propulsive hand motions are isolated, and the coefficients of lift and drag values are used to predict practical hand force measurements. The techniques for evaluating hand propulsion are similar to those of the aerodynamics engineer, who relies on background aero/hydrodynamic research to calculate wing and propeller forces. A survey of hand force measurements across a sampling of highly skilled competitors allows us to outline the mechanical foundations of propulsion in each of the four competitive strokes.

The results of this research offer a detailed and objective technique for evaluating swimming proficiency. We hope that this type of research will help coaches to gain a clearer understanding of effective stroke technique and thereby to direct swimmers with more certainty toward stroke perfection.

PART I: THE COEFFICIENT OF LIFT AND DRAG OF HAND MODELS AS MEASURED IN THE OPEN-WATER CHANNEL

The main objective here is to provide two critical parameters of force production in swimming: the coefficients of lift and drag for the hand. When we define their values, we will be able to predict swimming forces in accordance with the following equations:

$$L = \tfrac{1}{2}\rho V^2 C_L S \tag{1}$$

$$D = \tfrac{1}{2}\rho V^2 C_D S \tag{2}$$

where L = lift force, D = drag force, ρ = density of water, V = hand velocity, C_L = coefficient of lift of the hand, C_D = coefficient of drag of the hand, and S = hand plane area.

Procedures

Plastic resin models of the adult human hand were cast in a variety of finger-thumb orientations. The models were studied in the open-water channel of the Columbia University Fluid Mechanics Laboratory. Forces were measured by a cantilevered, strain-gauge balance-beam apparatus coupled with a carrier preamplifier and single-channel recorder. The principal model (hand No. 5) is shown in Figure 1.

The principal model was studied under steady-state flow conditions for angles of pitch ranging from 0° to 90° at 5° increments, and angles of sweepback ranging from 0° to 360° at 45° increments. Sweepback angles (ψ) defined the range in leading and trailing edge geometries inherent to the hand. Inspection of Figure 2 indicates that the shape of hand "seen" by the water flow will vary considerably with each sweepback angle.

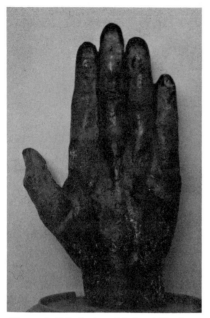

Figure 1. Principal model, hand No. 5.

Aerodynamic theory tells us that we can expect significant differences in lift/drag producing characteristics with these varying sweepback angles.

The next orientation angle of importance is angle of pitch. A hand positioned at any sweepback angle can be rotated between an angle of pitch (α) of 0° (flow slipping by parallel to plane of hand) to 90° (flow flat

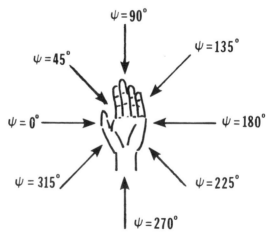

Figure 2. Sweepback angle convention.

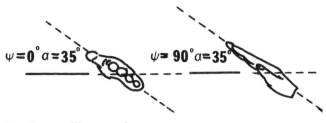

Figure 3. Two flow condition examples.

against the hand plane). A plot of lift and drag characteristics versus angle of pitch will yield the coefficient of lift and drag curves we seek to identify. In our analysis we of course consider both sweepback and angle of pitch to fully define the hand's position in space. An example of the interaction of α and ψ is shown in Figure 3.

Results and Conclusions

In the lab we conducted force measurements on the principal model for eight sweepback conditions and in each case for angles of pitch from $0°$ to $90°$. This yielded eight C_L-α and C_D-α curves, which are shown in Figure 4A and B.

When inspecting these curves it is important to notice two things. First, the lift characteristics certainly vary from curve to curve with each respective sweepback angle, and second, the general trend shows that C_L values increase up to an angle of pitch around $40°$ and then decrease. In general, these curves should supply a reference for any hand lift force calculation provided that the finger-thumb orientations are similar to the principal model.

These data confirm without doubt the publication of Counsilman (1971), which compared the principle governing hand propulsion with that of an airfoil. A direct comparison between our data and that of a NACA airfoil of similar aspect ratio (length/width factor) is shown in Figure 5.

Inspection of Figure 5 shows a similar curve shape between hand and wing, although the $C_{L\,max}$ for the hand is 20% lower than that of the wing. This might be expected because of the slightly irregular contour of the hand's surface.

Further comparison of hand values with wing data is difficult because the extremely low aspect ratios that accompany varying sweepback angles of the hand are outside the range of interest for typical airfoil studies. However, Pope and Harper (1967) published data for flat plates at very low aspect ratios, and a comparison of plate $C_{L\,max}$ values with hands for a similar range of aspect ratios is shown in Table 1.

In all C_D versus α curves (see Figures 6A, B) C_D increased with in-

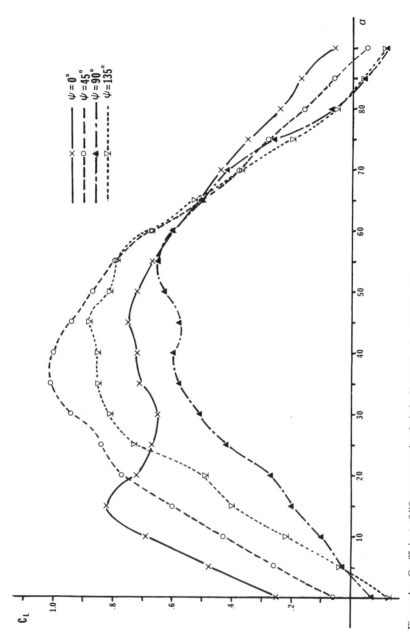

Figure 4a. Coefficient of lift versus angle of pitch. Hand No. 5, $\psi = 0°-135°$.

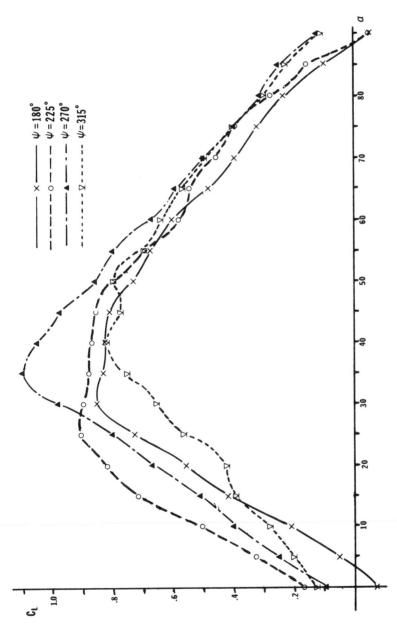

Figure 4b. Coefficient of lift versus angle of pitch. Hand No. 5, $\psi = 180°$-$315°$.

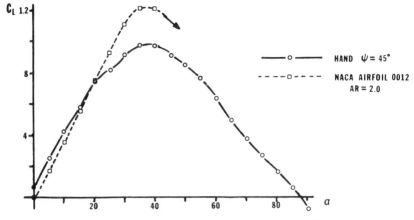

Figure 5. Lift characteristics, hand versus wing (Schleihauf, Jr., 1977).

creasing α as theory predicts. The C_D values that were measured for $\alpha = 90°$ ranged between 1.34 and 1.39. These values for C_D imply an effective resisting area of the hand as shown in Figure 7A. The extended perimeter of the hand may be caused by deflection of fluid streamlines as shown in Figure 7B.

The C_D of a flat plate at $90°$ is 1.28. The increase for the hand may be the result of the additional irregularities in the hand outline and/or of a slight concavity of the palm.

Finger-Spread Analysis

A secondary study was conducted to investigate the effect of finger spread on the lift/drag characteristics of the hand. The C_L-α curves in Figure 8 indicate that for $\psi = 0$, C_L values increase in indirect proportion to finger spread for $\alpha = 0°$-$60°$ (see Figure 8). $C_{L\,max}$ values were: fingers closed = 0.79, 1/8-inch spread = 0.71, 1/4-inch spread = 0.52, indicating a distinct advantage for finger-together hand positions for lift-producing motions.

C_D-α curves are shown in Figure 9. Here both finger-together and 1/8-inch spread positions appear superior to the 1/4-inch spread position.

Table 1. Comparison of $C_{L\,max}$ between hand and plates of similar aspect ratio

	$C_{L\,max}$	Aspect ratio
Hand	0.83–1.01	1.63–2.53
Plate	0.80–1.15	1.00–3.00

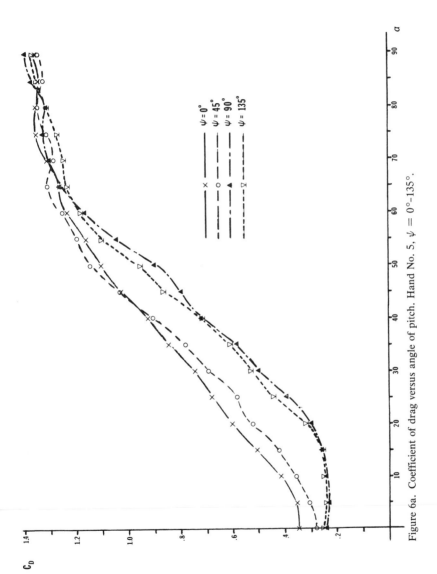

Figure 6a. Coefficient of drag versus angle of pitch. Hand No. 5, $\psi = 0°–135°$.

Figure 6b. Coefficient of drag versus angle of pitch. Hand No. 5, $\psi = 180°-315°$.

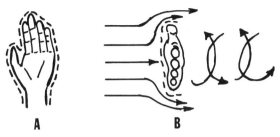

Figure 7. Hand drag-resisting area, $\alpha = 90°$.

Thumb Abduction Analysis

The results of a final study to investigate the effect of thumb position on lift characteristics for $\psi = 0°$ are shown in Figure 10. The curve for the model with the thumb 100% abducted into the plane of the fingers showed a $C_{L\,max}$ at an acute angle of pitch of only 15°. The models with 50% and 75% thumb abduction showed a $C_{L\,max}$ at more obtuse angles of pitch (45°-50°). Thus, it seems that for situations requiring a high lift/drag ratio a hand position with thumb fully abducted into the plane of the hand would be preferable to partially abducted thumb positions.

HAND LIFT/DRAG CAPABILITIES

Given the C_L and C_D curves for the hand, it will be interesting to examine their significance in more practical terms. For example, let us examine some vector force illustrations of the hand's lift/drag-producing capabilities.

Figure 11 shows three force configurations for a hand subjected to a uniform flow velocity at three selections of hand pitch. Looking at the lift forces we see that, in accordance with aerodynamic theory, lift force increases with pitch from "A" to "B," and then the hand "stalls," and the lift approaches zero with more obtuse angles of pitch. Looking at drag forces we see a continuous increase in drag with angle of pitch. These forces are drawn to scale. The largest force is the drag force in Figure 11C. For the conditions of this the maximum available drag is 30% higher than the maximum lift.

However, the conditions of the example that flow velocity is uniform at all angles of pitch is not particularly analogous to swimming situations. For example, in a swimming motion in which a large force is to be produced, the hand velocity will depend largely on the strength of the muscles most involved. In other words, the forcefulness of muscular contraction of the arm will balance water resistance to hand motion, and hand velocity will be determined as a byproduct. This implies that the strength of a swimmer's pull will determine hand velocity and not the reverse.

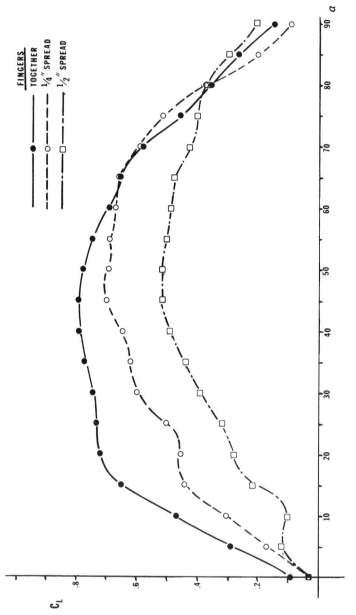

Figure 8. Finger-spread analysis. $C_L-\alpha$ curves, $\psi = 0°$.

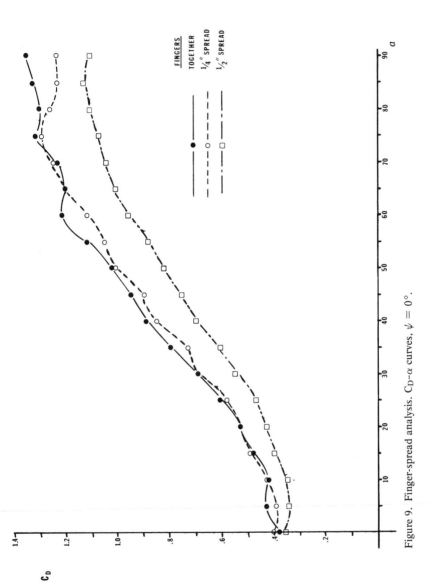

Figure 9. Finger-spread analysis. C_D-α curves, $\psi = 0°$.

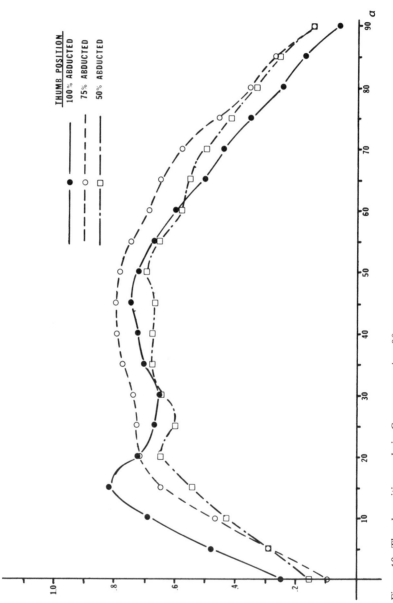

Figure 10. Thumb position analysis. C_L–α curves, $\psi = 0°$.

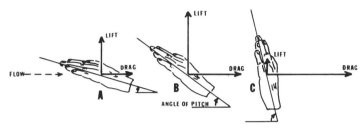

Figure 11. Lift/drag interaction. $\psi = 45°$.

To illustrate, suppose that in a given motion a swimmer is strong enough to deliver a 24-lb resultant force. He can do this in numerous ways, three of which are shown in Figure 12. In A, an acute angle of pitch has been selected. The hand speed generated to produce this force would be 12.0 ft/sec. In B, an equal interaction of lift/drag accompanies an angle of pitch of 35°, and a hand speed of 11.2 ft/sec would be used. In C, drag-dominated propulsion accompanies this obtuse angle of pitch, and a hand speed of 10 ft/sec would yield the 24-lb result.

Note that in each of the force configurations illustrated the resistance encountered by the hand is identical, and therefore, to a good approximation, the strength of muscular contraction of the arm should be similar. Actually, at higher hand speeds the physiological load may be slightly higher because of the inertial load of the mass of the hand and forearm, but in general the energy cost to the swimmer must be similar on the relatively narrow range of hand speeds shown.

It is obvious from this example that the hand has at its disposal various ways to create a given propulsive force. Therefore, hand velocity is, to an extent, arbitrary. In actual swimming situations we can expect that any of the propulsive force configurations shown in Figure 12 may be used, depending on the pulling situation. To investigate some realistic pulling situations, let us look at the cinematographic data.

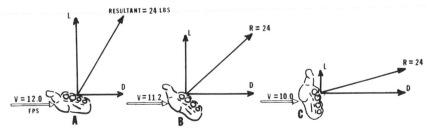

Figure 12. Resultant force production. $\psi = 0°$.

PART II: A MOTION PICTURE ANALYSIS OF HIGHLY SKILLED PROPULSIVE TECHNIQUES

The objective of this research segment is to break down the complex three-dimensional pulling patterns of skilled competitors so that force calculations can be made at key points in their strokes. We will use the coordinates of hand motion to give us measurements of hand velocity, sweepback angle, and angle of pitch. Given this information the relevant variables of the propulsive force Equations 1 and 2:

$$L = \tfrac{1}{2}\rho V^2 C_L S \qquad\qquad D = \tfrac{1}{2}\rho V^2 C_D S$$

can be determined, and force calculations are then possible.

Methodology

Film Analysis Procedure   All motion picture data were collected via biaxial techniques using the bottom and side views as principal viewing planes. Static camera position was maintained by underwater tripod supports, and the film speed used for the twin cameras was 45 frames/sec.

Films were taken on location at Indiana University, Central Jersey Aquatic Club, Bernal's Gator Swim Club, Long Island Swim Club, New York Athletic Club, and New Rochelle Aquatic Club. All subjects wore four miniature light bulbs on the hand to aid in subsequent data reduction.

The filmed results were combined with the coefficient of lift and drag values described in the previous discussion. The investigator was thus able to estimate the size and direction of the lift, drag, and resultant forces· used in hand propulsion. The variables that were drawn from the film for use in calculations included hand velocity, sweepback angle, plane of motion, and angle of pitch. The calculation procedures used to derive these variables were:

1. Hand velocity, which was calculated by a trapezoidal integral approximation of the displacement curve.
2. Sweepback angle (ψ) (defined earlier), which was measured relative to the front-view pulling pattern. Figure 13 shows a selection of four sweepback measures for a freestyle arm pull. Inspection of Figure 13 indicates that the sweepback angle at 1A is 90° (this is for flow from fingertip to wrist). At 1B we have $\psi = 0°$ (flow across palm, thumb leading). At 1C the sweepback angle is 180° (flow across palm, little finger leading), and finally at 1D the sweepback angle is 270° (flow from wrist to fingertip). This example shows that we can expect a wide range of sweepback angles to be used within the path of a single arm pull.
3. Plane of motion. The plane of motion at a point in the stroke may be

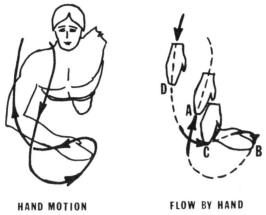

HAND MOTION   **FLOW BY HAND**
Figure 13. Freestyle sweepback angles.

thought of as a two-dimensional representation that best isolates the three-dimensional motion at that point. As a first approximation, this plane can be defined as the plane containing a line parallel to the Z axis and the asymptote to the front-view pulling pattern. A selection of viewing planes for a typical back stroke arm pull is shown in Figure 14. In each of the pattern diagrams the line of sight is chosen to be approximately normal to the motion at the point in question. This is done to minimize the foreshortening and distortion that normally occur with two-dimensional representation.

4. Angle of pitch (α). The hand's angle of attack was measured in the plane of motion for the point in question. The angle of pitch can be defined as the angle between the asymptote to the plane-of-motion pulling pattern and the plane of the hand. An example of an angle of pitch measure in back stroke is shown in Figure 15. (On occasion the plane-of-motion convention needs additional view rotation to isolate hand points near an edge view. This occurs most frequently with propulsive forces that are aimed to the side and upward, such as sideways hand motion used for body support.)

Through use of the above film analysis procedures, the investigator was able to obtain measurements of the essential characteristics of hand motion in three-dimensional space. The results of this analysis procedure when combined with the coefficient of lift and drag values from the lab will yield a quantitative basis for evaluating swimming propulsion.

Results

Test Experiments   Our hydrodynamic analysis procedure was first applied in three test experiment conditions to compare calculated forces

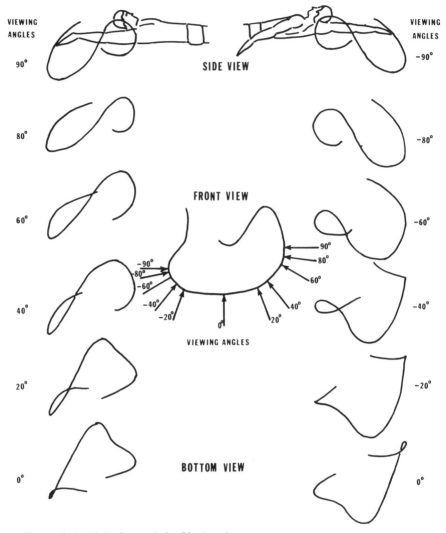

Figure 14. Multiple view analysis of backstroke.

with known loads. In each case a balanced condition was attained between a swimmer near maximal exertion and a dead load. The three variations of the test situation are shown in Figure 16.

In each case at least 10 trials were filmed, and a condition of equilibrium was sought in which the swimmer: 1) maintained a nearly constant position in space, neither gaining nor losing ground to the resisting load, and 2) maintained a position near the center of the range of view of both cameras. The single trial which best achieved the equilibrium condition was selected for analysis. In each case the propulsive effects of

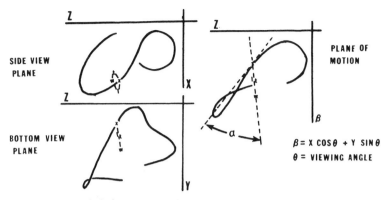

SIDE VIEW
PLANE

BOTTOM VIEW
PLANE

PLANE OF
MOTION

$\beta = X \cos \theta + Y \sin \theta$
$\theta = $ VIEWING ANGLE

Figure 15. Angle-of-pitch measurement.

the right hand and forearm were utilized in resultant force curve calculations.

Vertical Scull Experiment

When assessing the effective load carried by the swimmer the bouyant force of his body was taken into account. Also, each trial was conducted with the swimmer's head fully submerged to eliminate gravitational forces. Therefore, each trial was limited to 20 sec.

In the pull selected for analysis the equilibrium condition was nearly met, although a slight upward motion of the body was noted during the stroke cycle. This implies that the net force generated by the swimmer may be expected slightly to exceed the load being carried. This supposition agrees with the results shown in Figure 17, which indicate that the theoretically calculated force was 7.7 lb although the load was really 7.5 lb. Note that perfect correlation of results would rarely be expected because of the approximations in the procedure. We are only looking for a general correlation of results, and that seems to be indicated by the data.

Tethered Breaststroke

Force calculation in the tethered breaststroke experiment included hand and forearm resistance on the recovery as well as positive effects from the pull. The results indicated that R = 9.2 lb, while L = 9.0 lb. The results shown in Figure 18 agree with the observation that the body advanced slightly on the pulley during the pull selected for analysis (see Figure 18).

Tethered Freestyle

The results of the tethered freestyle experiment are shown in Figure 19. In the pull selected for analysis the swimmer was observed to drift backward slightly owing to the effect of the balancing load. This observation may account in part for the underestimated calculation of R_E shown in Figure 19.

Figure 16. Test experiments. A: vertical scull; B: tethered breaststroke; C: tethered freestyle.

Looking back at the swimming experiments we see that in three separate pulling circumstances the analytic procedure yields findings that agree generally with expected results. The findings support the contention that the film analysis procedure and lab data on C_L and C_D values can be combined to estimate the propulsive forces used in real swimming motions. Further studies, made in conjunction with films of free-swimming subjects, can also be expected to provide an objective basis for interpreting swimming propulsion.

Analysis of Skilled Propulsive Techniques

The following sampling of swimmers was analyzed in accordance with the calculation procedure previously detailed. Each swimmer made at least

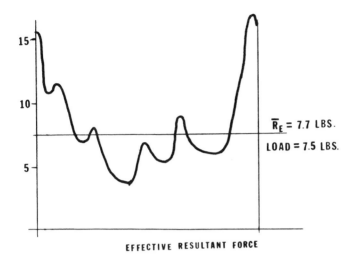

$\overline{R}_E = 7.7$ LBS.

LOAD = 7.5 LBS.

EFFECTIVE RESULTANT FORCE

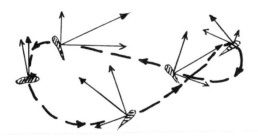

SUMMARY FORCE DIAGRAM

Figure 17. Vertical scull experiment.

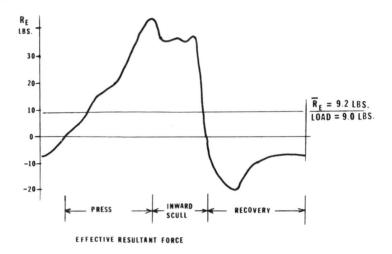

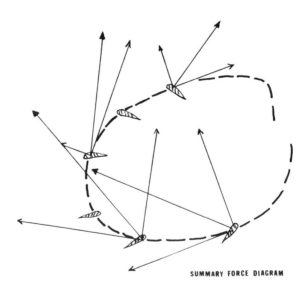

Figure 18. Tethered breaststroke experiment.

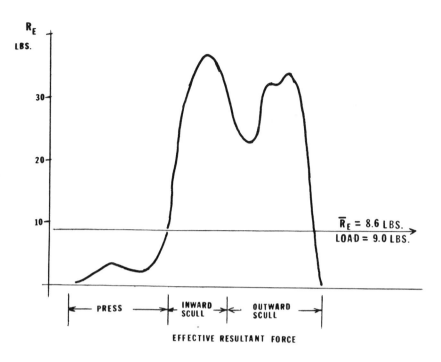

$$\overline{R}_E = 8.6 \ \text{LBS.}$$
$$\text{LOAD} = 9.0 \ \text{LBS.}$$

|←— PRESS —→|←— INWARD SCULL —→|←— OUTWARD SCULL —→|

EFFECTIVE RESULTANT FORCE

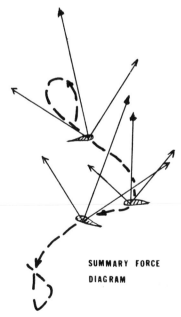

SUMMARY FORCE

DIAGRAM

Figure 19. Tethered freestyle experiment.

three passes by the camera for one or more of the four competitive strokes. The pass that best centered the lighted pulling hand in the film frame was selected for analysis.

The diagrams accompanying the analysis of each swimmer are intended to ease visualization of the mechanical foundations of key propulsive motions. To simplify the visualization process, all forces are plotted in one of the two principal viewing planes: side or bottom view. (In reality, all forces and orientation angles were calculated in the plane of motion and subsequently were superimposed on the nearest principal viewing plane.)

Breaststroke

Our first subject, Rick Thomas of Indiana University, exhibited classic breaststroke form, very similar to the model swimmer shown by Counsilman (1968). The key propulsive motions of the stroke are best isolated by the bottom-view diagram (see Figure 20, left).

The inward scull phase of the stroke contains the largest resultant forces by virtue of the acceleration of hand speed on the latter half of the positive propulsion. The drag force that is directed mainly to the side will have no effect on body motion because it will be effectively cancelled by the paired motion of the left and right hands.

A general comparison of the effect of hand propulsive forces on body velocity is shown in Figure 20, right. Inspection of the data indicates that peak body velocity occurs simultaneously with the inward scull phase of the stroke. This correlation between peak hand forces and peak body velocity would be expected theoretically provided forearm propulsion makes contributions in proportion to hand forces and extraneous inertial forces acting on the body are negligible. Given these restrictions, body velocity can be used to provide additional support for our data on hand propulsion.

The second subject in the breaststroke was Rick Hofstetter of Indiana University. The bottom-view diagram of his motion is similar to that of Thomas, although there is a slight variation in the orientation of the inward scull pattern (see Figure 21). The diagonally in and somewhat backward motion used by Hofstetter allows for a better orientation of the resultant force vectors on the inward scull than the motions of Thomas.

Summary results of seven other highly skilled breaststroke swimmers taken from Schleihauf (1977) show that all their pulling techniques include the predominant sideways motion of an outward press and inward scull to achieve propulsion (see Figure 22). Dalberg and Ball use the slightly inclined pulling pattern similar to Hofstetter, while Jastremski, Keating, McKenzie, Furniss, and Klinger have patterns more similar to that of Thomas. It is interesting now to consider the theoretical implications of the inclined pulling patterns discussed above.

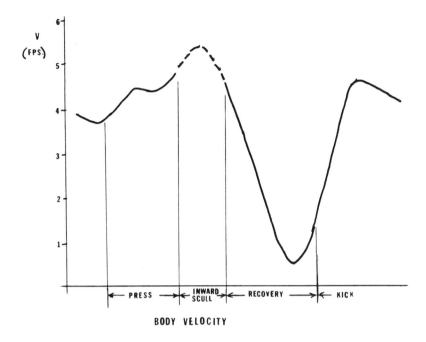

BODY VELOCITY

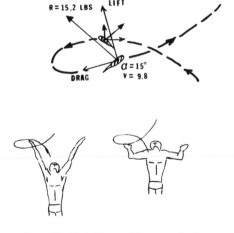

Figure 20. Rick Thomas' breaststroke form.

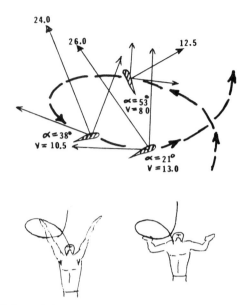

Figure 21. Rick Hofstetter's breaststroke form.

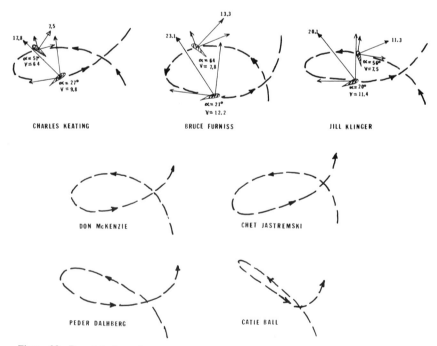

Figure 22. Breaststroke patterns.

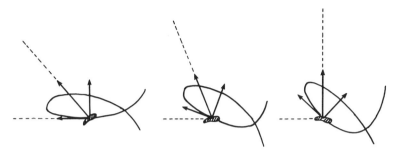

Figure 23. Breaststroke pull angles of inclination.

Mechanical Versus Spatial-Temporal Determinants of Efficiency

Thus far we have considered the effects of pulling motions from a mechanical point of view. For example, we have analyzed vector force diagrams in the breaststroke, and on the basis of the relative size and orientation of the resultant forces, we have established practical implications. According to this mechanical line of thinking, we may expect that in the breaststroke, the inclined pattern of Hofstetter would be more efficient than that of Thomas' straight-in pattern. For that matter, an even more steeply inclined pattern than Hofstetter's may be considered perfect because it would aim resultant forces directly forward (see Figure 23, right).

It is clear that the pull shown in Figure 23, right is mechanically efficient. However, why do highly skilled breaststroke swimmers seem to gravitate toward the techniques shown in Figure 23, left and middle, which appear less efficient? The answer may be found in an analysis which considers the spatial-temporal aspects of breaststroke pulling motions.

Consider the following theoretical example. Suppose a swimmer can move an outstretched arm to a fully contracted position (hand to shoulder) at the rate of 10 ft/sec relative to his body (see Figure 24A–F). The situation is analogous to a breaststroke pull made straight back (Figure 24A), with inward scull angles of inclination of 60°, 45°, and 30° (Figure 24B, C, D). It is interesting to compare these hand motions, which are identical in all respects except angle of inclination, with their effect as measured relative to still water in simulated swimming motions.

Figures 24G–L assume a constant forward body velocity of 5 ft/sec and show pulling patterns as they would appear relative to the water. Inspection of Figure 24 indicates that for a straight-back pull the standard 10 ft/sec hand motion relative to the body will translate only 5 ft/sec of hand speed to the water (Figure 24G). At the other extreme, a forward hand motion will translate 15 ft/sec hand speed to the water (Figure 24L). For angles of pull between these extremes, hand speed translation increases with decreasing angles of inclination.

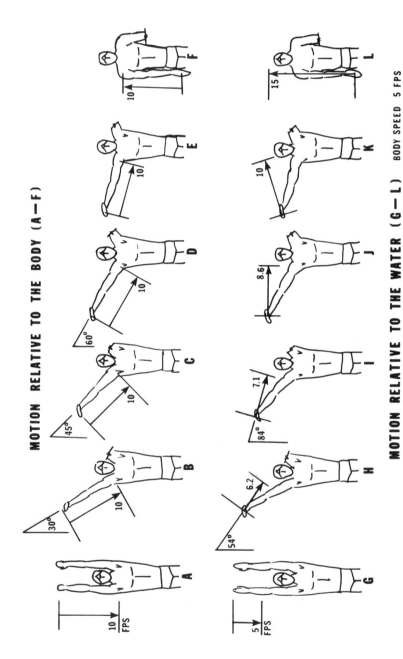

Figure 24. Spatial-temporal effects.

Figure 24J is comparable with a Rick Thomas type of inward scull, breaststroke pulling motion. Comparison of Figures 24J and 24G indicates that there is a 70% increase in effective hand speed for sideways hand motion as compared with straight-back motion. Bearing in mind that resultant forces vary as a function of hand velocity squared, the data imply that the forces produced by sideways motion will be about three times greater than those produced by backward hand motion. Of course, sideways hand motion will lose some force to the side, but typical $C_{L\ max}$ and $C_{D\ max}$ values imply that the effective propulsion shown in Figure 24J will still be twice that shown in Figure 24G. Thus, there is a spatial-temporal advantage to sideways hand motions in swimming situations with body translation.

Looking back at the sampling of breaststroke swimmers we see that spatial-temporal effects are clearly a dominant influence in the selection of pulling patterns. All of the breaststroke swimmers selected a wide pulling motion to maximize hand speed translation and resultant force magnitude. The variation that exists across the sample reflects flexibility and strength differences among subjects. In general, however, we can expect that either the Thomas or Hofstetter stroke styles will be used as effective stroke models in instructional problems.

Spatial-temporal effects will also influence pulling patterns in the remaining three competitive strokes. However, the results of our breaststroke study are unique in two respects. First, the paired-hand motions of breaststroke allowed neutralization of sideways force components. Such force neutralization would not be possible in strokes with alternate arm motions (e.g., freestyle and backstroke), and lateral body motion would result from large sideways force components. Second, the length of the breaststroke pull is significantly shorter than in the three remaining stroke disciplines. We can expect the extended length of the pulls of butterfly, backstroke, and freestyle will certainly influence selections of pulling pattern orientations.

In the final analysis we can expect that the efficiency of pulling motions will be determined by the interaction of numerous factors. Spatial-temporal effects, mechanical efficiency, and the specific strengths and flexibilities of the swimmer will all interact in selections of pulling motions. The exact formula for interaction of these factors will vary with the individual but will be revealed by further study of highly skilled competitors.

Butterfly

Our first subject in the butterfly stroke is Jim Montgomery of Indiana University. Data analysis indicates that Jim delivers two distinct pulses of power: the first on the inward scull (midstroke), and the second on the

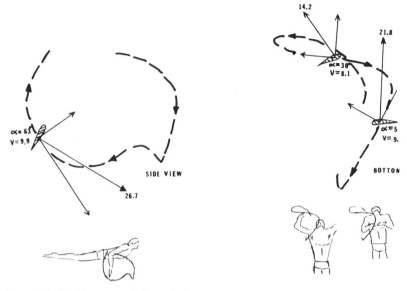

Figure 25. Jim Montgomery's butterfly form.

push-back and round-off portion of the stroke. The 14.2-lb resultant (see Figure 25, inward scull) appears similar to forces described above for the breaststroke. Here, Montgomery gets good hand speed translation to still water and uses the paired motions of the left hand to counter the sideways force components.

On the push-back phase of the stroke there is an excellent interaction of lift and drag force components to produce a straight-forward 21.8-lb resultant. These results indicate that the butterfly swimmer, unlike the breaststroke swimmer, can use the extra length of his pull to produce drag-dominated propulsive forces.

Finally, on the round-off portion of the stroke, we see a 26.7-lb resultant, angled forward and down. The downward component can be used to counter the upward thrust of the kick, and the forward component would contribute directly to propulsion. Here the lift force helps considerably in aiming the resultant in the proper direction.

A body velocity study was run on Montgomery, and the results are shown in Figure 26. Again the pulses in body speed seem to correspond with our calculated hand forces for this subject.

Our second subject is Jay Hershey of Indiana University. Hershey's style is similar to Montgomery's except that his inward scull uses a steeper angle of inclination and is narrower (see Figure 27). By virtue of this pattern his 7.8-lb force is aimed nearly straight forward, although the size of this force is not large, possibly because diminished hand speed translated

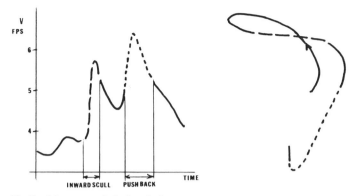

Figure 26. Jim Montgomery's body velocity.

to the water. On the push-back phase the 12.4-lb resultant is again nicely oriented by virtue of good lift/drag interaction. On the round-off we see an apparent improvement in Hershey's technique as compared with Montgomery's. Here, a large lift component keeps the 26.7-lb resultant aimed well forward. The downward component is small but should be sufficient to cancel kicking forces. (Preliminary research indicates that a typical kick delivers a 10–15-lb vertical force/ft.) As a result Hershey increases efficiency by flexing his wrist backward to attain acute angles of pitch and therefore lift-dominated propulsion on the finish of his stroke.

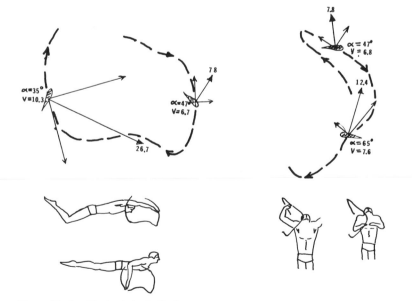

Figure 27. Jay Hershey's butterfly form.

A summary of other top butterfly swimmers (Schleihauf, 1977) is shown below. The sampling is divided into two groups. Those similar to Montgomery (Thomas, Hall, and Berry), and those similar to Hershey (Schwanhausser, Furniss, Troy, and Hickox) (see Figure 28).

In all cases we see that propulsion is derived from a range of similar propulsive techniques. On the inward scull effective techniques seem to cover the entire range between the styles of Montgomery and Hershey. Here, as in the breaststroke, there seems to be a tradeoff between the mechanical and spatial-temporal determinants of the stroke. On the push-back phase, drag forces dominate propulsion in all subjects. Finally, in the round-off, lift components play a critical role in effective force production.

Backstroke

Rick Thomas exhibits typical bent-arm backstroke technique. The side view shows a down-up-down pattern with a midstroke propulsive force of 27.1 lb (Figure 29). Here Thomas selects a hand angle of pitch that interacts with the pulling pattern orientation to produce a straight-forward resultant. In this instance both mechanical and spatial-temporal elements of the pull combine for maximal effectiveness. Both hand speed translation and force efficiency are high because of the skill of the subject.

The bottom view shows another effective sculling motion on the outward press. In this phase of the stroke the 28.8- and 23.1-lb resultants are aimed in a predominantly forward direction and are major contributors to propulsion. On the finish Thomas switches to drag-dominated propulsion with his 21.6-lb push-back phase resultant. The body velocity curve for Thomas again follows the trend outlined by our force analysis (see Figure 29).

A comparison of the other subjects studied (Schleihauf, 1977) indicates a broader range of swimming technique in backstroke than in breast or butterfly strokes. Comparison of side-view patterns shows two general stroke styles. Those with pronounced up-down-up sculling motions are shown in Figure 30A. (Hackett, Stamm, Hammer, and Stock); those with flatter side-view patterns (using more drag-dominated, push-back motions) are shown in Figure 30B (Furniss, Hall, Frankenbach, and Murphy).

Because all of these swimmers are highly skilled it would seem that either the Thomas or the Furniss style technique could be considered effective in backstroke. Each swimmer has apparently selected a pulling pattern that is best suited to his own particular strength and flexibility. The fact that they do not universally conform to a single stroke model is only an indication that they are for differing body types. Our data on freestyle generates similar conclusions.

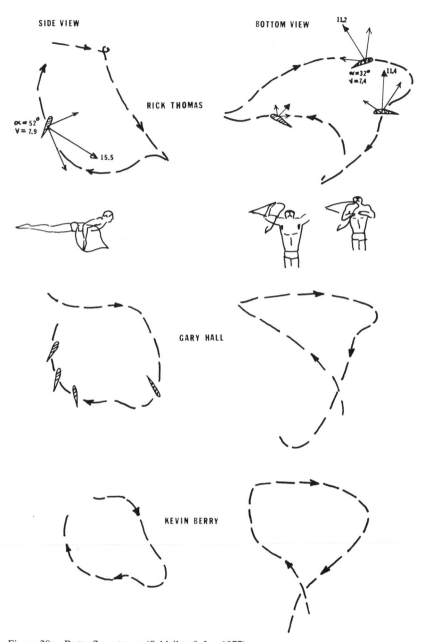

Figure 28a. Butterfly patterns (Schleihauf, Jr., 1977).

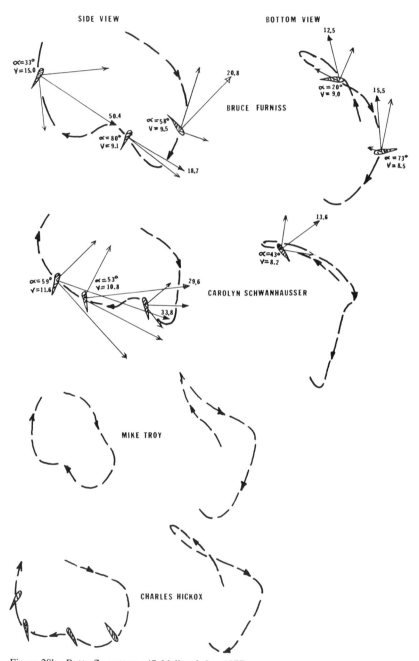

Figure 28b. Butterfly patterns (Schleihauf, Jr., 1977).

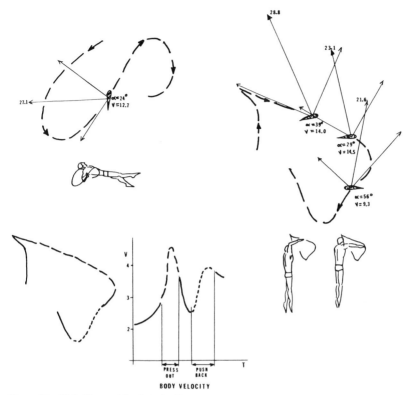

Figure 29. Rick Thomas' backstroke form.

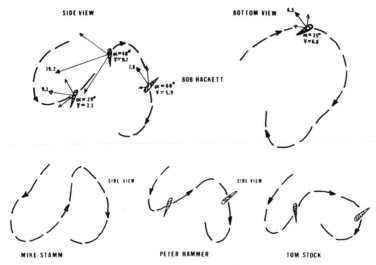

Figure 30a. Backstroke patterns (Schleihauf, Jr., 1977).

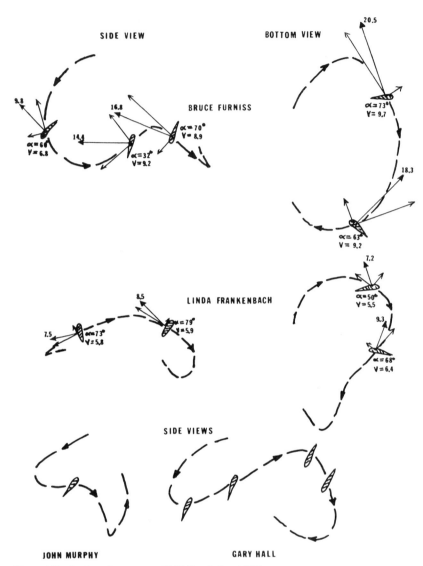

Figure 30b. Backstroke patterns (Schleihauf, Jr., 1977).

Freestyle

In freestyle three general styles of stroke technique were observed across the sampling of subjects. The first can be called classic technique and is shown by Rick Thomas of Indiana University.

The side view shows an initial pressing motion that relies heavily on the lift component for effective propulsion (see Figure 31, R = 13.0). The finishing motion is also isolated in the side view, and its 23.1-lb resultant

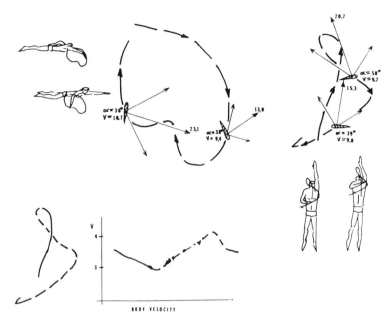

Figure 31. Rick Thomas' freestyle form.

is nicely oriented because of the interaction of lift and drag forces. As with Hershey's butterfly stroke, Thomas extends his wrist on the finish of the stroke to maximize the lift component.

The middle portion of Thomas' stroke is best isolated in the bottom view. The 20.7-lb resultant on the inward scull is aimed predominantly forward with a slight component to the side. This sideways component may be used in reaction to the inertial forces of the recovery. The outward scull phase produces a perfectly oriented 15.3-lb force.

The film indicates that Thomas continually adjusts his hand pitch according to the line of his pulling pattern. It is his extremely skillful hand manipulation that is responsible for the effectiveness of all phases of his stroke. His body velocity curve shows a smooth fluctuation of body speed in response to his nearly continuous application of force (see Figure 31). Other swimmers who use a stroke similar to that of Thomas are shown in Figure 32 (Furniss, Spitz, Hall, and Sintz).

A second style of freestyle is demonstrated by Carolyn Schwanhausser of Central Jersey Aquatic Club. Her high rate of turnover technique is characterized by a deep pressing motion, as shown in her side view (Figure 33). Here, key propulsive forces are generated by the upward and back sweeping motions of the finish. Both the 17.9- and 24.1-lb force are nicely oriented because of the interaction of lift and drag forces with the upward-swept pulling pattern.

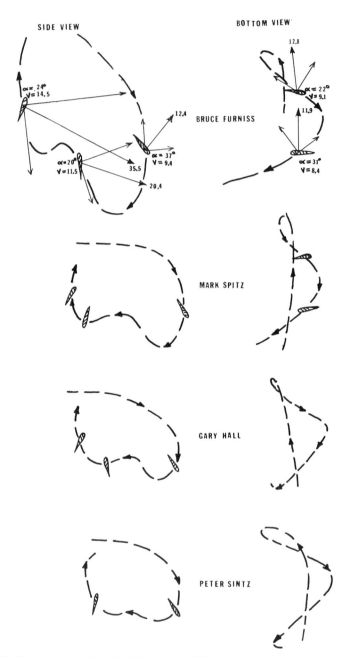

Figure 32. Classic freestyle form (Schleihauf, Jr., 1977).

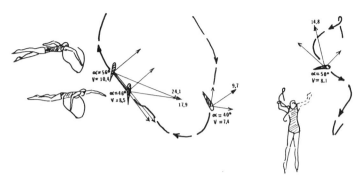

Figure 33. Carolyn Schwanhausser's freestyle form.

The bottom view for this style shows much less midstroke cross-over than that of the classic freestyler. It appears that Schwannhausser is eliminating in and out diagonal sculling motions, but she is compensating for their absence with increased turnover. In effect she is bypassing bicep-tricep strength motions and is substituting latissimus dorsi-originated power in her stroke. This technique will clearly be very efficient for swimmers with adaptabilities similar to Schwannhausser. Perry Daum of Long Island Swim Club is one such swimmer (see Figure 34).

A final classification of freestyle technique is exemplified by Olympic champion Jim Montgomery. The side-view pattern shown in Figure 35 indicates that Montgomery's press and finishing motion are similar to the classic style, although the midportion of the stroke is flatter and involves more direct push-back motions. The bottom view also shows a direct push-back motion at midstroke as indicated by the drag-dominated 15.0-lb resultant.

As a result it seems that at midstroke Montgomery is utilizing the mechanical advantage of push-back motions, and any loss of hand speed caused by spatial-temporal effects is compensated by the specific strengths of this particular swimmer.

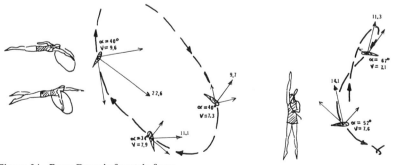

Figure 34. Perry Daum's freestyle form.

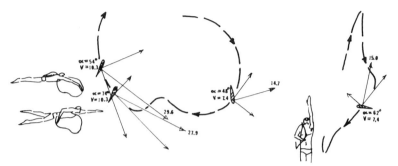

Figure 35. Jim Montgomery's freestyle form.

Another swimmer whose style is similar to Montgomery's is team-mate Jay Hershey (see Figure 36). Hershey uses a drag-dominated push-back motion at the 19.4-lb resultant. His major propulsive forces, however, show an equal interaction of lift and drag on the diagonal motions of the outward scull (35.7-lb resultant and finish (38.5-lb resultant).

In summary it seems that effective technique in freestyle can be generated for a broad range of swimming styles. Swimmers who exhibit skillful hand manipulation in sculling motions may be guided toward the so-called classic style. Others, who show a tendency toward a high rate of turnover and a deep press may choose to develop the qualities of the Schwanhausser technique. Finally, those best adapted to direct pushing motions may follow Montgomery's style.

Conclusions

The preceding results should provide a general understanding of highly skilled propulsive techniques to researchers, coaches, and swimmers. With this information the subjective coaching theories of the past may be replaced with more objective guidelines. Novice swimmers can be directed

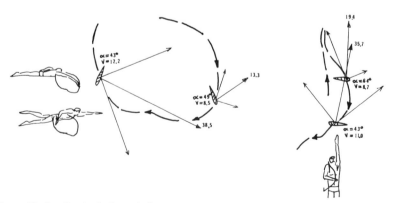

Figure 36. Jay Hershey's freestyle form.

with certainty toward swimming proficiency through the use of any of the highly skilled stroke models studied. Even the techniques of successful veteran competitors can be adjusted. Finally, our analytic technique may be of value in future research settings, with its potential influence limited only by the imagination of the researcher. We hope that continued research along this potentially fruitful line of inquiry will continue to expand our knowledge of swimming biomechanics.

ACKNOWLEDGMENTS

The author is indebted to Joseph Higgins, Teachers College, Department of Biomechanics, and to Joseph Castelli and Harold Thompkins (Columbia University Mechanical Engineering Department) for their cooperation in this project. We are also indebted to Coaches Counsilman, Elm, Bernal, and Davis for their cooperation in film sessions.

REFERENCES

Barthels, K. M., and Adrian, M. J. 1975. Three-dimensional spatial hand patterns of skilled butterfly swimmers. In: L. Lewillie and J. P. Clarys (eds.), Swimming II, pp. 154–160. University Park Press, Baltimore.

Counsilman, J. E. 1968. The Science of Swimming. Prentice-Hall, Inc., Englewood Cliffs, New Jersey.

Counsilman, J. E. 1971. The application of Bernouli's principle to human propulsion in water. In: L. Lewillie and J. P. Clarys (eds.), First International Symposium on Biomechanics of Swimming, pp. 59–71. Universite Libre de Bruxelles, Brussels.

Pope, A., and Harper, J. J. 1967. Low Speed Wind Tunnel Testing. John Wiley & Sons, Inc., New York.

Rackham, G. W. 1975. An analysis of arm propulsion in swimming. In: L. Lewillie and J. P. Clarys (eds.), Swimming II, pp. 174–179. University Park Press, Baltimore.

Schleihauf, R. E., Jr. 1974. A biomechanical analysis of freestyle. Swimming Tech. Fall: 89–96.

Schleihauf, R. E., Jr. 1976. A Hydrodynamic analysis of breaststroke pulling proficiency. Swimming Tech. Winter: 100–105.

Schleihauf, R. E., Jr. 1977. Swimming propulsion: a hydrodynamic analysis. In: R. Ousley (ed.), A.S.C.A. Convention, 1977, A.S.C.A., Fort Lauderdale, Fla.

Forces Acting on the Hand during Swimming and their Relationships to Muscular, Spatial, and Temporal Factors

R. Dupuis, M. Adrian, Y. Yoneda, and M. Jack

Because of the complex nature of fluid mechanics, research in swimming has not advanced as rapidly as it has in land sports. In particular there is a lack of information concerning measurement of the propulsive forces produced by a swimmer and the resistive forces that impede forward motion during the different phases of a stroke.

As early as 1933, Karpovich (1933) identified the resistance encountered by a body being towed through the water. Only recently has the effect of body position on the resistance been investigated (Kent and Atha, 1971; Van Manen and Rijken, 1975). The relationship of Bernoulli's principle to human propulsion in the water was described by Brown and Counsilman (1971). They asserted that both hydrodynamic lift and drag are components of the total propulsive force. Barthels (1975) and Barthels and Adrian (1975) demonstrated the existence of these lift and drag propulsive forces in the butterfly arm stroke but could not quantify such forces.

Several recent investigations have focused on the forces that act on the hand during swimming. These have been preliminary investigations of the front crawl stroke with minimal interpretation (Belokovsky, 1971; Van Manen and Rijken, 1975; Boicev and Tzvetkox, 1975). The purpose of this investigation was to examine the muscular forces and the forces acting upon the hand with respect to the kinematics of swimming the back crawl stroke and breaststroke.

PROCEDURES

The subjects for this investigation were three women intercollegiate swimmers. Data were obtained for each subject who performed the breast stroke at moderate and sprint paces and for two of these subjects who performed the backstroke under similar conditions of pace. The following techniques were used in data collection: 1) electromyography, 2) electrogoniometry, 3) dynamography, and 4) cinematography.

Electromyography

Surface electrodes were placed over the anterior and posterior deltoids, triceps, and wrist flexors to measure action potentials from these muscles. Electrode sites were determined by palpation during application of maximal resistance. Several types of adhesive tape were used to cover the electrodes to prevent water from interfering with the conductivity of the electrode (Figure 1, left). The wires were attached to a pole that was carried above the shoulder of the swimmer to prevent the wires from disrupting the subject's normal stroking pattern (Figure 1, right). The wires were connected to an ink-writing oscillograph (E&M Instruments physiograph), operating at 5 cm/sec.

Electrogoniometry

An elgon, similar to the type reported by Ringer and Adrian (1969), was taped over the right elbow joint of each swimmer (Figure 1-A). The 10-K potentiometer was encased in a rubber balloon which was secured with a silicone sealer. The wires from the elgon were connected by a 9-V double bucking circuit to a mirror galvanometric oscillograph (Honeywell visicorder 1508). Records were obtained at 2, 4, and 8 inches/sec (5.1, 10.2, and 20.3 cm/sec).

Dynamography

A waterproof Sensotic-bonded strain-gauge pressure transducer 8 mm in diameter was used to measure the forces acting on the right hand. The transducer was taped to a rubber glove worn by the subjects and placed between the first and second fingers at the metatarsal phalangeal joint. The wires from the transducer were attached to a pole and connected by an Accudata 113 amplifier to a visicorder, 1508 oscillograph. Records were obtained at 5.1, 10.2, and 20.3 cm/sec.

Cinematography

Motion pictures were taken from the front and right side at 25 frames/sec. A 16-mm Beaulieu camera was used for the front view, and a 16-mm LoCam camera was used for the side view films.

Synchronization of the Instrumentation Systems

A 12-V light bulb was placed in the field of view of both cameras and connected to the physiograph and to the visicorder by a basic electrical cir-

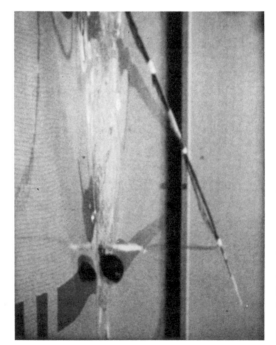

Figure 1. Testing situation showing pressure transducer, elgon, and electrodes attached to swimmer (front view) (*left*) and method of carrying wires (side view) (*right*). The underwater light for synchronization of cameras and recorders is depicted in front view.

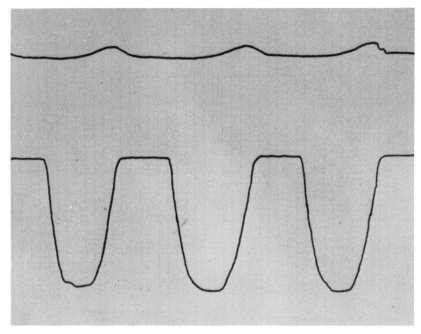

Figure 2. Typical pressure records and goniograms during the breaststroke. Top trace is pressure, and bottom trace is elbow angle. Upward direction depicts increased pressure and flexion, respectively.

cuit. The opened and closed status of the light bulb was recorded on the physiograph and visicorder. The circuit was closed manually, causing the light bulb to flash at approximately the start of each arm stroke.

Data Analysis

Pressure patterns for the three subjects in the breaststroke and the two subjects in the backstroke were compared.

RESULTS AND DISCUSSION

The curves generated by the pressure transducer on the palmar surface of the hand for the three subjects in the breaststroke were similar. Figure 2 shows a typical pressure recording with the corresponding goniogram. The maximum pressure on the palmar surface of the hand occurred at an elbow angle of approximately 120°. This was also the point of deepest penetration of the hand into the water. The pressure patterns obtained were similar to the exponential curves described by Belokovsky (1971) for the crawl arm stroke. The pressure was minimal when the hands were in the glide position and increased gradually, reaching a maximum value at

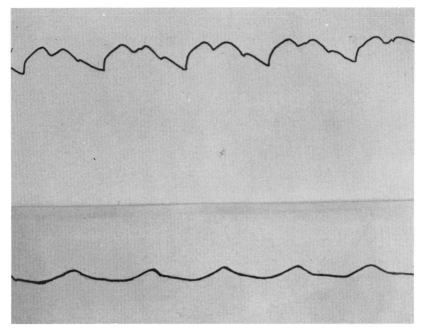

Figure 3. Typical pressure records for the backstroke and breaststroke. Top trace, "M"-shaped curve, was obtained during the backstroke. Bottom trace, exponentially shaped curve, was obtained during the breaststroke.

the point of deepest hand penetration. This was followed by a reduction in pressure until the glide position was reached. The time required to go from the minimal to maximal pressure was 0.34 sec, while the time from the maximal pressure to the minimal pressure was 0.16 sec.

As in the breaststroke, the pressure recordings for the two subjects in the backstroke were similar. However, the pattern for the backstroke differed from that for the breaststroke (Figure 3). The backstroke pressure curve was characterized by a maximal peak soon after hand entry into the water, followed by a reduction in pressure and then an increase in pressure, forming a second peak. This double-peaked pressure pattern could be described as an "M" curve. It has not been seen by previous investigators of pressures on the palm during swimming (Belokovsky, 1971; Van Manen and Rijken, 1975).

When the hand was lifted from the water, the transducer did not immediately record air pressure, but the curve "tailed" back toward the air baseline. Conversely, when the transducer was placed into the water, the response to the water pressure was immediate. The "tailing" shown in the latter part of the backstroke pressure recording is thus a function of the transducer and the fact that droplets of water were not immediately shed from the face of the transducer. In the breaststroke this same "tailing" was not evident because the hand always remains submerged.

As in the breaststroke, the maximal pressure in the backstroke coincided with the point of deepest penetration of the hand. The hydrostatic pressure on the transducer is given by the relationship:

$$\Delta p = -\gamma \Delta h \qquad \text{(Roberson and Crowe, 1975)}$$

where p = pressure, h = height below water surface, and $-\gamma$ = the specific weight of water (9790 N/m^3). Since, for both strokes, the maximal pressure occurred where the hydrostatic pressure was greatest, it seems that the hydrostatic pressure may be an important component of the total pressure recording. It is possible that the "M" curve pressure pattern shown in the backstroke was the result of changes in the hydrostatic pressure. The pressure reached its maximal value at the point of deepest penetration, decreased as the hand moved closer to the surface, and increased again as the hand moved deeper into the water.

There are other possible explanations, however, for this type of pressure variation. The pressure variation could be the result of inefficient stroke mechanics, the presence of a lift force, or a combination of these factors. Another factor that may have influenced the pressure recording was the effect of water turbulence on the transducer as the hand moved near the hip and thigh.

A comparison of the peak pressures in the breaststroke and backstroke for the same subjects showed greater pressure on the hand in the breaststroke. The reason for this could have been a greater depth of the hand in the breaststroke.

The maximum pressure for the sprint condition of the breaststroke was slightly greater than the moderate pace condition. Examination of the films showed that the kinematics of the stroke were so similar that the cause of this pressure difference could not be ascertained. At the sprint speed a higher wave may have been generated, thus increasing the hydrostatic pressure on the transducer, but there was no evidence to support this. In the backstroke there was no pressure difference between the moderate and sprint-paced strokes.

Electromyographic records were obtained for the breaststroke to relate muscle action to the pressure recordings and kinematics of the stroke. The posterior deltoid, wrist flexors, and triceps were active in the backward-downward-outward phase, and the anterior deltoid and wrist flexors were active in the backward-downward-inward phase with some slight activity in the posterior deltoid. These patterns agree with those presented by Yashizawa et al. (1976) for good breaststroke swimmers. Because the muscles were submaximally active, it was not possible to link the EMG to the pressure records. The magnitude of body resistance is such that maximum isometric force may not be necessary to propel the body forward. It would seem that three-dimensional cinematography would be of greater use than EMG in linking stroke mechanics to the pressure recordings.

Two of the subjects exhibited marked asymmetry in the first part of the recovery phase of the breaststroke. The arm with the electrodes and elgon attached showed an increased time and depth of recovery. When the subjects swam without the test apparatus, this same asymmetry existed. Therefore, the asymmetry was not caused by the test apparatus. It appears that, to obtain accurate measurements of the forces on the hands during swimming, measurements must be taken on each hand.

CONCLUSIONS

The use of strain-gauge pressure transducers is a valuable method for measuring the forces on the hand during swimming. Continuous force records can be obtained, and the subjects are not hindered by the test apparatus. However, the records obtained must be interpreted with care. The hydrostatic pressure as well as the propulsive force is a component of the total pressure recording. Pressure recordings may vary with the size and depth of the pool, with water temperature, with depth of hand placement, with the presence or absence of waves, or with any combination of these factors.

REFERENCES

Barthels, K. M. 1975. Three-dimensional kinematic analysis of the hand and hip in the butterfly swimming stroke. Ph.D. thesis, Washington State University, Pullman.

Barthels, K. M., and Adrian, M. J. 1975. Three-dimensional spatial hand patterns of skilled butterfly swimmer. In: L. Lewillie and J. P. Clarys (eds.), Swimming II, pp. 154-160. University Park Press, Baltimore.

Belokovsky, V. 1971. An analysis of pulling motions in the crawl arm stroke. In: L. Lewillie and J. P. Clarys (eds.), First International Symposium on Biomechanics in Swimming, pp. 217-222. Universite Libre de Bruxelles, Brussels.

Boicev, K., and Tzvetkox, A. 1975. Instrumentation and methods for complex investigations of swimming. In: L. Lewillie and J. P. Clarys (eds.), Swimming II, pp. 80-89. University Park Press, Baltimore.

Brown, R. M., and Counsilman, J. E. 1971. The role of lift in propelling the swimmer. In: John M. Cooper (ed.), Selected Topics on Biomechanics: Proceedings of the C.I.C. Symposium on Biomechanics, pp. 179-188. The Athletic Institute, Chicago.

Karpovich, P. V. 1933. Water resistance in swimming. Res. Q. 4:21.

Kent, M. R., and Atha, J. 1971. Selected critical transient body positions in breast stroke and their influence on water resistance. In: L. Lewillie and J. P. Clarys (eds.), First International Symposium on Biomechanics in Swimming, pp. 119–125. Université Libre de Bruxelles, Brussels.

Ringer, Lewis B., and Adrian, Marlene J. 1969. An electrogoniometric study of the wrist and elbow in the crawl armstroke. Res. Q. 40:353–363.

Roberson, John A., and Crowe, Clayton T. 1975. Engineering Fluid Mechanics. Houghton Mifflin Company, Boston.

Van Manen, J. D., and Rijken, H. 1975. Dynamic measurement techniques on swimming bodies at the Netherlands Ship Model Basin. In: L. Lewillie and J. P. Clarys (eds.), Swimming II, pp. 70–79. University Park Press, Baltimore.

Yashizawa, M., H. Tokurjama, T. Okamoto, and M. Kumamoto. 1976. Electromyographic study of the breaststroke. In: P. Komi (ed.), Biomechanics V-B, pp. 222–229. University Park Press Baltimore.

Analysis of Acceleration as a Measure of Swimming Proficiency

I. Holmér

Velocity fluctuations within a single stroke cycle in swimming are the result of accelerating and decelerating actions on the body exerted by propulsive movements and water resistance. Analysis of the relationship of the swimmer's acceleration and velocity versus time presents information about the way in which the different movements contribute to changes in swimming speed. Further, the magnitude of variation should indicate motion efficiency because less energy is wasted with a more uniform velocity. The precise nature of this relationship in swimming, however, has not been determined. Kornecki and Bober (1978) suggested that the deviation between extreme velocities and the mean velocity within a stroke cycle of a swimmer would be a useful measure of efficiency. The crucial problem has been to obtain data on single-stroke cycle kinematics in a way that makes more sophisticated analysis possible. Although time consuming and expensive, high speed cinematography is a classical method. Cavanagh (1976), however, has recently questioned the accuracy of acceleration data derived from such an analysis. Other instruments for recording velocity fluctuations have been presented (Karpovich and Karpovich, 1970; Kent and Atha, 1974). In the present study a linear accelerometer was used to determine the forward motion of the swimmer's body. The purpose was to develop a technique for reliable acceleration measurements and to analyze the data obtained for different swimmers and strokes.

METHODS AND PROCEDURES

Acceleration was measured with a linear accelerometer (Kulite, Ridgefield). The signal was recorded on an FM instrumentation tape recorder (Tandberg, series 100). The acceleration and velocity signals (obtained

Study supported by grants from the Research Council of the Swedish Sports Federation.

from analog integration) were recorded again on a polygraph together with the frame markings from a movie camera. The acceleration signal was analyzed for its spectral components with a frequency spectral analyzer (Bruel & Kjaer) using a technique similar to Broch's (1972). Similar frequency analysis techniques have been increasingly applied to low frequency signals (e.g., EMG). The velocity frequency spectrum was derived from the corresponding acceleration spectrum. Root mean square (RMS) values were calculated for each acceleration sample as

$$\text{RMS} = \sqrt{\Sigma a_i{}^2} \quad ; i = 0.25, \ldots, 10\,\text{Hz}$$

where a is acceleration in m/sec^2.

The experiments were performed in a swimming flume (Åstrand and Englesson, 1974) in which water speed could be controlled. The accelerometer was attached to the swimmer in three different ways. The swimmer wore a belt around his waist (method I) or his neck (method II). The belt was connected, via a nylon cord and a pulley system, to a small weight (100 g) and the accelerometer. The horizontal movement was thereby transferred to a vertical movement and registered with the accelerometer. The accelerometer was also taped to the back of the swimmer at the level of the fifth lumbar vertebra and secured with a belt (method III). In this way the accelerometer measured the forward movements of the swimmer directly. The resonance frequency of the measurement system was checked and found to be well above the interval of interest (0.25–10 Hz).

During the acceleration recordings, the swimmer was filmed from the side window of the flume with a movie camera (Fujica ZC1000). The camera frame rate was 72 frames/sec, and each frame produced a mark on a separate channel of the tape recorder.

Three swimmers—one recreational, one middle class, and one elite—participated in the study. They swam for 1–2 min each at several different velocities up to their maximal velocity. Recordings of 30-sec duration were made only after steady-state velocity and stroke rate were reached.

RESULTS AND DISCUSSION

Measurements with the line-pulley system (methods I and II) produced very similar results for corresponding stroke patterns; thus, the acceleration seemed to be relatively independent of the belt position. The slight deviations that were detected could probably be attributed to the extra movement of the head caused by breathing. Figure 1 depicts the curves obtained for one subject during front crawl and breaststroke swimming. The actions of the arms and legs were easily identified with the corresponding curves on the recording.

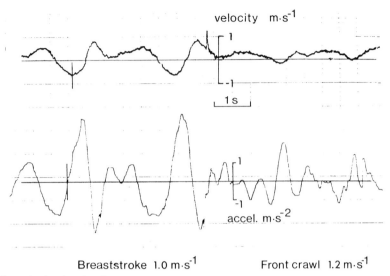

Breaststroke 1.0 m·s⁻¹   Front crawl 1.2 m·s⁻¹

Figure 1. Acceleration (lower curve) and velocity (upper curve) recordings for one swimmer during breaststroke and front crawl swimming. The velocity curve is shifted about 2 mm to the right compared with the acceleration curve because of the polygraph pen interaction.

In the breaststroke, the leg recovery phase produced a pronounced retardation of forward motion, while the following leg kick sharply accelerated the body. Acceleration caused by arm action was much less extensive. The concomitant velocity fluctuations are seen in the upper trace of Figure 1. The magnitudes of the velocity and acceleration fluctuations were much less in the front crawl than in the breaststroke, despite the higher swimming velocity (Figure 1).

The recordings with the accelerometer taped to the back displayed a slightly different pattern, although the main curvature and the arm and leg pattern were similar. The acceleration signal was probably mixed with vertical gravitational acceleration produced when the back (and the position of the accelerometer) performed rotational movements up and down in the sagittal plane during the stroke cycle. The errors caused by changes in position were not quantified but seem to diminish at higher velocities. The reliability of velocity measurements needs to be evaluated more carefully.

The acceleration and velocity curves offer significant information about stroke biomechanics. However, more detailed analysis of these kinds of data is beyond the scope of this article.

The most complete set of data was obtained with the accelerometer on the back. Accordingly, these data were used for the frequency spectrum analysis. The results obtained for the three swimmers illustrate the

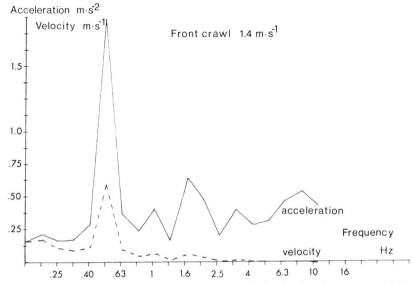

Figure 2. Frequency spectra for the acceleration and velocity signal during front crawl swimming in one swimmer. The ordinate displays the total amount of acceleration and change in velocity at different signal frequencies of the recording. The values between 0.25 and 10 Hz were considered for the analysis.

application of this kind of technique to the analysis of swimming movements.

Figure 2 depicts the frequency spectrum of the middle-class swimmer obtained at 1.4 m/sec in the front crawl. This type of diagram illustrates the contribution to the total acceleration of the movement at various frequencies from 0.25 to 10 Hz (i.e., from one total cycle every 4 sec to 10 cycles/sec). The very pronounced peak is derived from the arm action and thus occurs at a frequency identical to mean arm stroke rate. The peak is shifted to the right with increasing speed, resulting from progressively higher arm stroke rates. The data emphasize the importance of the arm action. The force exerted and the acceleration produced result in a significant change in velocity (Figure 2, lower curve).

At higher swimming velocities a second peak emerges, which can be attributed to the action of the legs (Figure 3). The frequency of the leg peak seems to be approximately three times greater than the frequency of the arm peak. Again this peak coincides with the mean kick rate; this swimmer was a six-beat kicker. The diagram in Figure 3 illustrates the effect of leg kicking. In this swimmer, leg action is pronounced only at maximal or near maximal speed. Apparently, the change in velocity caused by leg action at maximal intensity in this swimmer is very small compared with the effect of arm action. Accordingly, this swimmer generates most of

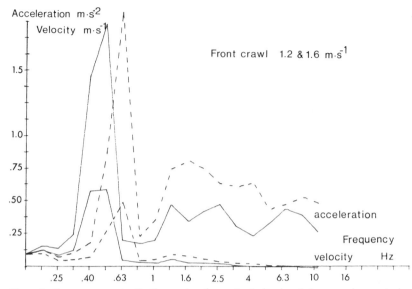

Figure 3. Frequency spectra for the acceleration and velocity signals for one swimmer during front crawl swimming at two different velocities. Note the shift to the right of the peaks as a result of the higher stroke rate with increased velocity and the pronounced acceleration peak at 1.6 m/sec as a result of increased leg action.

his propulsion through his arm action. It would be interesting to analyze in the same way swimmers with more powerful leg-kicking patterns.

The frequency spectra of the middle-class and the elite swimmer are compared at the same velocity in Figure 4. Apart from the differences in frequency response accounted for by the variations in swimming technique, the elite swimmer displays smaller acceleration and velocity peaks. Theoretically, a uniform velocity requires less energy and is more efficient (Belokovsky and Kuznetsov, 1976). It seems reasonable to assume that one significant way to obtain a superior swimming technique would be to minimize intracycle velocity fluctuations. The result here agrees with the observations presented by Miyashita (1971) and Kornecki and Bober (1978).

Different methods have been proposed to assess swimming efficiency from determinations of the intracycle velocity fluctuations (Miyashita, 1974; Kornecki and Bober, 1978). In the present study, the mean square root value (RMS value) was computed for the whole frequency interval (0.25 to 10 Hz). The RMS value for the elite swimmer was 30–40% lower than for the middle-class swimmer at 0.8–1.6 m/sec (Figure 5), confirming the better economy of the elite swimmer. The time integral of the acceleration signal gives results with the same trend.

In summary, intracycle acceleration analysis seems to provide a

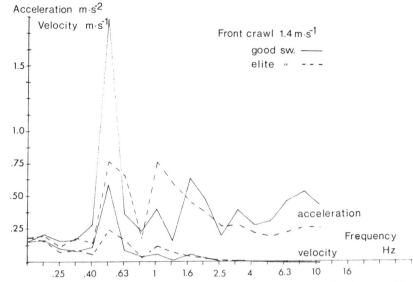

Figure 4. Frequency spectra for the acceleration and velocity signals during front crawl for two swimmers of different abilities. Note the smaller values of the elite swimmer as a result of less fluctuation in acceleration during swimming.

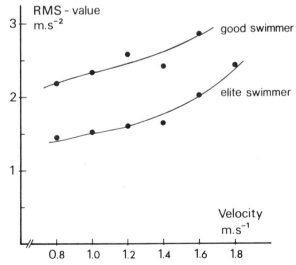

Figure 5. Root mean square values (RMS) for two swimmers during front crawl swimming at different velocities. The RMS value gives some indirect evidence of the extra energy spent because of acceleration and deceleration within the stroke cycle.

useful instrument for exploring swim stroke kinematics. When fully developed, the method should be able to give:

1. Accurate and continuous recordings of the accelerations within the stroke cycle
2. Velocity versus time relationships for the stroke cycle through integration of the acceleration signal
3. Quantification of the uniformity of swimming velocity
4. Information about the relative contribution to propulsion from arm and leg action

ACKNOWLEDGMENTS

The author is indebted to Bengt-Olov Wikström and Björn Sköldström for technical assistance and data evaluation and to Flygt AB, Solna, Sweden, for providing the swimming flume.

REFERENCES

Astrand, P.-O., and Englesson, S. 1974. A swimming flume. J. Appl. Physiol. 33:514.
Belokovsky, V. V., and Kuznetsov, V. V. 1976. Analysis of dynamic forces in crawl stroke swimming. In: P. V. Komi (ed.), Biomechanics V-B, pp. 235–242. University Park Press, Baltimore.
Broch, J. T. 1972. Mechanical vibration and shock measurements. Bruel and Kjaer, Copenhagen.
Cavanagh, P. R. 1976. Recent advances in instrumentation and methodology of biomechanical studies. In: P. V. Komi (ed.), Biomechanics V-B, pp. 399–411. University Park Press, Baltimore.
Karpovich, P. V., and Karpovich, G. P. 1970. Magnetic tape natograph. Res. Q. 41:119–122.
Kent, M. R., and Atha, J. 1974. A device for the on-line measurement of instantaneous swimming velocity. In: J. P. Clarys and L. Lewillie (eds.), Swimming II, pp. 58–63. University Park Press, Baltimore.
Kornecki, S., and Bober, T. 1978. Extreme velocities of a swimming cycle as a technique criterion. In: B. O. Eriksson and B. Furberg (eds.), Swimming Medicine IV, pp. 402–407. University Park Press, Baltimore.
Miyashita, M. 1971. An analysis of fluctuations of swimming speed. In: L. Lewillie and J. P. Clarys (eds.), First International Symposium on Biomechanics in Swimming, pp. 53–58. Universite Libre de Bruxelles, Brussels.
Miyashita, M. 1974. Method of calculating mechanical power in swimming the breast stroke. Res. Q. 45:128–137.

Analysis of Swimming Techniques

A Kinematic Investigation of Movement Patterns in Swimming with Photo-optical Methods

K. Reischle

This study deals with hip displacement in one stroke cycle and with the associated movement patterns of the butterfly, crawl, and backstrokes. The efficiency of the pull-push phase and of the kick phase depends on the speed fluctuations, the movement patterns, and the angle of attack of the hand and foot during the respective phases. The main purpose of this study was to find kinematic parameters that: 1) determine the performance of the swimmer, and 2) support quantitatively the biomechanical model of an optimal movement pattern in swimming.

METHODS

Sixty highly skilled age-group swimmers—36 females and 24 males (group 1)—and 44 untrained physical education (PE) students (group 2) were tested and compared. Table 1 shows the differences in swim times and stroke frequencies for 15 m.

Lightstreak photography, a simple method for recording movement patterns reported earlier (Reischle, 1978), was used to measure the limb movement patterns. The system utilized two 2.4-V light bulbs, one attached to a swimmer's wrist and one to his ankle. A rechargeable Ni-Cd battery (Varta 2.4 V) served as a power source. The batteries were waterproofed by embedding them in a polycasting resin.

The hip displacement in one stroke cycle was recorded with a light bulb attached to the swimmer's hip, which glowed during the pull-push phase. This bulb was switched on when the hand entered the water, and it was switched off when the hand reached the surface again (see Figure 1). Therefore, during competition and training, coaches can determine the hip distance covered in one stroke cycle with the help of the nomogram that has been developed (see Figure 2).

Table 1. Differences in mean times (15 m) and stroke frequencies between highly skilled swimmers (group 1) and PE students (group 2)

Variable	Stroke	Group	Sex	N	Mean	SD	t ratio	Two-tail prob.
Time (15 m)	Crawl	1	m	24	7.8 (sec)	0.48	-7.01^a	0.000
		2	m	24	12.2 (sec)	3.02		
Frequency		1	m	24	50 (ft/min)	5.07	1.65	0.112
		2	m	19	45 (ft/min)	12.28		
Time (15 m)	Crawl	1	f	28	8.5 (sec)	0.54	-11.82^a	0.000
		2	f	19	13.1 (sec)	1.63		
Frequency		1	f	26	49 (ft/min)	5.40	6.21^a	0.000
		2	f	17	40 (ft/min)			
Time (15 m)	Butterfly	1	m	24	8.4 (sec)	0.74	-4.95^a	0.000
		2	m	23	14.8 (sec)	6.17		
Frequency		1	m	24	53 (ft/min)	4.80	8.10^a	0.000
		2	m	17	39 (ft/min)	6.20		
Time (15 m)	Butterfly	1	f	27	9.1 (sec)	0.53	-5.22^a	0.000
		2	f	19	16.4 (sec)			
Frequency		1	f	26	54 (ft/min)	4.30	10.21^a	0.000
		2	f	16	39 (ft/min)	5.90		
Time (15 m)	Back	1	m	23	10.5 (sec)	0.98	-10.61^a	0.000
		2	m	23	14.8 (sec)	1.65		
Frequency		1	m	24	38 (ft/min)	4.19	3.03^a	0.000
		2	m	18	34 (ft/min)	4.63		
Time (15 m)	Back	1	f	28	11.2 (sec)	1.15	-6.61^a	0.000
		2	f	18	14.6 (sec)	1.94		
Frequency		1	f	28	39 (ft/min)	4.04	3.19^a	0.003
		2	f	16	35 (ft/min)	4.86		

^{a}Significant at 0.05 level of probability.

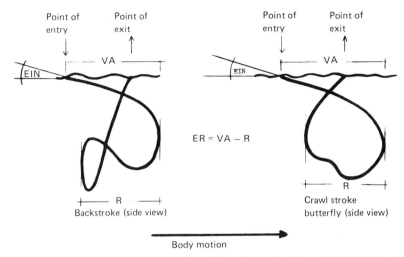

$$ER = VA - R$$

Figure 1. Pull-push phase of the back, butterfly, and crawl strokes relative to still water. EIN (angle of entry), VA (forward-downward phase, R (backward phase), ER (difference between VA and R).

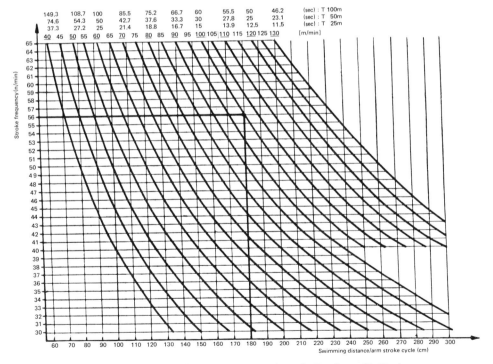

Figure 2. Nomogram for swimming distance per arm stroke cycle, L_{zr}. $L_{zr} = Vs/f$, where: Vs = swimming velocity and f = stroke frequency.

The traces were recorded with an underwater camera (Nikonos III). This camera was equipped with a lens that was modified for underwater conditions with a shutter speed set at 3–6 sec at an f-11 stop. Kodak Tri X Pan (27 Din or ASA 400) film gave good results.

The camera was placed 8.75 m from the plane of motion with the lens axis aligned perpendicular to the direction of swimming. A reference scale located in the plane of motion was visible in the photographic field. The swimmers were instructed to swim at maximum speed, and the stroke frequency was measured with a special stroke-frequency meter.

The pull-push and the kick phases, which were recorded in the side view, gave a two-dimensional model of the three-dimensional movement pattern. Correction for perspective errors was not considered necessary, and, therefore, was not done. The recorded movement pattern represented the motion relative to still water and not the swimmer's body. The data were treated statistically by an independent t-test and a correlation analysis.

RESULTS

The hip displacement in one stroke of the highly skilled swimmers was significantly greater for butterfly, backstroke, and crawl stroke. These results have been reported previously by Reischle (1978). The pull-push phase and the kick phase of the two groups differed in the following kinematic parameters. For the highly skilled swimmers the angle at the point of entry was significantly smaller, and the distance between the point of entry and the end of the forward-downward phase was significantly greater (see Tables 2 and 3). If the forward-downward phase is multiplied by the stroke frequency, this significant difference is even more pronounced.

The complete path of the backward phase (backward-downward and backward-upward) of highly skilled swimmers was significantly shorter. The ratio of backward phase to stroke frequency makes this significant difference even more distinct. The difference between the forward-downward phase and the backward phase of highly skilled swimmers was also significantly greater than this same difference in the less skilled subjects (see Table 4).

The Pearson correlation coefficients show for all groups a high, negative correlation between angle at the point of entry and the forward-downward phase (Table 5).

The angles of the downward phases of butterfly kick, crawl kick, and the upward phase of the backstroke kick of the highly skilled swimmers were significantly smaller than the respective kicks of the PE students (see Table 6). The butterfly kick of the poorer swimmers had a mean angle of

Table 2. Differences in mean angles of entry (EIN) between group 1 and group 2 in crawl, butterfly, and backstrokes

Variable	Stroke	Group	Sex	N	Mean (°)	SD	t ratio	Two-tail prob.
Angle of entry (EIN)	Crawl	1	m	22	25.9	11.35	−1.66	0.105
		2	m	23	32.7	15.95		
	Crawl	1	f	36	26.6	10.27	−1.81	0.076
		2	f	19	32.3	12.30		
Angle of entry (EIN)	Butterfly	1	m	24	25.9	16.7	−3.17[a]	0.003
		2	m	20	53.5	20.08		
	Butterfly	1	f	36	31.6	11.49	−4.40[a]	0.000
		2	f	16	47.7	13.58		
Angle of entry (EIN)	Back	1	m	20	34.5	11.17	−4.06[a]	0.000
		2	m	10	54.5	15.43		
	Back	1	f	35	33.9	12.2	−4.73[a]	0.000
		2	f	10	55.0	13.1		

[a]Significant at 0.05 level of probability.

Table 3. Differences between group 1 and group 2 in mean forward/downward phases (VA) and backward phases (R) in crawl and back strokes

Variable	Stroke	Group	Sex	N	Mean (cm)	SD	t ratio[a]	Two-tail prob.
Forward/downward phase (VA)	Crawl	1	m	22	50.9	20.4	2.56	0.014
		2	m	23	36.1	18.4		
		1	f	36	51.3	15.2	3.79	0.000
		2	f	19	36.4	16.0		
	Back	1	m	21	44.7	14.3	5.38	0.000
		2	m	10	17.8	9.4		
		1	f	35	39.4	14.2	4.10	0.000
		2	f.	10	19.0	12.7		
Backward phase (R)	Crawl	1	m	22	42.6	6.2	−3.31	0.002
		2	m	23	52.5	12.9		
		1	f	36	39.9	9.1	−3.18	0.002
		2	f	19	48.5	10.2		
	Back	1	m	20	45.2	8.2	−3.70	0.001
		2	m	10	57.8	9.9		
		1	f	35	45.1	6.7	−2.70	0.010
		2	f	10	52.0	8.5		

[a]Significant at 0.05 level of probability.

Table 4. Differences in mean performances between group 1 and group 2 (ER = VA − R)

Variable	Stroke	Group	Sex	N	Mean (cm)	SD	t ratio[a]	Two-tail prob.
VA − R (ER)	Crawl	1	m	22	8.3	20.1	3.52	0.001
		2	m	23	−16.5	24.5		
		1	f	36	10.8	16.2	4.68	0.001
		2	f	19	−14.0	10.2		
VA − R (ER)	Back	1	m	20	−2.3	16.4	6.05	0.000
		2	m	10	−38.2	12.8		
		1	f	35	−5.1	15.3	5.27	0.000
		2	f	10	−34.2	15.8		

[a]Significant at 0.05 level of probability.

Table 5.   Pearson correlation coefficients

Group[a]	Stroke	Sex	N	Coefficient (r)
1	Crawl	m	22	−0.75
1	Crawl	f	36	−0.73
2	Crawl	m	18	−0.80
2	Crawl	f	16	−0.69
1	Back	m	20	−0.73
1	Back	f	34	−0.73
2	Back	m	8	−0.77
2	Back	f	8	−0.76

[a]Group 1 = highly skilled, group 2 = PE students.

over 90°. This fact points to an active flexion of the shank by the poor swimmers.

Table 6 also shows that the distance between the first and the second butterfly kick of the highly skilled swimmers was significantly greater than for the less skilled group. This fact provided evidence of the well-timed co-ordination of the two kicks with the pull-push phase—i.e., the less skilled swimmers didn't kick during the second half of the pull-push phase; instead they kicked before this phase was initiated.

DISCUSSION

The empirical results corresponded with the conceptual biomechanical model of an optimal movement pattern. The relatively small angles at the point of entry together with a relatively long forward-downward phase indicate a high swimming velocity but with a low hand acceleration at the beginning of the pull-push phase. In other words, skilled swimmers avoid slippage, which often occurs when poor swimmers accelerate too much at the beginning of the pull-push phase. Thus, the body's inertia is not overcome. According to Schleihauf (1974), "A poor swimmer will obtain positive hand speed earlier in the stroke cycle ... thus indicating slippage."

The shorter backward phases of skilled swimmers indicates a higher efficiency of the pull-push phase, which is achieved when the swimmers utilize drag and lift forces for propulsion by outward and inward movement with a corresponding angle of attack (Counsilman, 1969; Schleihauf, 1974; Barthels and Adrian, 1975; Reischle, 1976). The difference between forward-downward phases shows that "the resultant motion of the hand relative to the water is forward not backwards," as stated by Schleihauf (1974).

The point of exit is in front of the point of entry as reported by Coun-

Table 6.   Differences in mean performances between group 1 and group 2 including the downward phases of the kicks (AB, AB_1, AB_2), the upward phases of the kick (AUF) stroke and the distances ($X_{1/2}$) between kick 1 and kick 2 of the butterfly

Variable	Stroke	Group	Sex	N	Mean	SD	t Ratio[a]	Two-tail prob.
AB	Crawl	1	m	22	57.5°	11.85	-2.66	0.011
		2	m	23	69.7°	18.40		
		1	f	35	64.3°	10.50	-2.77	0.011
		2	f	18	76.6°	17.20		
AB_1	Butterfly	1	m	20	85.6°	8.90	-2.83	0.012
		2	m	15	107.3°	28.70		
AB_2	Butterfly	1	m	21	61.2°	16.82	-6.02	0.000
		2	m	15	99.9°	21.82		
		1	f	33	55.6°	20.62	-5.79	0.000
		2	f	14	93.9°	21.07		
X_{12}	Butterfly	1	m	20	75.6 (cm)	10.07	5.61	0.000
		2	m	15	46.7 (cm)	8.45		
		1	f	33	75.0 (cm)	14.00	5.24	0.000
		2	f	13	48.0 (cm)	20.00		
AUF	Back	1	m	20	68.7 (cm)	10.65	-2.47	0.020
		2	m	8	80.5 (cm)	13.38		

[a]Significant at 0.05 level of probability

silman (1969), Clarys, Jiskoot, and Lewillie (1973), Schleihauf (1974), and Reischle (1976).

CONCLUSION

The significant differences described were observed in both males and females. This result indicates the reliability of the method described and shows that the kinematic parameters, described objectively, determine swimming performance.

REFERENCES

Barthels, K. M., and Adrian, M. J. 1975. Three-dimensional spatial hand patterns of skilled butterfly swimmers. In: J. P. Clarys and L. Lewillie (eds.), Swimming II, pp. 154–160. University Park Press, Baltimore.
Clarys, J., Jiskott, J., and Lewillie, L. 1973. L'emploi de traces lumineuses dans l'analyse biomećanique de differents styles de natation (Use of the lightstreak method in the biomechanical analyses of different swimming styles). Kinanthropologie 5:127.
Counsilman, J. E. 1969. The role of sculling movements in the arm pull. Swimming World 10(12):6–7, 43.
Reischle, K. 1976. Das antriebsproblem beim Schwimmen (The problem of propulsion in swimming). Leistungssport 6(4):302–310.
Reischle, K. 1978. Lightstreak photography: a simple method for recording movement patterns. In: B. Eriksson and B. Furberg (eds.), Swimming Medicine IV, pp. 408–414. University Park Press, Baltimore.
Schleihauf, R. 1974. A biomechanical analysis of freestyle. Swimming Tech. 11.89.

Modeling of
Lower Extremity Forces
in the Dolphin Kick

R. K. Jensen and J. McIlwain

Little is known about the contribution of the dolphin kick to changes in the horizontal and vertical momentum of the swimmer. Counsilman (1968) asked if the dolphin kick is propulsive. He observed that the first kick may accelerate the swimmer and elevate the hips (p. 69). Data collected by Barthels and Adrian (1975) suggest that during the reach and early outsweep phases for the arms, the downbeat of the legs is accompanied by a forward acceleration of the hip. The horizontal and vertical forces produced by movement of the body segments through water can be estimated from modeling techniques. The purpose of this study was to model the lower extremity of the swimmer and to estimate the joint reaction forces for the dolphin kick.

In the past, modeling studies of swimming strokes have been theoretical and were based on input functions for the motions of the segments. Analytical studies were done by Seireg and Baz (1971), Gallenstein and Huston (1973), Jensen and Blanksby (1975), and Jensen and Tihanyi (1978). These studies indicate the relative contributions of the segments to the stroke. In the present investigation empirical data were collected and used to estimate the segmental forces and moments of force.

PROCEDURE

Two swimmers of international caliber, a female (WH) and a male (GM), were filmed from the side and below the surface at 48 frames/sec. Anthropometric measurements taken of the lower extremity of the swimmers were used to formulate a geometric representation of the segments. The model assumes that each segment can be represented as a frustrum of a cone (Hanavan, 1964).

Displacement data for the model were obtained by determining for each frame the rectangular coordinates for the hip and the angular coordinates for the thigh, lower leg, and foot using a PCD digital analyzer. The raw displacement data were filtered using a low pass Butterworth digital filter with a cutoff frequency of 8 Hz, and velocity and acceleration arrays obtained using finite difference equations (Pezzack, Norman, and Winter, 1977).

Segmental size parameters were calculated and used with the mean densities reported by Clauser, McConville, and Young (1969) to give the inertial parameters needed for the kinetic analysis. The kinematics of the segmental mass centers and joint centers for the model were calculated (Jensen and Blanksby, 1975). To estimate the drag force acting on each segment, the procedure of Gallenstein and Huston (1973) was followed. The segments were assumed to be mean diameter cylinders, and the drag coefficients reported by Hoerner (1958) were assumed to hold for the nonsteady-state conditions experienced by the swimmers. Horizontal and vertical components of the joint forces and the moments of force were then calculated using equations of motion reported previously (Jensen and Bellow, 1976; Jensen and Blanksby, 1975), and the required kinematic and kinetic curves were plotted.

RESULTS AND DISCUSSION

The size and inertial parameters for the lower extremity segments of the two swimmers are given in Table 1. The dimensions were similar, with the female (WH) having slightly greater mass in the foot and less mass in the thigh and the male (GM) having a longer lower leg and foot.

The phases in the stroke are the upbeat and the downbeat as characterized by the absolute angular displacement for the lower leg

Table 1.   Size and inertial parameters for the lower extremity segments of the two swimmers

	WH			GM		
Swimmer Segment	Thigh	Lower Leg	Foot	Thigh	Lower leg	Foot
Length (m)	0.363	0.387	0.255	0.363	0.440	0.276
Volume (m³ × 10³)	6.05	2.73	0.92	6.36	2.73	0.77
Mass (kg)	6.35	2.97	1.01	6.67	2.95	0.84
Weight (N)	62.2	29.1	9.9	65.4	29.1	8.2
Buoyancy (N)	59.3	26.7	9.1	62.3	26.7	7.6
I_G (kg/m² × 10³)	75.3	37.2	5.5	76.9	48.3	5.3

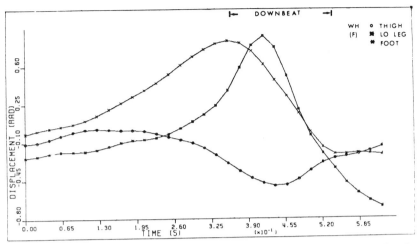

Figure 1. Absolute angular displacements for the lower extremity segments of the female (WH).

(Figures 1 and 2). It is evident that the lower-leg downbeat or clockwise rotation, as seen from the left side of the swimmer, was preceded by a similar but smaller rotation of the thigh that starts from approximately the horizontal position. The downbeat was followed by an extended rotation of the foot. Differences between the two swimmers are noticeable at this point in that WH started her foot rotation at a greater angle and delayed the movement more than GM. As shown by the slopes of the

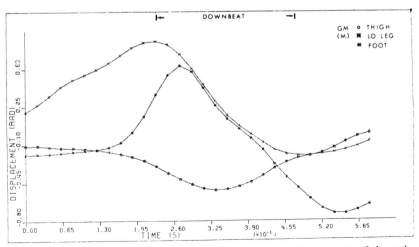

Figure 2. Absolute angular displacements for the lower extremity segments of the male (GM).

curves, the angular velocities for WH's foot and lower leg were greater than for GM's.

For the two swimmers the drag force acting on each segment depended on the dimensions of the segment, the square of the relative velocity between the fluid and the segment, and direction of the relative-velocity vector. Relative velocity is attributable to translational and rotational velocity. The translational velocity of the foot is caused by the velocities of the thigh and lower leg. To this is added the velocity attributable to the rotation of the foot. If the direction of the relative velocity vector for the mass center approaches the normal to the segment, the velocity component for the drag force is high. If the relative velocity vector approaches the tangent to the segment, the velocity component and thus the drag force are low. The sequence of high rotational velocities for the thigh, lower leg, and foot produced a high relative velocity, which was primarily normal to the foot. The result was the high drag force for the foot (Figures 3 and 4). Further, in keeping with the angular velocities, the drag force curves for WH were larger than for GM.

The results for the foot can be contrasted with the drag forces for the lower leg. It is generally supposed that the lower leg sets up drag forces than are used for propulsion. Figures 3 and 4 show that the drag forces during the downbeat were small. This can be attributed to the directions of the velocity vectors, which approached tangential, and to the smaller magnitudes of the relative velocities. Positive drag forces for the thigh and negative drag forces for the lower leg precede the downbeat (Figures 3 and 4). Figures 1 and 2 show, however, that because of the angular position of these two segments, the component of the drag was added to the

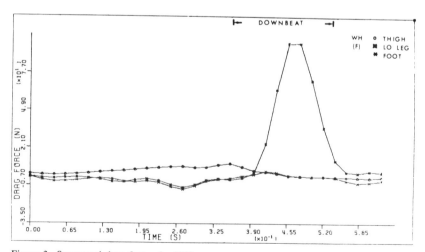

Figure 3. Segmental drag forces for WH.

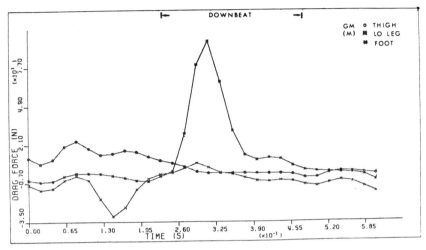

Figure 4. Segmental drag forces for GM.

resistance acting against the swimmer. It is evident from the curves for drag that the only drag forces of consequence were those acting on the foot during the downbeat.

The horizontal reaction forces for the three segments of the two swimmers are shown in Figures 5 and 6. As the swimmers were moving from right to left, negative values indicate propulsion and positive values indicate resistance. The curves for the hip show that during the downbeat the lower extremity contributed to the propulsion of the swimmers. This contribution can be analyzed by considering the relative magnitudes of the

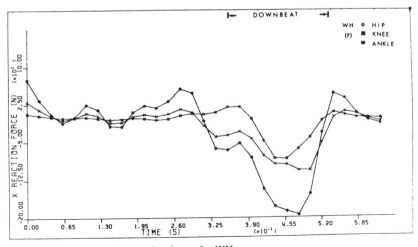

Figure 5. Horizontal joint reaction forces for WH.

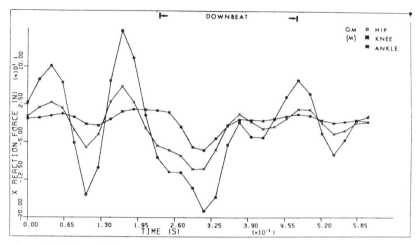

Figure 6. Horizontal joint reaction forces for GM.

viscous and inertial force components at the ankle, knee, and hip. As expected from the calculated drag forces (Figures 3 and 4) the horizontal component of the drag force for the ankle was large and reached a peak of -48.3 N for WH and -42.7 N for GM. However, the calculated ankle drag impulses for the two swimmers were similar. The differences between the two curves for the ankle (Figures 5 and 6) can be explained in terms of the inertial forces. The inertial impulse for WH was greater than that for GM.

The differences between the force curves for the ankle and knee (Figures 5 and 6) can be almost totally explained in terms of inertial forces because the horizontal component of the drag force was effectively zero. Differences between the force curves for the knee and hip can be explained in the same manner. Impulse calculated for the hip indicated that despite the shorter duration of her downbeat, WH produced a slightly greater impulse than GM.

The effects of the upbeat on the horizontal forces for the two swimmers are different. The curves for GM were large and fluctuated around zero. For WH the curves were smaller. For both there was a net effect on resistance. Once again these curves are largely the result of inertial forces with a limited component of drag for the lower leg just before the downbeat.

It is evident from the vertical force curves for the hip in Figures 7 and 8 that the lower extremity made a net contribution to the vertical momentum of the hip during the downbeat. The drag component exceeded the inertial component for the ankle and reached peak values of 97.3 N for WH and 87.4 N for GM. The contributions of the remaining segments were almost totally inertial. The inertial forces were positive during the in-

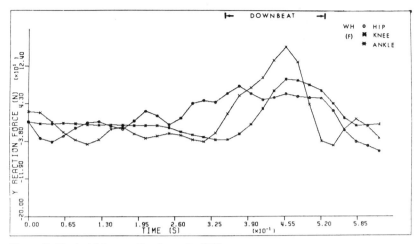

Figure 7. Vertical joint reaction forces for WH.

itial phase of the downbeat but then fluctuated between negative and positive to give the force patterns of Figures 7 and 8. The curves for the hip also indicate that during the upbeat there was a net positive effect, which can be attributed largely to the thigh. In general it can be said that the drag force through its action on the foot had a greater influence on the vertical component of force than on the horizontal component.

The patterns of movement for the segments of the lower extremity were produced by the moments of force at the three joints. The moments for the ankle during the downbeat were small (Figures 9 and 10) compared with the moments for the knee and hip. Given the relative sizes of

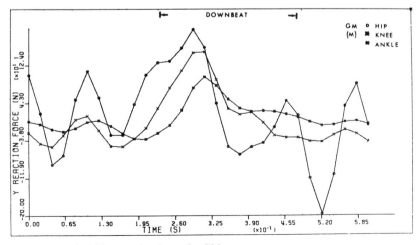

Figure 8. Vertical joint reaction forces for GM.

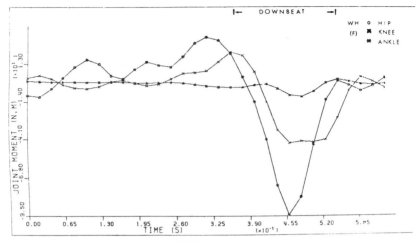

Figure 9. Joint moments of force for WH.

the drag forces (Figures 3 and 4) the moment curves indicate once again the importance of the inertial components in the actions of the lower extremity. The moments required to produce the upbeat were smaller than the moments for the downbeat. The timing of the moments is also of interest, with the hip moments preceding the knee moments and in the downbeat the knee moments preceding the ankle moments. Comparison of the two figures shows that the moments for GM during the upbeat were greater than for WH but less during the downbeat.

The outcome of greatest interest to the swimmer and coach is the forward velocity of the swimmer. Hip velocities are given in Figures 11 and

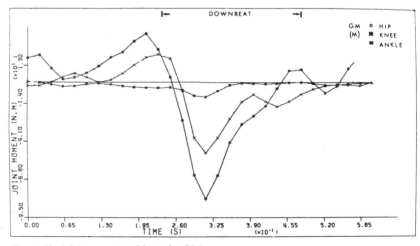

Figure 10. Joint moments of force for GM.

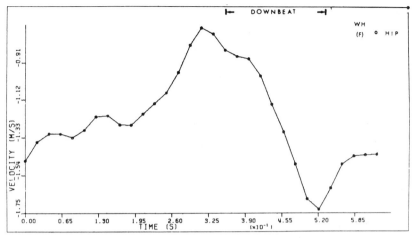

Figure 11. Hip horizontal velocity for WH.

12. Presumably because of the actions of the remaining body segments, the velocity for GM before the downbeat was greater than for WH. Following the downbeat, the hip velocities for the two swimmers were very similar. The mean forward acceleration for WH during the downbeat was -3.62 m/sec,[2] and for GM it was -2.23 m/sec.[2]

CONCLUSIONS

In general it can be concluded that Counsilman's observations are correct (1968). In the interest of improving performance, however, it is important

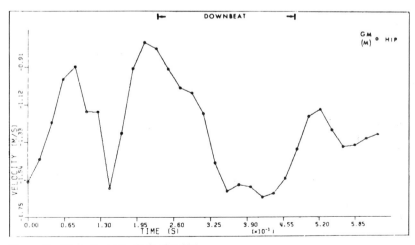

Figure 12. Hip horizontal velocity for GM.

to know why the dolphin kick accelerates the swimmer and elevates the hip. As a result of muscle contraction across the hip, knee, and ankle joints, moments of force were produced that gave the upbeat and downbeat movements of the kick. The moment curves were timed so that they followed a sequence from hip to knee to ankle. There was also a substantial decrease in the magnitudes of the curves from hip to knee to ankle. The moments for the hip and knee were almost totally accountable in terms of inertial forces because the drag forces acting on the thigh and lower leg during the downbeat were negligible. The insignificance of the drag forces was largely the result of the direction of the relative velocity vectors. Drag forces for the foot were comparatively large and played a significant role in the moments for the ankle and the horizontal and vertical reaction force components for the ankle. The horizontal forces for the ankle were augmented by the inertial forces for the lower leg and thigh to give the reaction forces at the hip. The reaction forces provided propulsion for the swimmers during the downbeat and resistance during the upbeat. An increase in forward velocity was noted for the hips during the downbeat. The downbeat also produced vertical reaction force curves, which affected the vertical momentum of the lower extremity.

The force curves for the female, WH, indicate that her dolphin kick was more effective than that of the male, GM. The results of the study could be used as the basis for a further study designed to improve the performance of the dolphin kick. It is further suggested that the mathematical model could be improved by using an elliptical-zone fragmentation of the segments (Jensen, 1978) in place of the whole-segment representation used in this study.

ACKNOWLEDGMENT

The assistance of the Canadian Amateur Swimming Association and the two swimmers, Wendy Hogg and Gary MacDonald, who served as subjects is gratefully acknowledged.

REFERENCES

Barthels, K., and Adrian, M. 1975. Three-dimensional spatial hand patterns of skilled butterfly swimmers. In: J. P. Clarys and L. Lewillie (eds.), Swimming II, 154-60. University Park Press, Baltimore.

Clauser, C. E., McConville, J. T., and Young, J. W. 1969. Weight, volume and center of mass of segments of the human body, pp. 69-70. AMRL Technical Report, Wright Patterson AFB, Ohio.

Counsilman, J. E. 1968. The Science of Swimming. Prentice-Hall, Inc. Englewood Cliffs, New Jersey.

Gallenstein, J., and Huston, R. L. 1973. Analysis of swimming motions Hum. Fac. 15:1:91-98.

Hanavan, E.P. 1964. A mathematical model of the human body, pp. 64-102. AMRL Technical Report, Wright Patterson AFB, Ohio.

Hoerner, S. F. 1958. Fluid Dynamic Drag. Hoerner, Midland Park, N. J.

Jensen, R. K. 1978. Estimation of the biomechanical properties of three body types using a photogrammetric method. J. Biomech. 11:349-358.

Jensen, R. K., and Bellow, D. G. 1976. Upper extremity contraction moments and their relationship to swimming training. J. Biomech. 9:219-225.

Jensen, R. K., and Blanksby, B. 1975. A model for upper extremity forces during the front crawl underwater phase. In: J. P. Clarys and L. Lewillie (eds.), Swimming II, pp. 145-153. University Park Press, Baltimore.

Jensen, R. K., and Tihanyi, J. 1978. Fundamental studies of tethered swimming. In: F. Landry and W. Orban (eds.), Biomechanics of Sports and Kinanthropometry, pp. 143-148. Symposium Specialists, Miami.

Pezzack, J. C., Norman, R. W., and Winter, D. A. 1977. An assessment of derivitive determining techniques used for motion analysis. J. Biomech. 10:377-382.

Seireg, A., and Baz, A. 1971. A mathematical model for swimming mechanics. In: L. Lewillie and J. P. Clarys (eds.), Biomechanics in Swimming, pp. 81-103. Universite Libré de Bruxelles, Brussels.

Relationship between Stroke Asymmetry and Speed of Breaststroke Swimming

B. Czabański and T. Koszczyc

Predomination of one side of the human body over the other side is a well-known phenomenon. Various methodical studies reveal bilateral differentation to be a common feature in human motor development. Both endogenous and exogenous fibers are generally thought to form in a bilateral manner. However, the lateralization process has not been fully explained. The asymmetry of the hemispheres of the brain is observed in individual development (ontogenesis) from the fetal period on. Greater efficiency of the right hand as compared with the left hand is a recognized characteristic in the functional asymmetry of man, and similar differences are found in the lower limbs (Szczebiotko, 1975). There is significant asymmetry in the length of the bones of the lower limbs, with preference to the left leg, and differences in the circumference of the thighs and calves (Artemeva, 1964; Czabański, 1975; Drozdowski, 1975). Alterations in the functional scope of the respective limbs, combined with morphological changes, are observed (Kurachenkov, 1966). According to some researchers the right lower limb performs functions that require speed and precision, while the left lower limb is used more often in movements requiring great dynamic strength (Wolański, 1962; Dolja, 1973; Starosta, 1975). The superiority of the right hand and left leg is a type of lateralization characteristic for women, whereas higher efficiency of the right hand and right leg predominates in men (Koszczyc, 1977).

The problem of lateralization is particularly significant in sports: such as running, cycling, and swimming, which are symmetrical in nature. Of special interest here are the leg movements in breaststroke swimming. The human structure is not precisely symmetrical, and most human movements are asymmetrical. The following questions arise:

1. Are the requirements for absolute symmetrical motions justified?
2. Will the attainment of symmetry result in improved swimming performance?

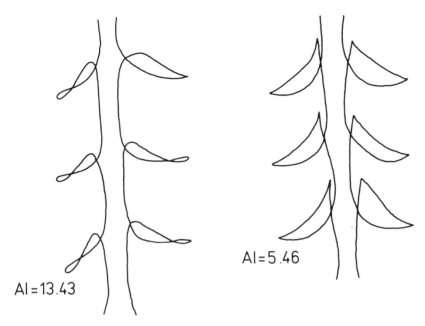

Figure 1. Typical breaststroke leg kick patterns.

The purposes of this study were: 1) to verify the extent of asymmetry in the motion of the lower limbs in the breaststroke, 2) to define possible differences in the degree of asymmetry for women and men, and 3) to examine the relationship between asymmetry and swimming speed, assuming the latter to be the best indicator of swimming efficiency.

METHOD

The subjects selected for investigation were 30 female and 27 male students of ages 19 to 22 years. Asymmetry of the lower limb movements was measured by cyclophotography. The subject swam 10 m at maximum speed with his hands supported by a float. At the starting point he rested his legs on a rope to eliminate any velocity resulting from his pushing off from the swimming pool wall. Small bulbs connected to a power supply were mounted on the swimmer's heels. Three successive breaststroke kick cycles for each subject were analyzed. Two typical leg kick patterns are presented in Figure 1.

Figure 2 identifies the components used to calculate the asymmetry index (AI). The places where the curves are nearest to each other were identified as the beginning and termination points and are connected by straight lines (z'_1-z_1 and $z'_{31}-z_{31}$). The midpoints of these lines were con-

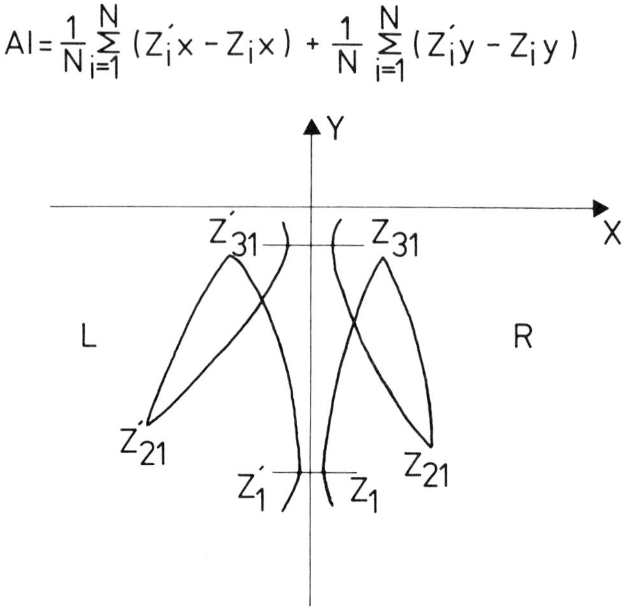

$$AI = \frac{1}{N}\sum_{i=1}^{N}(Z_i'x - Z_ix) + \frac{1}{N}\sum_{i=1}^{N}(Z_i'y - Z_iy)$$

Figure 2. Components used in calculating the asymmetry index.

nected by a straight line (Y) that represented the axis of symmetry for both curves.

A second line was drawn perpendicular to the axis of symmetry, resulting in an x,y coordinate system for identifying selected points in the movement pattern. The asymmetry index for the lower limb motion in the breaststroke was calculated from the formula:

$$AI = \frac{1}{N}\sum_{i=1}^{N}(z_i'x - z_ix) + \frac{1}{N}\sum_{i=1}^{N}(z_i'y - z_iy)$$

where, N = number of points determined in one motion cycle, $z_i'x$ = length of the given straight line from x axis to z_i' point, z_ix = length of the given straight line from x axis to z_i point, $z_i'y$ = length of the given straight line from y axis to z_i' point, and z_iy = length of the given straight line from y axis to z_i point.

The absolute values of differences in the lengths of the given straight lines are under the Σ sign. The asymmetry index was calculated from the arithmetic mean of three successive motion cycles, with a value of 0 indicating perfect symmetry.

RESULTS AND DISCUSSIONS

The group of women and men observed had similar swimming efficiency, which was expressed in the approximate average speed of swimming by

Table 1.   Average asymmetry index for women and men

	Asymmetry index (mean ± SE)	Significance
Men (N = 26)	11.32 ± 4.82	P < 0.01
Women (N = 30)	9.55 ± 3.33	P < 0.01

use of the lower limbs only. The mean for women was 0.57 m/sec, and for men it was 0.66 m/sec. The speed for women ranged from 0.5 to 0.7 m/sec, and for men it ranged from 0.5 to 0.93 m/sec. Not one swimmer demonstrated full motion symmetry. The lowest index for women was 3.95, and for men it was 5.75, indicating greater asymmetry for men (see Table 1).

To explain the relationship between speed and asymmetry, the average asymmetry index was calculated for the group of women and men who had similar efficiency—i.e., who swam at a similar speed. The results presented in Table 2 indicate that similar asymmetries for men and women occur when they swim at the same velocity. Furthermore both groups increased in asymmetry as velocity increased. This was substantiated by the results of the correlation analysis, which revealed a moderate, statistically significant correlation of $r = 0.59$ (see Table 3).

Table 2.   Asymmetry index: means and standard deviations for women and men for the breaststroke leg kick

	0.5–0.6 m/sec		0.61–0.7 m/sec	
	N	mean ± SE	N	mean ± SE
Women	7	9.13 ± 2.91	7	9.82 ± 2.79
Men	9	9.28 ± 2.57	9	9.54 ± 2.61

Table 3.   Relationship between the degree of asymmetry and speed for the breaststroke ($r = 0.59$)

	N	mean ± SE
Leg velocity (m/sec)	56	0.59 ± 0.18
Asymmetry index	56	10.33 ± 4.04

The following conclusions are based on the results of this experiment:

1. Asymmetry in leg kick patterns is present for most breaststroke swimmers.
2. In general, men are more asymmetrical than women, but this difference diminishes when they swim at the same speed.
3. A positive relationship exists between the leg kick asymmetry and speed.
4. Coaches should not emphasize symmetry in their training program, and swimmers should not concentrate on this aspect of their performance.

REFERENCES

Artemeva, L. S. 1964. On the problem of flat-foot in sportsmen. Theory and Practice of Sports 7:42-44. (In Russian)
Bober, T., and B. Czabański. 1974. The influence of different swimming speeds on changes in the technique of the breaststroke. Performance Sports 12:4-8. (In Polish)
Czabański, B. 1975. Asymmetry of the lower limbs in breaststroke swimming. In J. P. Clarys and L. Lewillie (eds.), Swimming II, pp. 207-213. University Park Press, Baltimore.
Dolja, G. V. 1973. The asymmetry of the development of the strength of the leg muscles, and the sports results in the high jump. Theory and Practice of Sports 12:25-27. (In Russian)
Drozdowski, S. 1975. From research on the asymmetry of muscle development in the limbs of competing athletes. [Monograph] Physical Education Academy, Poznan, Poland. (In Polish)
Koszcyzc, T. 1977. The rhythm and the process of the asymmetric movement of the lower extremities in classical style swimming. Fourth Polish Symposium on Biomechanics. [Monograph] Physical Education Academy, Poznan, Poland. (In Polish)
Kurachenkov, A. J. and Vietergalter, O. V. 1966. Manifestation of asymmetry in the development of the support and movement apparatus. Theory and Practice of Sports 8:42-43. (In Russian)
Starosta, W. 1975. Symmetry and asymmetry of movement in sports. Sports and Tourism, Warsaw. (In Polish).
Szczebiotko, Z. 1975. The asymmetry of upper and lower extremities in women who practice handball playing. [Monograph] Physical Education Academy, Poznan, Poland. (In Polish)
Wolanski, N. 1962. The influence of the extremities on the formation of the asymmetry of body shape in the phylogenic and ontogentic aspect. Anthropology Review 28:27-61. (In Polish)

Telemetric EMG of
the Front Crawl Movement

G. Piette and J. P. Clarys

The electromyographic signals of several muscles were analyzed to assess
the extent of their involvement in the front crawl movement. The electromyographic recordings from a group of top and a group of average swimmers were compared, using a standardizing procedure, for isometric and
dynamic contractions. The qualitative and quantitative analyses revealed
some interesting electromyographic patterns.

Although the front crawl movement in swimming is one of the most
thoroughly investigated, the amount of information now available is far
from sufficient for a definite statement as to which muscles are involved in
this swimming stroke and the extent of this involvement. Indeed the total
number of electromyographic (hereafter referred to as EMG) investigations of muscle movements occurring in water is small. This is probably
because of: 1) the difficulty in fixing surface electrodes to the skin, and
2) the complexity and sophistication of the equipment needed to transmit
and to record EMG signals from subjects while they are immersed in
water.

Two distinct methods of recording muscle potentials in water are
presently in use by the scientific research community: 1) the combination
of surface electrodes and wire transmission (Ikai, Ishii, and Miyashita,
1964), and 2) the combination of surface electrodes and telemetric
transmission (Lewillie, 1967).

Despite supplementary electronic requirements and the limitation of
a two-channel recorder, a telemetric recording method was chosen
because this method does not hinder the movements of the subject. Thus
far, it has been determined that eight muscles and/or muscle parts make
a significant contribution to the front crawl movements.

PROCEDURES

Recording Procedures

Using telemetric transmission methods, the muscle potentials were broad-
casted from a transmitter (fixed on the subject) to an amplifier, and re-

corded on a two-channel recorder, according to the test setup described by Lewillie (1967) and previously used in EMG studies of swimming movements by Lewillie (1968, 1971, 1973), Clarys, Jiskoot, and Lewillie (1973), Maes, Clarys, and Browwer (1975), Loyens (1975), and Piette (1977). The surface electrodes were fixed on the skin with elastic adhesive bandage that was waterproofed with a plastic spray. The locations of the electrodes on the body were chosen according to the recommendations of Basmajian (1967) and Goodgold (1974).

During the first pool length, the amplification was adapted to the signal intensity for each individual, and during the second pool length the EMG signals were recorded. After the experiment, the transmitter channels of each muscle were calibrated with a known microvoltage.

Muscle Selection

Muscles were selected according to several criteria: 1) the importance of the relative subdermal muscle surface (Maes, Clarys, and Browwer, 1975) (muscles with a subdermal surface less than 10 cm² were omitted because of the possible increase in faulty recordings); 2) the existing fundamental EMG knowledge of a specific muscle, including the experimentally determined optimum contraction; and 3) the results of previous EMG investigations relating that muscle to the front crawl movement.

Eight muscles or anatomical muscle parts satisfied these criteria— namely, the m. biceps brachii, the m. latissimus dorsi, the pars clavicularis and stenocostalis of the m. pectoralis major, the superior and inferior parts of the m. gluteus maximus, and the m. rectus abdominis (above and under the umbilicus).

After each swim in which data were recorded, the maximum isometric effort was measured for each muscle separately. This contraction pattern was subsequently used as a relative standard for quantitative evaluation and comparison.

Selection of Subjects

Male subjects (N = 12) with a mean age of 20 years, were selected, and divided into six competitive swimmers and six noncompetitive swimmers. The first group, the competitive swimmers, were able to swim 100 m in less than 60 sec. The second group, all PE students, swam the same distance in about 1 min 20 sec.

Methods for Data Comparison

Comparison of data in electromyographic research has proved to be difficult unless such data are standardized. First, the surface of the EMG patterns of 1) the dynamic contractions, 2) the isometric contractions, and 3) the calibration signals were measured over a known time period (in sec) with a planimeter (type OTT 113). Thus, it was possible to express a microvoltage signal in terms of surface values (in cm^2) to simplify the calculation of the results.

By dividing the dynamic and the isometric contraction values by the calibration value (CV), normalized dynamic contractions (DC) and a normalized (relative 100%) isometric contractions (IC) were obtained.

$$\frac{DC\,(cm^2\,sec)}{CV\,(cm^2\,sec)} \quad and \quad \frac{IC\,(cm^2\,sec)}{CV\,(cm^2\,sec)}$$

Second, all normalized dynamic contraction values were expressed as a percentage of the individual normalized isometric contraction values. Such a simple procedure permitted the comparison of quantitative EMG data for a single individual and between individuals on a relative basis.

RESULTS AND DISCUSSION

The mean values of muscle activity, expressed as a percentage of the maximum isometric contraction for each muscle (100%) studied, both for all subjects and for the competitive and noncompetitive swimmers separately, are shown in Table 1. These data constitute a summary of the initial results of the investigations.

It is common knowledge that the main propulsive force in swimming the front crawl is derived from the arms and shoulder girdle (De Goede,

Table 1. Mean muscle activity as a percentage of the maximum isometric contraction [a]

Muscle	All subjects (activity in %)	Noncompetitive swimmers (activity in %)	Competitive swimmers (activity in %)
m. Biceps brachii	30.86 ($\pm$16.20)	26.57 ($\pm$16.54)	34.45 ($\pm$15.23)
m. Latissimus dorsi	61.12 ($\pm$75.68)	23.66 ($\pm$ 8.19)	92.34 ($\pm$91.23)
m. Pectoralis major pars clavicularis	31.91 ($\pm$14.50)	26.10 ($\pm$10.96)	36.75 ($\pm$37.46)
m. Pectoralis major pars sternocostalis	41.64 ($\pm$31.44)	39.68 ($\pm$39.80)	43.27 ($\pm$22.00)
m. Rectus abdominis above umbilicus	60.94 ($\pm$47.62)	37.86 ($\pm$13.68)	83.13 ($\pm$57.65)
m. Rectus abdominis under umbilicus	70.14 ($\pm$51.37)	48.37 ($\pm$32.00)	91.96 ($\pm$57.42)
m. Gluteus maximus pars superior	60.47 ($\pm$34.68)	41.40 ($\pm$15.50)	79.52 ($\pm$37.94)
m. Gluteus maximus pars inferior	76.71 ($\pm$74.18)	31.18 ($\pm$10.40)	122.41 ($\pm$82.00)

[a]($\pm$ SD) = standard deviation.

Jiskoot, and Van der Sluis, 1971). However, it appears from the records in this investigation that the m. latissimus dorsi, the m. rectus abdominis, and the m. gluteus maximus clearly have a higher mean activity than the biceps and pectoralis muscles. Further, the competitive swimmers' results were significantly different from those for noncompetitive swimmers.

In addition, an overall increased activity for all muscles investigated was noted, both for competitive swimmers and for noncompetitive swimmers. This confirms previous observations of Ikai, Ishii, and Miyashita (1964), Barthels and Adrian (1972), and Yoshizawa et al. (1975). However, considering the large standard deviation values, the individual variation in muscular activity is important.

These findings substantiate the theory that competitive swimmers make better use of their muscular efforts but also suggest that there is significant participation by the trunk and pelvic girdle musculature. It seems that the differences in swimming performance are not only a matter of swimming skills (i.e., techniques) but also a result of more efficient use of abdominal, back, and gluteal muscles in the swimming movements.

m. Biceps Brachii

The action of the m. biceps brachii in these swimmers during one complete arm cycle was characterized by two separate contraction peaks, one during the glide and one at the moment of the propulsive phase. This pattern remained identical in a series of consecutive cycles for each individual subject and, apart from some differences in intensity and duration, was similar for all subjects. These results agree with the findings of Ikai, Ishii, and Miyashita (1964), Clarys, Jiskoot, and Lewillie (1973), and Maes, Clarys, and Browwer (1975). Differences in technique, such as a wide or high recovery, long or short glide, and variations in the pull-push trajectory, did not seem to affect the contraction pattern. Indeed, similar EMG tracings were also found for the water polo players in the front crawl arm movement in previous studies (Clarys, Jiskoot, and Lewillie, 1973). With regard to the two-peak pattern, the inter-individual variation remained relatively small.

m. Latissimus Dorsi

The EMG pattern for 10 of the 12 subjects demonstrated regularly recurring patterns in the consecutive swimming cycles with regard to the m. latissimus dorsi. The other two (noncompetitive) swimmers showed very irregular EMG tracings. Among the regularly recurring recordings, two types of contraction patterns were observed: single and double peaked. The single-peaked pattern appeared in five subjects, and the double-peaked pattern appeared in the other five. Most of the competitive swimmers showed one peak only.

With regard to the graphic form of the EMG recordings, the contributions of the m. latissimus dorsi to the front-crawl movement were in accord with those found by Ikai, Ishii, and Miyashita (1964), Vaday and Nemessuri (1971), and Belokovsky and Ivanchenko (1975). The activity of the m. latissimus dorsi recorded for the competitive swimmers was four times higher than for noncompetition swimmers, and interindividual variations were much more important than was observed in the non-competitive group (Table 1).

m. Pectoralis Major (pars clavicularis and sternocostalis)

The m. pectoralis major was active in the swimming action studied. However, in general, the pars sternocostalis participated more intensively in the front crawl movement than the pars clavicularis (Table 1). The ster-nocostalis component worked with greater regularity, and all subjects had recurring graphic patterns in a series of consecutive arm cycles. For the pars clavicularis, eight of 12 subjects demonstrated EMG muscle signals that were repeated in a regular pattern.

Three distinct pattern types were found for the overall activity of the pectoralis major muscle: single-, double-, and triple-peaked contractions. The pars clavicularis was recorded either with a double-peaked contrac-tion (observed in six subjects) or with a single-peaked contraction (two subjects). Similar results were found in the studies of Ikai, Ishii, and Miyashita (1964), Vaday and Nemmessuri (1971), and Belokovsky and Ivanchenko (1975). On the other hand, the pars sternocostalis demon-strated alternatively single-peaked contractions (two subjects), double-peaked contractions (nine subjects), and a triple-peaked contraction (one subject).

For both parts clavicularis and sternocostalis recordings, the non-competitive swimmers always exhibited a double-peaked contraction. Strangely, the single-, double-, and triple-peaked contractions all ap-peared in the recordings of the competitive swimmers.

m. Rectus Abdominis (above and below the umbilicus)

As with the m. pectoralis major, a different percentage of activity (Table 1) was observed between the two parts of the abdominal muscle studied. This difference was reflected in the regularity of the recurring contraction pattern. The recording of abdominal muscle activity under the umbilicus demonstrated less irregularity if it were measured over a longer time. Fur-ther, the m. rectus abdominis indicated greater activity below the um-bilicus than above. These findings contradict the results of Maes, Clarys, and Browwer (1975). Nevertheless, the graphic form of these EMG signals agreed with Ikai, Ishii, and Miyashita (1964) and Maes, Clarys, and Browwer (1975).

Single-peaked contractions (two subjects—under umbilicus; one sub-ject—above umbilicus), double-peaked contractions (six subjects—under umbilicus; five subjects—above umbilicus), and a triple-peaked contraction (one subject and only above the umbilicus) were found. Again, the activity measured in the competitive swimmers was markedly higher, although the interindividual pattern was variable.

m. Gluteus Maximus (pars inferior and superior)

The two parts of the gluteal muscle showed irregular recordings for most of the test, and judging by the percentage of activity (Table 1) both groups studied demonstrated a highly varied degree of activity. The inferior part of the muscle was more dominant than the superior part in competitive swimmers, while the reverse was true for non-competitive swimmers. In any case, it was clear that this irregularity in the combined action of both parts of the gluteal muscle was very important in the crawl, especially for swimmers in competition.

The irregularity of the electromyogram can be explained by the interindividual variation of the leg kick (two to six beats, single and double cross-kick, and so forth). It should be noted that the significant activity found appears to contradict the use of the legs in the whole crawl stroke. All the subjects demonstrated a regular EMG recording with a double-peaked contraction pattern, except for one triple-peaked pattern by a noncompetitive swimmer. Both muscle parts demonstrated the same pattern, but at different moments, because the peaks did not correspond to identical phases of the leg movement. Obviously this muscle needs to be studied more thoroughly. Ikai, Ishii, and Miyashita (1964) did not register significant gluteal activity, while Vaday and Nemessuri (1971) did find gluteal muscle participation.

CONCLUSIONS

1. All muscles investigated in this study are used in the front crawl movement.
2. The overall muscle intensity is more pronounced for the contractions demonstrated by the competitive swimmers. The difference in intensity between competitive and noncompetitive swimmers is most evident for the m. latissimus dorsi, rectus abdominis, and gluteus maximus.
3. The number of contraction peaks recorded during the arm cycle (single, double, and triple peaks) demonstrate that great interindividual variation occurs among competitive swimmers.

ACKNOWLEDGMENTS

The authors are grateful to R. Robeaux for his technical assistance and to J. Sumner for his advice.

REFERENCES

Barthels, M. K., and Adrian, M. J. 1972. Variability in the dolphin kick under four conditions. In: L. Lewillie and J. P. Clarys (eds.), First International Symposium on Biomechanics in Swimming, pp. 105-118. Universite Libre de Bruxelles, Brussels.

Basmajian, J. V. 1967. An analysis of pulling motions in the crawl arm stroke. In: L. Lewillie and J. P. Clarys (eds.), First International Symposium on Biomechanics in Swimming, pp. 217-221. Universite Libre de Bruxelles, Brussels.

Belokovsky, V., and Ivanchenko, E. 1975. A hydrokinetic apparatus for the study and improvement of leg movements in the breaststroke. In: J. P. Clarys and L. Lewillie (eds.), Swimming II, pp. 64-69. University Park Press, Baltimore.

Clarys, J. P., Jiskoot, J., and Lewillie, L. 1973. A kinematographical, electromyographical and resistance study of water polo and competition front crawl. In: S. Cerquiglini, A. Venerando, and J. Wartenweiler (eds.), Biomechanics III, pp. 446-452. S. Karger Verlag, Basel.

De Goede, H., Jiskoot, J., and Van der Sluis, A. 1971. Over stuwkracht bij zwemmers (On the propulsion of swimmers). De Zwemkroniek 48(2):77-90.

Goodgold, J. 1974. Anatomical Correlates of Clinical Electromyography. Williams & Wilkins Company, Baltimore.

Ikai, M., Ishii, K. and Miyashita, M. 1964. An electromyographical study of swimming. Res. J. Phys. Educ. 7:47-54.

Lewillie, L. 1967. Analyse télémetrique de l'electromyogramme du nageur (Telemetric analyses of the electromyogram of the swimmer). Trav. Soc. Med. Belge l'Educ. Phys. Sport, fasc. 20:174-177.

Lewillie, L. 1968. Telemetrical analysis of the electromyograph. In: J. Wartenweiler, E. Jokl, and M. Hebbelinck (eds.), Biomechanics I, pp. 147-148. S. Karger Verlag, Basel.

Lewillie, L. 1971. Quantitative comparison of the electromyograph of the swimmer. In: L. Lewillie and J. P. Clarys (eds.), First International Symposium on Biomechanics in Swimming, pp. 155-159. Université Libre de Bruxelles, Brussels.

Lewillie, L. 1973. Muscular activity in swimming. In: S. Cerquiglini, A. Venerando, and J. Wartenweiler (eds.), Biomechanics III, pp. 440-445. S. Karger Verlag, Basel.

Loyens, R. 1975. Zewmmen met paraplegen (Swimming with paraplegics). Masters thesis, Vrije Universiteit Brussels, Brussels.

Maes, L., Clarys, J. P., and Browwer, P. J. 1975. Electromyography for the evaluation of handicapped swimmers. In: J. P. Clarys and L. Lewillie (eds.), Swimming II, pp. 268-275. University Park Press, Baltimore.

Piette, G. 1977. Electromyografie van de borstcrawl (An electromyographical study of the front crawl). Masters thesis, Vrije Universiteit Brussels, Brussels.

Vaday, M., and Nemessuri, N. 1971. Motor pattern of free style swimming. In: L. Lewillie and J. P. Clarys (eds.), First International Symposium on Biomechanics in Swimming, pp. 1967-1973. Université Libre de Bruxelles, Brussels.

Yoshizawa, M., Tokuyama, H., Okamoto, T., and Kumamoto, M. 1975. Electromyographic study of the breaststroke. In: P. V. Komi (ed.), Biomechanics V-B, pp. 222-229. University Park Press, Baltimore.

Underwater Recording of Electromyographic Activity Using Fine-wire Electrodes

T. Okamoto and S. L. Wolf

The first electromyographic (EMG) studies designed to analyze swimming motions in adults were performed by Ikai, Ishii, Miyashita (1964) using surface electrodes. Subsequently the technique was developed to analyze movement patterns in children and infants (Okamoto, 1976; Okamoto et al., 1976), still using surface electrodes. Most studies of aquatic movements in man have used amplification systems that are suspended out of the water some distance from the subject. As a result, investigators have had to contend with various technical problems, including movement artifact incurred by unstable leads between surface electrodes and recording equipment.

It would seem that the provision for waterproof amplifiers, located close to the sight of pickup, could minimize such recording problems. Additionally, the use of indwelling electrodes could help to isolate activity from specific muscles. In preparing to monitor underwater muscle performance for both swimming behavior in children and ambulation in rehabilitation patients we have developed an inexpensive, effective, and rapid method for recording EMG underwater using fine-wire electrodes. Although fine-wire electrodes have been used to record underwater activities in amphibians (Osse, 1969), to the best of our knowledge this clinical technique has not been reported previously. This paper describes our methodology and demonstrates its potential application.

METHOD

After thoroughly shaving and cleansing the area selected for needle insertion, fine-wire electrodes (nylon-karma alloy, 25μ in diameter) are injected using the method described by Basmajian (1974). Briefly, this technique involves the placement of fine-wire leads, insulated to within 1

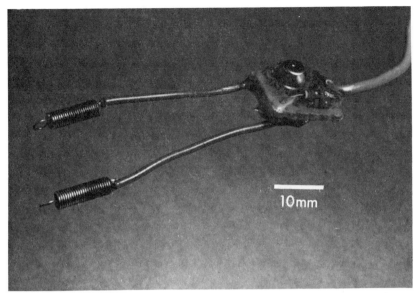

Figure 1. High impedance dual-source followers with slender insulated leads connecting to phono springs.

mm of their tips, through a 27-gauge hypodermic needle. The tips are barbed and staggered so that they remain within the muscle after the needle is withdrawn.

The wires are taped to the skin surface, and their remaining uninsulated ends are connected to phono springs (4.76 mm in diameter), which, in turn, are led to a high impedance dual source follower (Basmajian and Hudson, 1974) by slender insulated leads (Figure 1). This source follower is about the diameter of an American penny and is insulated with an epoxy resin (Twin Tube, Radio Shack). The phono springs are carefully wrapped in surgical waterproof tape (Blenderm, 3M Co.) for preliminary insulation (Figure 2). Each spring is then placed within an ink-dropper cap (3 cm long, 1 cm in diameter), sealed with petroleum jelly, and closed in place with a pencil eraser (Figure 3). Well-insulated shielded leads connect the dual source follower to a DC differential amplifier with audio amplifier accessories. EMG along with other signals (electrogoniogram, foot contact switch) are stored on FM tape (Tandberg-Sangamo series 100). The output from this tape recorder is viewed on a storage oscilloscope (Tektronix 5111). A Beckman surface electrode placed on well-abraded skin serves as an excellent ground, which is easily insulated by waterproof tape.

It is essential that the fine-wire leads adhere to the skin surface because failure to take this step may result in considerable movement

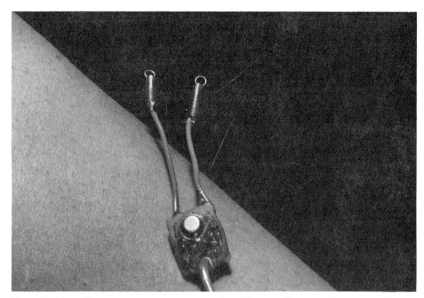

Figure 2. Tape about to enwrap one phono spring. Note the fine-wire electrode leads.

Figure 3. Two ink-dropper caps, each encasing phono springs and each sealed with petroleum jelly and closed with a pencil eraser.

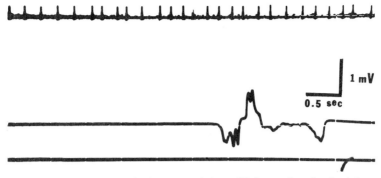

Figure 4. Upper trace: isolated single motor unit from tibialis anterior when leg is in water (left), and removed from water (right). Middle trace: DC change incurred by breaking contact of an uninsulated lead (placed at level of fine-wire insertion) with water. Lower trace: goniogram record. Note that there is no ankle movement. Amplitude calibration in this and all subsequent figures refers to EMG traces.

artifact. Additionally, attempts to join the fine-wire ends to uninsulated terminals leading to the source followers by using a silver paint contact, subsequently covered by petroleum jelly and waterproof tape, seemed successful. This method, however, can become messy if the investigator must "trouble-shoot" for an electrode recording problem. As described above, with minimal practice this technique requires between 5 and 10 min of preparation time for each electrode site. Each recording channel, exclusive of oscilloscope and tape recorder, can be constructed for under $75 (American) and can be checked for procedural errors without complete disassembly of each recording array.

RESULTS

To evaluate the fidelity of EMG signals in air and beneath the water, single-motor units (SMUs) were isolated through minimal contractions of the tibialis anterior muscle. Recording at both fast and slow (Figure 4) sweep speeds showed that signal characteristics of SMUs in water (Figure 4, left) and during removal of the leg from the aqueous medium (Figure 4, right) were similar. Activity patterns remained consistent in both environments during progressive recruitment of SMU (Figure 5) and during a strong contraction of the muscle (Figure 6).

The activity shown in Figure 7 was recorded from tibialis anterior using both fine-wire (upper trace) and surface (second trace) electrodes during ambulation in a therapeutic pool. Excellent temporal correlations between activity from the fine-wire and surface electrode pairs can be seen during the swing phase of gait (upward deflection of goniogram record, lowest trace). A small electrical artifact occurs on the foot contact record (third trace) just before heel strike (upward deflection).

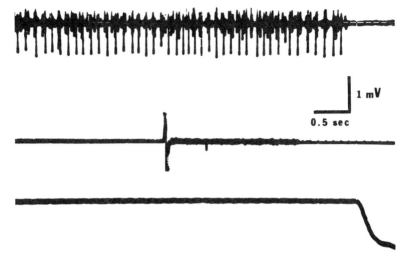

Figure 5. Same as in Figure 4 but slight contraction recruiting a few more motor units. Note plantar flexion (end of lowest trace, downward deflection) silences the motor unit activity.

Figure 8 depicts EMG activity recorded from fine-wire electrodes in tibialis anterior (upper trace) during stepping movements in the water. Bursts of muscle activity are synchronized with ankle dorsiflexion movements (upward deflection, lowest trace), which occur between the break (small spike) and contact (large spike) of the foot with the pool surface, as seen on the middle trace.

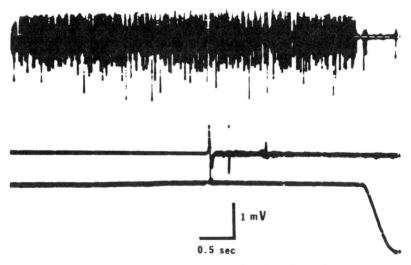

Figure 6. Same as in Figure 5 but with strong contraction of tibialis anterior.

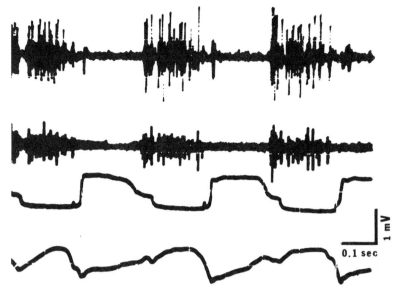

Figure 7. Tibialis anterior activity during walking beneath water surface. Top trace: fine-wire electrode recording. Second trace: miniature Beckman surface electrode recording. Third trace: foot contact switch (floor contact, upward deflection). Fourth trace: goniogram record with upward deflection, indicating ankle dorsiflexion.

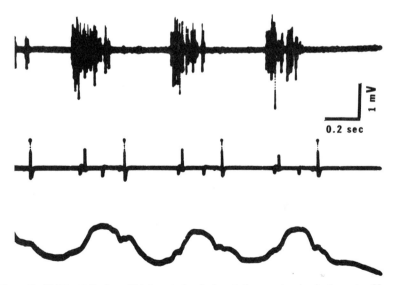

Figure 8. EMG activity from tibialis anterior during stationary stepping in the water. Upper trace: fine wire electrode recording. Middle trace: foot contact switch. Lower trace: goniogram (dorsiflexion, upward deflection).

DISCUSSION

To date, few problems concerning movement artifact have been encountered when the methodology described here has been used. Recording sessions can last for several hours without interruption. The only major difficulty observed has been the occasional "shorting out" of fine-wire electrodes—i.e., uninsulated tips making contact within the muscle. This situation will be observed as a flattened or blank trace on the EMG channel during muscle contraction. The problem is easily rectified by a gentle pull on the fine wires near their insertion into the muscle.

Since percutaneous recordings from muscle afford the investigator the benefit of assuming pickup from a specific muscle, this technique will enable one to monitor precise muscle behavior during various aquatic activities. The insulation and placement of source followers near the muscle greatly attenuate the burdensome difficulties inherent in other underwater recording techniques.

Specific plans to use our methodology to record swimming activities are already underway. This technique will also allow us to compare normal and pathological gait patterns on land and in an aquatic environment. The possibility of combining the resistance offered by the water during ambulation in stroke patients (Baker et al., 1977; Wolf, 1978) with the audio feedback provided from the amplifier and the visual feedback from the oscilloscope or pen-writing device to help these individuals reacquire motor control presents an avenue for future rehabilitation research.

REFERENCES

Baker, M., Regenos, E., Wolf, S. L., and Basmajian, J. V. 1977. Developing strategies for biofeedback applications in neurologically handicapped patients. Phys. Ther. 57:127-132.
Basmajian, J. V. 1974. Muscles Alive: Their Functions Revealed by Electromyography, 3rd Ed. Williams & Wilkins Company, Baltimore.
Basmajian, J. V., and Hudson, J. E. 1974. Miniature source-attached differential amplifier for electromyography. Am. J. Phys. Med. 53:234-236.
Ikai, M., Ishii, K., and Miyashita, M. 1964. An electromyographic study of swimming. Jap. Res. J. Phys. Educ. 7:55-87.
Okamoto, T. 1976. Yoshoji no suiei-shidokatei no bunseki (A kinesiological study of swimming). J. Health Phys. Educ. Rec. 26:409-414.
Okamoto, T., Tokuyama, H., Yoshizawa, M., Kodaira, A., Tsujino, A., and Kumamoto, M., 1976. Yoshoji no suiei no kindenzuteki kenkyu (An electromyographic study of swimming in children). Shintai Undo no Kagaku I (The Science of Human Movement I), pp. 115-126. Kyorin Shoin, Tokyo.
Osse, J. W. M. 1969. Functional morphology of the head of the perch (Perca fluviatilis L.): An electromyographic study. Neth. J. Zool. 19:289-392.
Wolf, S. L. 1978. Essential considerations in the use of muscle biofeedback. Phys. Ther. 58:25-31.

Electromyographic and Cinematographic Study of the Flutter Kick in Infants and Children

H. Oka, T. Okamoto, M. Yoshizawa, H. Tokuyama, and
M. Kumamoto

Electromyographic studies of swimming movements in infants and children have been performed by Tokuyama, Okamoto and Kumamoto (1976) on the breaststroke and the crawl stroke. In these experiments, the process by which the flutter kick is learned was analyzed electromyographically to elucidate how a child who could not swim without support first behaved in the water and then spontaneously acquired the technique of the flutter kick, which was similar to that seen in skilled adults.

PROCEDURES

The subjects were 31 infants and children, ranging from a 10-month old to a 12-year old, and eight skilled adults who served as controls. Three of the children were tested for three consecutive years to study their learning process, with the same subject serving as his own control. The muscles studied were the tibialis anterior, the gastrocnemius, the vastus medialis, the rectus femoris, the biceps femoris, and the gluteus maximus. EMGs were recorded with an 18-channel multipurpose electroencephalograph (San-ei Sokki Co. Ltd., Tokyo) using waterproofed surface electrodes, 10 mm in diameter. The movements of the subjects were photographed with a 16-mm movie camera from the side (32 frames/sec) through an underwater window. A signal in each frame of the film and the electrogoniograms of the knee joint were recorded simultaneously with the electromyograms.

RESULTS AND DISCUSSION

In the case of the 10-month-old to 1-year-old infants who could not swim without support the lower limbs were excessively flexed when their bodies were immersed in the water for the first time. As they became more experienced in the water, reciprocal flexion and extension movements of the lower limbs were observed, but some of them showed simultaneous flexion and extension movements. The discharges of the gastrocnemius, the vastus medialis, and the rectus femoris showed co-contraction. Motion picture analysis showed that the knee was extended with the foot plantar flexed instead of the whip-like leg movements that are characteristic of the skilled adults. These findings seemed to suggest that the extensors and flexors were alternatively contracted in the infants.

Figure 1 shows the EMGs of a 2-year-old who was in the initial period of learning to swim and could swim only about 2 m without support. The infant's body was kept in a nearly upright position, while the knee and hip joints were completely extended from the acutely flexed position. The angular changes in the knee and hip joints indicated that the infant did not perform the whip-like action of the lower limbs similar to the skilled adults. The knee and hip joints in the infant were simultaneously extended and flexed, and a "pedaling" movement was observed.

According to Okamoto (1970), it is a characteristic of infants that the knee is not completely extended at the end of the kicking phase in walking, running, and jumping. He pointed out that the knee extension and hyperextension of the hip seen in the adult are not performed until about 7 years of age. The complete extension of the knee and hip joints at the end of the kicking phase in the 2-year-old mentioned previously might be possible only in the water and maybe effective in keeping the body afloat.

As to the EMGs, the discharge patterns of the tibialis anterior, the gastrocnemius, the vastus medialis, and the rectus femoris of the 2-year-old were similar to those of the 1-year-old infants. A marked discharge of the gluteus maximus was observed in the kicking phase. According to Wheatley and Jahnke (1951) and Okamoto (1966), the gluteus maximus does not contract unless there is a resistance to movement. Thus, the discharge of the gluteus maximus observed in the kicking phase suggests that the "pedaling" movement was performed forcefully to keep the body afloat in the water.

When the upper body reached a position parallel to the surface of the water, the discharge of the gluteus maximus diminished and that of the other extensors in the lower limbs tended to decrease.

In the case of a 6-year-old child, who could swim about 10 m without any special aid, the range of the hip joint angle was much less compared with the skilled adult, and the knee and hip joints were simultaneously flexed and extended.

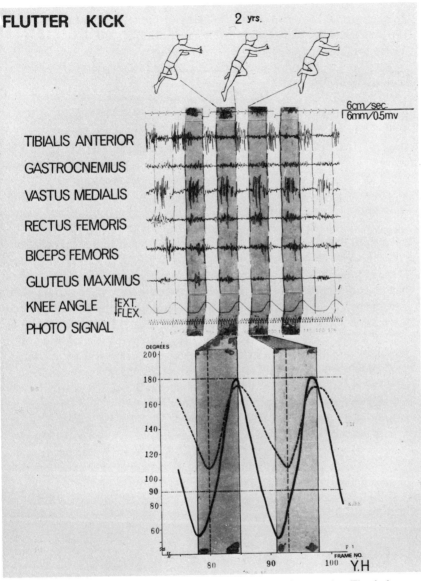

Figure 1. EMGs of a 2-year-old in the initial period of learning to swim. The dark zone shows the kick phase, and the white zone shows the recovery phase. The solid and dotted lines in the lower panel show the angular curves of the knee and hip joints, respectively.

The discharge patterns of the vastus medialis, the rectus femoris, and the biceps femoris observed in the kicking phase were similar to those of the skilled adult. The child showed only little or no discharge in the gastrocnemius but had discharge in the tibialis anterior at the end of the kicking phase. In contrast, the skilled adult showed marked discharge in the gastrocnemius and only a small or no discharge in the tibialis anterior. These findings indicate that the child performed the leg kick with the ankle flexed and could not perform the up-and-down action at the ankle seen in the skilled adult.

One year later, the subject was trained for 2 weeks with appropriate instruction based on electromyographic observations obtained from skilled adults. The strong discharge of the gluteus maximus appeared in the latter part of the kicking phase as seen in the skilled adult, and the movement of thigh became stronger. The angular changes in the knee and hip joints showed the whip-like action, but the marked discharge of the gastrocnemius at the end of the kicking phase was not yet observed. This showed that the up-and-down movement at the ankle was not performed.

The following year, when the subject was 8 years old, she had practiced until the she was able to swim 25 m or more without special aid. After this prolonged practice, a strong discharge in the gastrocnemius appeared at the end of the kicking phase, and the acquisition of the up-and-down action at the ankle was confirmed. When another 12-year-old child had learned to swim 25 m or more without aid, this subject also acquired the up-and-down movement at the ankle at the end of the kicking phase.

In a 5-year-old who was specially trained for about 2 years at a swimming school and could swim 100 m or more, the forms and the discharge patterns were fairly similar to those of the skilled adult as seen in the left panel of Figure 2. However, the strong discharge of the biceps femoris was scarcely observed in the early part of the recovery phase, and the hyperextension of the hip joint was not performed.

In learning to walk, run, and jump, the hyperextension of the hip joint is not developed until about 7 years of age. This seems to suggest that the hyperextension of the hip joint may not be a part of the movement and pattern without a certain maturity of the locomotive system, even in an infant under 7 years of age who is trained to perform an exercise such as swimming with great proficiency.

CONCLUSIONS

1. The 10-month-old to 1-year-old infants who could not swim, flexed their lower limbs excessively when they were supported in the water for the first time, but as they became more experienced, they showed reciprocal or simultaneous flexion and extension movements of the lower limbs.

2. For the 2-year-olds, who were in the initial period of learning to swim, the muscular discharge pattern and motion analysis showed that

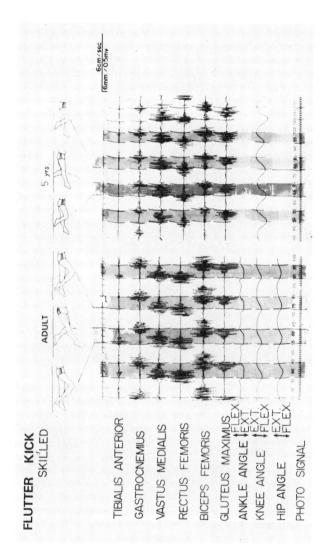

Figure 2. EMGs of the flutter kick of one of the skilled adults used as a control (left) and of the 5-year-old child who was specially trained for about 2 years (right).

"pedaling" movements of the lower limbs were actively performed with the upper body in a nearly upright position.

3. Children from 5 to 6 years old, in the initial period of learning to swim with their bodies supported nearly parallel to the surface of the water, flexed or extended their knee and hip joints simultaneously but did not show a whip-like action of the lower limbs. The movements of their thighs were insufficient, and the up-and-down movements at the ankles were not observed.

4. In the case of one of the 6-year-olds who was trained with appropriate instruction based on the electromyographic observations obtained from the skilled adult, the form of the flutter kick was much improved, and the discharge patterns approached those of the skilled adult. One of the effective suggestions was to disregard the knee movement and to make the movement of thighs stronger.

REFERENCES

Okamoto, T. 1966. Jitensha-sohkoh ni kansuru kindenzuteki kenyu (Electromyographic study of bicycle exercise). J. Liberal Arts Dep. Kansai Med. School 1:55–61.

Okamoto, T. 1970. Nyuyohji (1 saiji) oyobi yohji (2 saiji) ni okeru hokoh no shutoku shujyuku katei no kindenzuteki kenkyu (Electromyographic study of the learning process of walking in 1- and 2 year-old infants). Liberal Arts Dep. Kansai Med. School 3:19–65.

Tokuyama, H., Okamoto, T., and Kumamoto, M. 1976. Electromyographic study of swimming in infants and children. In: P. V. Komi (ed.), Biomechanics V-B, pp. 215–221. University Park Press, Baltimore.

Wheatley, M. D., and Jahnke, W. D. 1951. Electromyographic study of the superficial thigh and hip muscles in normal individual. Arch. Phys. Med. 32:508–515.

Biomechanical Principles Applied to the Halliwick Method of Teaching Swimming to Physically Handicapped Individuals

K. Nicol, M. Schmidt-Hansberg, and J. McMillan

In 1949 James McMillan taught a group of severely handicapped girls, most of whom were afflicted with cerebral palsy, to swim. The method that was devised and developed was named after the institution where it was originally developed—Halliwick School in London. Support for this venture was received from an orthopaedic surgeon, Oliver J. Vaughan-Jackson, now a Visiting Professor at Newfoundland University. The method is now practiced in every continent of the world.

In the development of the teaching technique, consideration was given to the various needs and abilities of the handicapped so that they could control the movement of their asymmetrical body shapes and densities. In this regard, no two people are alike. The physical requirements cannot be dissociated from mental reaction that may result from a situation involving loss of balance.

By observing any child who is learning physical movement or an adult who is acquiring a new physical skill (e.g., ice skating), a noticeable pattern of human learning can be seen. It starts with a mental adjustment to the elements or environment of the activity. This is followed by efforts in gross patterns of movement, which can be referred to as balance restoration. Success in this phase leads to the prevention of movement while holding a starting position or posture—inhibition. Finally, a mentally pleasing and physically controlled movement—facilitation—is accomplished.

THE HALLIWICK METHOD

In the Halliwick method, a teaching program has been developed that allows individuals with various handicaps to be taught in one group. The method incorporates the principles of mental adjustment, balance restoration, inhibition, and facilitation with those of physiology, psychology, and biomechanics.

The method, like the human body, has a skeletal structure around which the form is developed. The form comprises games/activities, group dynamics, music and movement, and so forth, which can be freely used, but a semblance of order is maintained by the skeletal structure. This structure, outlined in a 10-point program, is a guide to progression; unlike the 10 Commandments, it is a positive structure, stating, "Thou shalt DO" rather than "Thou shalt NOT."

The 10-point program is outlined in the four phases of human learning that are associated with physical movement. It is essential that the phases are considered in a specific order to avoid the common error that so often exists: teaching a complex swimming movement to a person whose mind is focused on one objective only—survival.

The time taken for each phase depends entirely on the degree and nature of the individual handicap. The 10 points can be defined briefly as follows:

1. Mental adjustment. An appreciation of the differences in the elements—land versus water; the comparison of posture and movement on land and in water; the realization that there are two effective forces in action, gravity and buoyancy.

2. Disengagement. The encouragement to use any newly developed ability without mental or physical assistance.

3. Vertical rotation control. The control of balance and movement around a transverse axis (sitting to lying).

4. Lateral rotation control. A control of balance and movement around a longitudinal axis (rolling from a prone to a supine position).

5. Combined rotation control. Control around a diagonal axis. This is usually essential for the more asymmetric body to control changes in its shape and/or posture.

6. Mental inversion. A psychological step involving an attempt to stay under water, opposing the effect of the buoyant force of the water. It is also an adequate response to the points previously taught.

7. Balance is stillness. The ability to maintain a posture in water against the disturbing forces.

8. Turbulent gliding. An expression that covers the activity of the body that is moved in the supine position through the water. The body is not touched and no propulsive movement is performed by the swimmer.

9. Simple progression. The body is now required to make a simple movement, establishing a progression through the water.

10. Basic movement. The application of a defined, larger-patterned movement of progression. It is based on hydrodynamic principles and can be used by some 70% of the handicapped population.

One year ago, the Halliwick method began to be used at Frankfurt University to teach the handicapped to swim. The swimming class consisted of seven physically handicapped children, aged 8 to 9 years, and an equal number of students who acted as teachers. Since it was desirable to have the teachers act in a specific way, according to the children's specific handicap, an instructional method based on the demonstration of the behavior of a model of the human body in the water was developed to illustrate the biomechanical principles involved in swimming instructions.

FACTORS AFFECTING BUOYANCY

Any object that has a density less than that of the water can float without movement, which means that a part of the body is always above the water. The ability of the human body to float depends on several factors:

1. The temperature of water (an increase of 1 °C lowers the density by 0.3%).
2. The content of salt in the water (1% salt increases the density by 2.3%).
3. The density of the swimmer as determined by the somatotype (it varies by approximately 10%).
4. The volume of air in the lungs (1 liter, corresponding to about 20% of the vital capacity, changes the body density by about 1.5%).

Usually therefore, in water of about 20 °C, having a low salt content, the normal body type during normal inspiration can float in a vertical position. The immersed volume displaces sufficient water to support a position of the head out of the water, but the extent varies with body build. In most cases one is unable to breath in this position; therefore, the task is to look for a stable position that enables the individual to breathe and to survive in water.

For simplicity, let us examine the behavior of a rectangular cube of wood. As is the case with nearly all objects placed in water, this piece of wood has several stable floating positions, which indicates that it will return to its original position when it is displaced slightly and released. When the displacement exceeds a certain limit, the object will not return to its original position but will continue to move to a new position of stability. The more stable the position, the greater will be the force that is required for this transition.

To look for a stable breathing position for the vertically floating subject, lift his feet so that he is floating horizontally. The position should be supine with legs extended, the hands at the hips, and the face out of the water. In this position we hope that the subject can breathe comfortably and will be stable. The result of this experiment may vary. Some persons can remain in the horizontal position with a certain degree of stability. Others will rotate around their longitudinal axis so that they retain the horizontal position but with their face down in the water. Most people will return to the vertical or near vertical position. The result is that the human body, when it is extended and the hands are at the hips, may have one, two, or even more stable positions in water. However, only one of these will enable the subject to breathe comfortably without movement of any kind.

BIOMECHANICAL PRINCIPLES APPLIED TO THE FLOATING BODY

It was necessary to develop procedures to put the body of all subjects into the desired position and to demonstrate these techniques to swimming teachers. Two different methods were utilized to accomplish this. First, a capacitance-type force platform was waterproofed (Nicol and Krüger, 1979) and placed on the floor of the pool under the floating body of subjects to demonstrate buoyancy or buoyant forces and the influence of changes in body shape on the supporting force that is required to keep the body afloat. Second, a wooden model of the human body was constructed. To create the variations of the overall body density, some of the wood was replaced by air and lead, respectively. These additions were made so that the various parts of the model were related to the mass and densities of the various segments of the human body.

First, let us analyze what can be done to assist the subjects who are unable to remain in a horizontal position. They move to a vertical position because the density of their legs is about 1.2, whereas the density of their trunk is about 0.8, generating an angular moment. There are three ways to compensate for this moment, as illustrated in Figure 1.

1. The moment is decreased when the lever arm is decreased; therefore, the legs are flexed.
2. The angular moment of the legs can be counteracted partly by another moment created by the arms (also having a density of 1.2) which are lifted over the head.
3. The counter moment of the arms can be increased if the hands or parts of them are raised above the water, thus reducing the buoyant force and increasing the apparent weight.

The second problem is to prevent rotation around the longitudinal axis of the subject. In such movements the moment of inertia is small compared with that of the transverse axis, so the body is in a state of critical equilibrium when it is displaced from the symmetrical position by more than 15°. Therefore, balance of the paraplegic (asymmetric about the pelvic axis) is much easier to maintain than that of the hemiplegic

Figure 1. Standard swimming position.

(asymmetry around the spinal axis). Massive amputation or a similar abnormality in shape and/or density leads to a need for simultaneous control around both spinal and pelvic axes to maintain a controlled posture.

When rotation starts, parts of the body will move upward and may even come out of the water if their distance from the axis of rotation is great enough. In this case, the buoyant force on these parts becomes zero, and an additional force is generated. When this force is multiplied by the perpendicular distance from the axis, a restoring moment is generated that tends to stabilize the body. This stabilizing force can be increased greatly if the subject spreads his arms and/or legs and thus increases the distance and the stabilizing angular moment (see Figures 2 and 3).

The second way to prevent longitudinal rotation is to compensate for the asymmetry—e.g., by lateral flexion of the hip to the side that tends to move downward; by doing this, parts of the arms and legs that have a higher density are moved to the lighter side.

Another way to prevent rotation is to put the arm of the heavier side (say the left side) across the chest. In Figure 4, this is demonstrated for a hemiplegic. When this is done, the subject will rotate to the heavier side if he does not place his arm far enough to the right. Only when his elbow is placed near or across the center line will the angular moment caused by the asymmetry be counteracted. The reason for this is that parts of the arm come out of the water when it is placed across the chest, so the buoyant force on these parts is zero, and an additional angular moment is

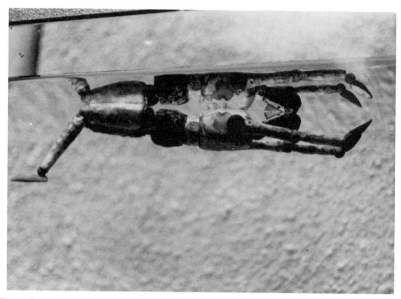

Figure 2. Overcompensation of the moment around the pelvic axis in a one-sided amputation of the lower leg.

Figure 3. Reduction of overcompensation.

Figure 4. Compensation of hip flexion by the crossing of one arm over the chest.

generated. When the elbow is placed across the center line, the additional moment results in an overcompensation, thus balancing the moment caused by asymmetry. A similar result can be obtained if the subject crosses the leg of his heavier side over his other leg; by doing this, the result of asymmetry is compensated for, and the body is stabilized. This method can be used, for example, to stabilize the position of a single-leg amputee who tends to roll to the side of his remaining leg. When the forearm of the same side is crossed over the chest, that part of the forearm that comes out of the water stabilizes the body (Figures 5 and 6).

In this way, the swimmer can lie on his back and breathe safely. To increase his safety and to make him independent from the teacher, it is necessary to enable him to: 1) restore the supine position when he has come to a prone position by accident, 2) come to a standing position in shallow water, and 3) return to a swimming position.

Restoring the body to a supine position from the prone position is achieved by lifting an arm out of the water (preferably on the heavier side)

Figure 5. Rotation around both axes in a one-sided amputation of the thigh.

and crossing it over the back. An angular moment is generated (by the same mechanism as previously described), thus, turning the body onto the back.

Most people achieve the standing position simply. They need only to reverse the procedures that they followed to retain the horizontal position. When this is not successful, the hands should be brought to the sides at the hips, they should then be slightly out of the water, and they should be maintained in that position until a vertical attitude is achieved.

The final task—that of getting the subject into a swimming position without the help of the teacher—is achieved simply by the subject laying back into the water, placing his hands over his head, and flexing his knees, if necessary.

In this way, teachers were able to have these handicapped children restore their balance according to their individual needs. After 30 hr of instruction, five of seven children were able to stay in deep water without undue risk.

Figure 6. Compensation of both rotations.

REFERENCES

McMillan, J. 1978. The role of water in rehabilitation. Fysioterapeuten 2:43–46, 3:87–90, 6:236–240.
Nicol, K., and Krüger, F. 1979. Impulses exerted in performing several kinds of swimming turns. In: J. Terauds (ed.), Swimming III, pp. 220–230. University Park Press, Baltimore.

An Evaluation Procedure for Competitive Swimmers

U. J. J. Persyn, R. G. C. Hoeven, and D. J. Daly

To evaluate a swimmer's style, an efficient practitioner relies on his observations of the swimmer's movement and his ability to judge other physical capacities of the swimmer. When his observation is, however, aided by objective film data and when he has adequate instrumentation to measure specific anthropometric, motor, and physiological parameters, the effectiveness of his evaluation should be increased. The key to this evaluation is not only the establishment of factors governing proper swimming techniques (e.g., synchronization, flexibility, etc.) but obtaining and, most important, applying relevant measurements (Hochmuth, 1967; Miller and Nelson, 1973).

In swimming, the lack of visibility of the movement remains a particular problem for both researcher and practitioner; as a result, interpretations of the hydromechanical aspects of the movement are still a source of controversy. Because of this situation, some specific temporal and spatial data have been collected from films of world-class swimmers. Methods were developed at the same time to present this information on one graph. From this study, reported earlier, some hypotheses regarding "optimal" stroke mechanics have been formed. With few exceptions, such as the backstroker Stamm (see later), champion swimmers use uniform patterns as compared with intermediate swimmers. Naturally, the hypotheses developed needed confirmation through further research. With this in mind, in the following work, good swimmers simulated (while being filmed) some correct and incorrect movements or positions (e.g., no roll, extreme inclinations of the trunk, exaggerated sideways movements of the hips, etc.).

With the insights gained from this work and the information gained from the champions' patterns, the testing of the validity of an evaluation procedure for swimmers was started (Persyn, 1974; Persyn, De Maeyer, and Vervaecke, 1975; Persyn and Vervaecke, 1975 a, b; Persyn, Vervaecke, and Verhetsel, 1976). First, the patterns of 18 swimmers of the

National Belgian Team were studied, using videotape, but their physical capacities were controlled only roughly (Persyn, Thewissen, and Vervaecke, 1976). Later we were fortunate to have a group of seven young swimmers (12-14 years old), coached by a postgraduate specialist. These young swimmers had been trained in a wide range of skill variations, increasing greatly the ease of correction. The cooperation and patience of these subjects and their coach were very helpful in controlling the correction process.

PROCEDURE

The complete evaluation procedure involved a number of steps that can be accomplished in 1 day. Underwater 16-mm films were first taken from front and side views while the subjects performed the particular skills of interest. Films were also made while they swam with their arms and legs alone and sometimes while they used a one-arm crawl pull. Top speed was always filmed first. A series of anthropometric and motor tests were given, and other information about training schedules and best times for various skills was collected.

The films were analyzed to establish the following time and space parameters: 1) positions of body segments in relation to the water level, to the trunk, or to each other, 2) paths of hands and feet and of a fixed point on the trunk, and 3) phases delimited by spatial points of reference. These parameters were combined and placed along a single time base in a synchronization diagram. Certain time and space parameters of the limbs and the corresponding body positions and fluctuations of velocity were thus measured. These data then allowed interpretations concerning propulsion and resistance. When one observes, for instance, an important acceleration of the body while the legs are squeezed together in the breaststroke and in addition an external rotation, a flexion, and a supination of the feet, only a propeller-like propulsion can be induced. Analogous empirical reasonings, based on some time and space data, together with some somatic information, can sometimes be found in the popular literature.

From the various parameters in the synchronization diagram from patterns of top swimmers, style deviations within intermediate swimmers can be localized, and the search for their origin can begin. Such deviations are, however, not necessarily the result of a real fault but can also be a result of a shortcoming in capacities. An example of a fault is an extension of the feet during the squeezing of the legs in the breaststroke. A shortcoming could be the inability to supinate the foot sufficiently during this phase. In addition to flexibility, another motor factor that can be limiting is power (e.g., of the latissimus dorsi and triceps brachii, etc.). Anthropometric factors will also be important here (e.g., width of the pelvis, surface and shape of the feet, etc.). Motor shortcomings can sometimes be drastically improved through specific (land) conditioning, while faults in technique must be corrected through specific training in the pool. A morphological factor that determines the efficiency of longer efforts to a large extent is the distance between the center of buoyancy and the center of gravity. This distance results in a torque that can cause drag. Although this factor (as well as most anthropometric factors) is hardly trainable, we are now preparing to measure this in the future.

When individually adequate instructions in relation to the movement or to the quantity and intensity of the training for longer distances must be proposed, not only the hydromechanic and motor/anthropometric interpretations but physiological ones must be made. A breaststroker could, for example, cover a short distance, swimming with his arms alone, at a high speed and be very slow for longer distances, thus lacking local endurance. Velocity/distance curves of various strokes, patterns, and analytical skills, such as only pulling or kicking, are thus important at this point, as practical information relating to efficiency (Figure 3). More accurate measurements are obtained by gas analyses (Douglas-bag method) and telemetric cardiotachometry. It must be remembered that the corresponding synchronization diagrams are always a necessary control for the movements. (Various data can be collected simultaneously in a swimming treadmill (flume), which will be incorporated in the instructional pool.)

When cinematographic, anthropometric, motor, physiological, and medical data can be obtained in a single day, immediate discussion with the trainer and sometimes with the swimmer is possible. Following this "external" evaluation, a choice of individually appropriate instructions is proposed for the swimming pool, in collaboration with the personal trainer. After a few weeks of practice at home, the evaluation procedure is repeated until one is unable to offer further corrections. The following evaluation takes place after a period of time in which one expects the growth process to alter some physical capacities.

To illustrate this practical system, some examples are given. First, two top swimmers (about whom some particular hypotheses were confirmed) and a good age-group individual medley swimmer (J. A.) are used as illustrations. In these cases the propulsion principles are not stressed (hand and foot concept) but mainly body velocity fluctuation and some balance problems.

RESULTS AND DISCUSSION

The Backstroke of Stamm

The arm movement of the backstroke of Olympic silver medalist Michael Stamm was described in a photographic series by Counsilman (1977). Although the patterns of top backstrokers are homogeneous, the synchronization of Stamm's arms with his legs is a striking exception. At first look, the style of this swimmer showed some discontinuity. From a closer observation (without analysis) of Counsilman's film, it appeared not only that he used a four-beat kick instead of a six-beat kick, but that (instead of a crossed synchronization) he used a parallel synchronization, with the left arm pressing down after the entry while the left leg kicked down (Figure 1). To gain better insight into this deviation, a synchronization diagram was set up, including phases, paths of the movements of hands and feet, fluctuation of the swimming velocity, and longitudinal body roll. This diagram has been compared with that of Gary Hall, which we consider a "normal" one (Figure 2).

The fluctuation in Stamm's velocity seemed a convincing argument for establishing the diagnosis of a "faulty" style: the greatest deviation is 50% of the mean velocity and only 28% for Hall (Figures 1 and 2). In principle this fluctuation must be limited in the crawl and back crawl strokes.

Two hypotheses are confirmed by Stamm's pattern:

1. A function of the kick that follows the downward push phase of the arm is that of rolling the body. In Hall's pattern we observed that the roll coincided with these two actions. In Stamm's pattern the roll to the left was initiated by the downward push of the right arm but was retarded by the left downward kick. The crossed kick took place during the pull and push phases, allowing additional roll. Finally, the downward kick of the left leg together with the downward push of the left arm caused a late but rapid roll to the right.

2. A function of the kicks is, in our opinion, to maintain a uniform velocity of translation within each cycle of the movement. In Hall's pattern the legs closed during the least propulsive entry and upward lift phases of the arms, thus limiting the decrease in velocity (Figure 2, C-D). In Stamm's pattern this closing of the legs occurred during the propulsive pull phase, increasing the already important acceleration, which followed the excessive deceleration caused by the previous spreading of the legs (Persyn, De Maeyer, and Vervaecke, 1975).

As a matter of course, it must be specified that interpretations of patterns are limited without any anthropometric or motor information.

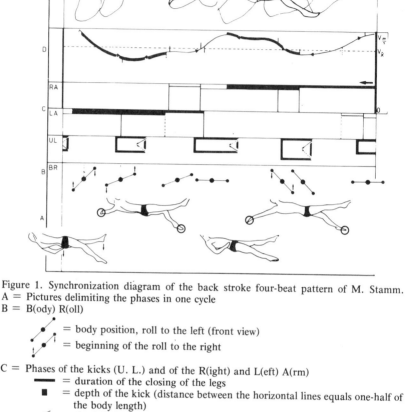

Figure 1. Synchronization diagram of the back stroke four-beat pattern of M. Stamm.
A = Pictures delimiting the phases in one cycle
B = B(ody) R(oll)

    = body position, roll to the left (front view)

    = beginning of the roll to the right

C = Phases of the kicks (U. L.) and of the R(ight) and L(eft) A(rm)
    ━━ = duration of the closing of the legs
    ■ = depth of the kick (distance between the horizontal lines equals one-half of
    the body length)
    < = the right leg moves downward

    = delimitation of the phases (side view) from right to left:
    ━━ = entry and downward press to 45°, defined by a straight line between
    wrist and shoulder with regard to the horizontal
    ━━ = pull from 45° to 90°
    = first-part push, from 90° to the bottomward action
    ■ = second-part push, bottomward action
    ⊏ = upward lift from deepest hand position to water level
    ── = recovery

D = Velocity fluctuation of the body displacement ($V\frac{m}{s}$)

    ------ = mean velocity
    = fluctuation corresponding to pull and push phases
    ► ◄ = fluctuation corresponding to closing of the legs
E = Path of the movement of hands and feet (M. P.)

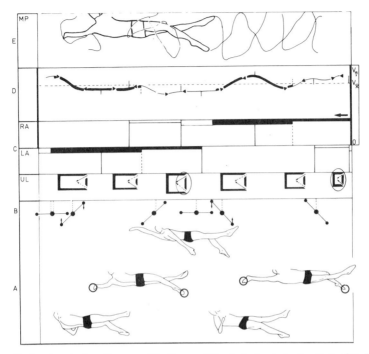

Figure 2. Synchronization diagram of the "normal" back stroke six-beat pattern of G. Hall.

Two Strokes of a National Age-Group Champion

A global evaluation of patterns of the swimmers within our experimental club is, of course, more reliable than with top swimmers that have been seen only on film and is much more representative of the level of swimmer with whom we will usually be dealing. The case of one such swimmer (J. A.), 13 years old, is worked out here for the crawl and breaststroke.

The Crawl Stroke

A simple above-water observation of this swimmer showed a right lateral displacement of the pelvis, after right-side inhalation in the six-beat crawl. This displacement was accompanied by a jerky forward movement. The velocity/distance curve of this swimmer showed relatively weak performances in long distances (Figure 3). Despite the jerky movement on one side, his performances were equivalent when he swam with the left or the right arm alone. Moreover, specific pulling strength and flexibility tests indicated a symmetric development of the two shoulder girdles. His ankle flexibility was limited (without overstretching), and his propulsion, when only kicking, was not particularly effective.

Based on this simple information, the swimmer was advised to

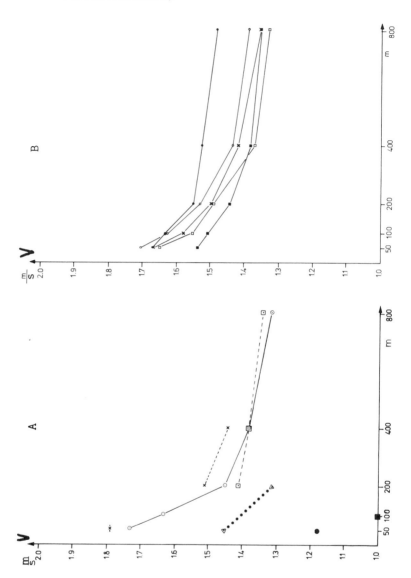

Figure 3. Velocity/distance curves of various subjects.
A = J. A.
      O—O = original six-beat pattern curve, breathing to the right
     D·····◁ = original pulling only
      ● = original one-arm pulling, right and left
     ■ = original kicking
   ▢-▢ = two-beat with alternating breathing after 3 weeks
   x--x = two-beat with alternating breathing after 6 weeks
    -x- = six-beat with alternating breathing after 6 weeks
B = Five swimmers (women) of the national Belgian team in their best stroke

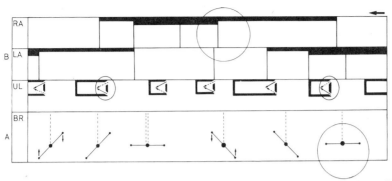

Figure 4. Synchronization diagram of the "normal" six-beat crawl pattern of G. Hall. Symbols: see Figure 1, except for the arm phases in B.

= from right to left:
—— = entry of the hand from the water level to the beginning of the maximum arm extension
▬ = pressing down from the end of the entry to an angle of 45°
▬ = pull, from 45° to 90°
▬ = push, from 90° to 135°
▬ = upward lift from 135° to the water level
—— = recovery
♀♀♀ = duration of breathing
•━━•━━• = body position, roll to the left (rear view)

change from his normal six-beat kick to a two-beat crossover kick to counterbalance the movement of his pelvis. To eliminate the jerky movement, alternating breathing was proposed, to the right or left every three arm actions. This breathing is learned easily, but the two-beat crossover pattern demands a totally different synchronization and is not attained as easily as the straight two-beat kick. Each adaptation resulted in an increase in velocity a few weeks later: the six-beat with alternating breathing in the sprint and the two-beat in distances longer than 400 m (Figure 3). However, while breathing on the right side, the wiggling movement remained with the six-beat kick, and the jerky movement remained with both kicking patterns.

The synchronization diagrams were then drawn, in a certain sense a posteriori (Figures 4 to 7). When breathing on the right side, a glide stroke type entry of the left arm was seen, coupled with a two-beat arm synchronization; while rolling on the other side, a two-beat high elbow entry was seen, with a glide stroke arm synchronization (Figure 5D). The entry of the right arm was so rushed that the pull and push phases of this arm nearly overlapped these two phases of the left arm; their paths almost crossed each other. The body roll occurred relatively late in relation to this arm entry (Figures 4 and 5, A-B). Following this action, the deepest kick was seen on the opposite side, rolling the body even further than at the left side. (Nevertheless, the right kick should be deeper for rolling further at

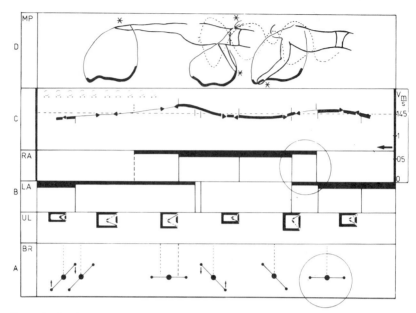

Figure 5. Synchronization diagram of the six-beat crawl pattern of J. A.
✱ = Synchronization of the arms, right and left hand entry, respectively.

the breathing side). In the "normal" pattern, the roll on the right is in-itiated during the pull and push phases of the left hand and is achieved by the kick at the left side and not as much by the arm entry at the right side. The lateral inward path of the hand (with a slightly inclined angle of in-

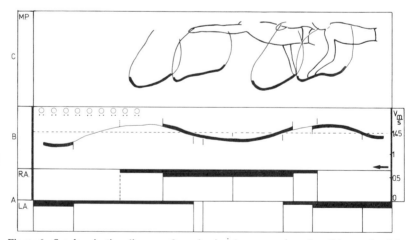

Figure 6. Synchronization diagram of crawl swimming, arms alone, breathing on the right (J.A.).

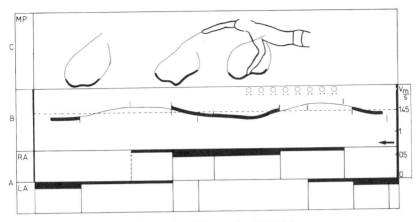

Figure 7. Synchronization diagram, breathing on the left (J.A.).

cidence) in the pull and push phases causes the body to roll (as a reaction to this propeller-like movement).

The combination of this deep (slightly across the midline) arm entry with the deep kick pushed the pelvis to the right. This deviation was corrected by the lateral closing of the bottom leg in the two-beat crossover pattern, but the roll was increased (Persyn, 1974; Persyn, DeMaeyer, and Vervaecke, 1975).

The alternating breathing resulted in a more fluent body displacement in the two patterns, shortening the glide and lengthening the high elbow entry. When not breathing (swimming arms alone), the subject showed correct synchronization of the arms. While breathing on the right side (arms-alone diagram, Figure 6), the subject had more velocity fluctuations (30%) than during left breathing (18%) (Figure 7), but an equal average velocity was attained (even without previous training). To make sufficient breathing possible in the six-beat crawl and to obtain a more uniform velocity fluctuation, breathing on the left side exclusively was proposed.

Two hypotheses were confirmed by J. A.'s pattern:

1. In comparison with arms-alone swimming, right breathing, we still observed less velocity fluctuation (18%) and more space between the hand paths for the six-beat pattern, right breathing. This again seemed to explain an important function of the kick in maintaining the continuity of the body displacement.

2. It was interesting to specify that when the subject swam with arms alone, the maximum velocity occurred during the pressing-down and upward-lift phases of the arms, phases without backward displace-

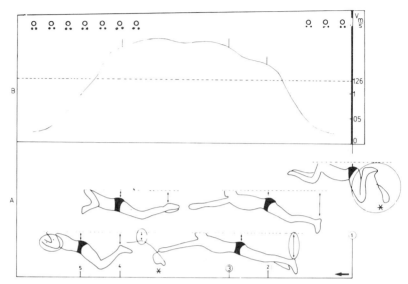

Figure 8. Synchronization diagram of the initial "faulty" breast stroke (J.A.).
A = 1 = beginning of extension of the legs (feet turned outward)
    2 = maximum spreading of the legs
    3 = end of the accelerated squeezing of the legs
    4 = beginning of arm recovery (hands return forward)
    5 = ± 90° bend in the knees
    ✶ = movement paths of the feet and hands
B = Velocity fluctuation of a fixed point on the body

ment of the hands. This strengthened the hypothesis of the propeller principle of propulsion (Counsilman, 1969) in these phases.

Further maturation of this young swimmer will determine the choice of six- or two-beat kicking. After a few weeks of automatizing the skill, his performances over 400 m were equal. Since he was still relatively weak in pulling power and not particularly flexible in the ankle (which is not easy to improve), it was assumed that once the arm action was adapted to this pattern, his performances in the two-beat pattern would surpass those in the six-beat pattern, even in shorter distances (e.g., 200 m). In fact, 6 weeks later, using the two-beat pattern, he improved his six-beat personal records by 6 sec in 200 m and by 13 sec in 400 m (without bettering his performances in the six-beat pattern) (Figure 3).

Physiological tests provide more help in the still-empirical selection of the appropriate pattern. The efficiency during swimming with arms or legs alone and in various patterns of the whole stroke will give the coach an idea of the subject's actual potential. In the adaptation period of his two beat, J. A., for example, attained a lower pulse rate in a 400 m all-out effort than when he used a six beat. However, in this continuous evolution

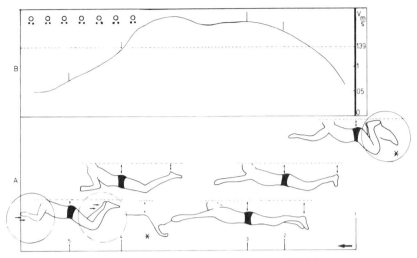

Figure 9. Synchronization diagram of the adapted breaststroke (J.A.).

of his crawl performances an optimal combination of the four strokes remains the ultimate goal in preparation for the medley event.

The Breaststroke

If J. A.'s performance was not extremely weak in the breaststroke (1.24 in 100 m), his style was technically poor (an interesting situation for a technical trainer). In this stroke, diverse fundamentals were neglected, mainly those related to balance:

1. The couple action caused by the drag forces applied on the forearm and the lower leg during the first part of the recovery did not occur. This action served to lift the head out of the water for breathing (Figure 9A).

2. The elbows were dropped near the trunk during the last part of the pull, retarding the first part of the recovery and excluding the possibility of this couple action (Figure 8A).

3. The breathing occurred, therefore, too early in the pull and lasted too long because the abdominal and thoracic muscles were still contracted.

4. The early lift of the head resulted from a deep arm action, starting from near the surface (Figure 8A, 3).

5. The hip flexion was exaggerated, placing the feet too low in relation to the buttocks. As a result, the propulsive extension of the legs brought the feet too deep, lifting the pelvis (Figure 8A, 1).

6. Finally, the lifting of the straight legs caused an inclined position of the body (Figure 8A, 3).

The correction of those deviations was largely obtained automatically by having the subject swim with his head continually out of the water, using extremely late (contra) breathing (cf. Wilkie). In 1 month, this swimmer lowered his 100-m time by 7 sec. Although his arm pull remains relatively narrow and his kick wide, we prefer to wait until further adaptations occur in his shoulder girdle strength. Then he might improve by broadening his pull and by kicking in a narrower pattern, eventually partially overlapping the leg and arm actions.

CONCLUSION

At first, Cureton (1930), but later Schramm (1959), Counsilman (1968), Krüger (1972), Malzahn and Stafenk (1973), Boičev (1974), and Miyashita (1974) pleaded for a combination of observation and measurement methods and proposed steps in a multidisciplinary approach to swimming skills. Their strategy, which we have tried to apply in this study, is useful as an operational basis in our postgraduate program for a technical trainer but, of course, the coaching ability can be developed only by a close collaboration with successful practitioners.

REFERENCES

Boičev, K. 1974. Methods of Control in Swimming. Medicina and Phyzcultura, Sofia. (Translation of the original title into English.)

Counsilman, J. E. 1968. The Science of Swimming. Prentice-Hall, Inc., Englewood Cliffs.

Counsilman, J. E. 1969. The role of sculling movements in the arm pull. Swimming World 10:6-7.

Counsilman, J. E. 1977. Competitive Swimming Manual. Counsilman, Bloomington.

Cureton, T. K. 1930. Mechanics and kinesiology of swimming. Res. Q. 1:87-121.

Hochmuth, G. 1967. Biomechanik Sportlicher Bewegungen (Biomechanics of Sport Movements). Limpert Verlag, Frankfurt-Main.

Krüger, F. 1972. Diagnostische Möglichkeiten der sportmotorischen Leistung im Schwimmen (Diagnostic possibilities for motor performances in swimmers). Informations. Training 12:100-108.

Malzahn, K., and Stafenk, W. 1973. Zur Effektivität verschiedener Bewegungsvarianten im Brust-und Kraulschwimmen (Effectiveness of different movements in breast and crawl stroke swimming). Teor. Prakt. Körperkult. 22:724-735.

Miller, D. I., and Nelson, R. C. 1973. Biomechanics of Sport. Lea & Febiger, Philadelphia.

Miyashita, M. 1974. Methods of calculating mechanical power in swimming the breaststroke. Res. Q. 45:128-137.

Persyn, U. 1974. Technisch-hydrodynamische benadering van de bewegende mens in het water (Technical-hydrodynamic approach of human motion in water). Hermes VIII (3-4):5-136.

Persyn, U., De Maeyer, J., and Vervaecke, H. 1975. Investigation of hydrodynamic determinants of competitive swimming strokes. In: J. P. Clarys and L. Lewillie (eds.), Swimming II, pp. 214-222. University Park Press, Baltimore.

Persyn, U., Thewissen, M. and Vervaecke, H. 1976. Conceptions de l'évaluation du mouvement aquatique, en relation avec une stratégie de formation d'enseignants (A conception of swimming movement evaluation, in relation to teachers' training). International Congress on Physical Education. Jyväskylä. In press.

Persyn, U., and Vervaecke, H. 1975a. Functional research on the technical initial swim situation in physical education students. In: D. Schmüll, J. Groenman, and J. W. de Vries, ICHPER, Vol. 18, pp. 296-307. Jan Luiting Foundation, Zeist.

Persyn, U., and Vervaecke, H. 1975b. A model for a functional evaluation of full-synchronization data in the crawl stroke. Hermes IX:425-435.

Persyn, U., Vervaecke, H., and Verhetsel, D. 1976. Mesure technique du niveau de départ dans la nage du crawl (Technical measurements of the beginners' level in the crawl stroke). International Congress on Physical Education. Jyväskylä. In press.

Schramm, E. 1959. Untersuchungsmethoden zur Bestimmung des Widerstandes, der Kraft und der Ausdauer bei Schwimmsportlern (Research methods of drag, power, and endurance within P.E. competitive swimmers). Wiss. Zeitschr. DHFK 2:161-180.

Swimming
Starts
and Turns

Biomechanical Analysis of Starting Techniques in Swimming

V. M. Zatsiorsky, N. Zh. Bulgakova, and N. M. Chaplinsky

The start is generally acknowledged to be an important element for success in competitive swimming, especially in the short events. Various techniques have been developed by coaches and swimmers and investigated by researchers to evaluate their efficiency. Parfionov (1959) and Torre (1976) recommended a starting technique in which the arms are swung forward from a hyperextended position. Studies by Nivandi (1963), Moverson (1964), and Maglischo (1969) reported that the best technique involved a full arm swing. More recently the grab, or grip, start has become increasingly popular, and a number of studies have shown it to be superior to others (Hanauer, 1967, 1972; Roffer and Nelson, 1972; Michaels, 1973; Van Slooten, 1975; Lowell, 1975). The latter two studies reported that some swimmers performed better using the conventional arm swing method. Finally, the use of a modified track start has been suggested by Fitzgerald (1973).

No study has been reported in which all four of these starts have been compared. It is important that such a project be carried out, utilizing a reasonably large sample of highly skilled swimmers. The purposes of this study were: 1) to compare the efficiencies of these four swimming start techniques, and 2) to identify the key factors that affect starting performance.

PROCEDURES

This investigation involved two experiments and a total of 105 swimmers. In the first experiment the subjects were 45 highly skilled male swimmers, ranked as Masters of Sport, comprised of 15 from each specialty (free style, butterfly, and breaststroke). After completion of three or more daily training sessions, each swimmer completed four trials of each start technique on one day, resulting in a total of 16 starts. The four techniques

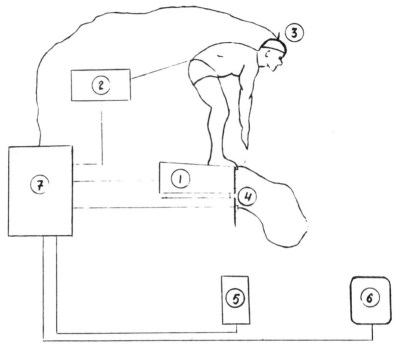

Figure 1. Instrumentation system. 1. Dynamographic starting block; 2. speedograph; 3. head entry time recording device; 4. device for measuring time over 5.5 m; 5. camera for above water filming; 6. camera for underwater filming; 7. Oscillograph.

were: 1) forward arm swing, 2) full arm swing, 3) grab, and 4) track start. The order of starts was randomized using a 4 × 4 Latin square design, and the best start for each technique, based on time to 5.5 m, was selected for analysis.

In the second experiment 60 swimmers of different levels (20 Masters of Sport, 20 first grade sportsmen, and 20 second grade sportsmen) participated as subjects. The mean age was 17.5 ±1.7 years; height, 172.0 ±10.3 cm, and weight, 63.5 ±13.0 kg. They each completed a three-trial vertical jump test and executed three grab starts. The best trial for each was selected for analysis. Results of these tests were combined with height and weight data in the analysis of the relevant factors affecting successful performance.

An instrumentation system, comprised of a number of measurement devices, was used. These components, shown diagrammatically in Figure 1, were: 1) force-measuring starting block, 2) velocity indicator, 3) device for recording head entry, 4) line unit for determining time over 5.5 m, and 5) two motion cameras for above-water and underwater filming.

In the first experiment the analysis was based primarily on the time

Table 1. Summary of ANOVA for starting technique and swimming stroke based on swimming efficiency ($N = 45$)

Source of variance	SS	df	EMS	F ratio
Starting technique (A)	0.3112	3	0.1037	4.95[a]
Swimming stroke (B)	0.0190	2	0.0095	0.45
Interaction (A $\times$ B)	0.0542	6	0.0090	0.43
Error	3.5184	168	0.0209	
Total	3.9028	179		

[a]Significant at the 0.05 level.

from the starting gun until the swimmer covered 5.5 m. The data were treated statistically using analysis-of-variance techniques. The starting movements were further divided in the second experiment to include the times for: 1) support (block clearance), 2) flight, and 3) glide. In addition, selected biomechanical and performance variables were incorporated in the correlation, and regression analyses were used to identify the most important biomechanical factors in the grab start.

RESULTS

First Experiment

Results of the ANOVA, shown in Table 1, indicate that the time required to cover the first 5.5 m depends on starting technique but not on the swimming stroke to be performed. Further statistical analysis of the data, presented in Table 2, revealed that the significant difference was the result

Table 2. Analysis of mean differences in starting time for four start techniques ($N = 45$)

Starting technique	X (sec)	σ (sec)	Significance of differences 1	Significance of differences 2	t Criteria 3	t Criteria 4
Forward arm swing	2.759	0.108	x			
Full arm swing	2.748	0.106	—	x		
Grab	2.737	0.176	—	—	x	
Track	2.845	0.127	a	a	a	x

[a]Indicates significant differences ($P < 0.05$) between means.

of the relatively poor performance in the track start. The differences among the other three starts were not statistically significant, indicating that they were efficient. However, differences among the starts were observed for certain biomechanical indicators. For example, in the grab start the magnitude of the ground reaction force was less and the duration of take off was greater than in traditional arm-swing starting techniques (Figure 2). At the same time the ground reaction impulse was approximately equal for all three starting techniques.

Second Experiment

Because equal efficiency was observed for the three main starts, the biomechanical features may be more important than the specific techniques. The second experiment was designed to evaluate and to compare selected biomechanical components in the grab start to determine their effect on starting performance.

The first step in this analysis was to divide the time of start, which was from start signal to 5.5 m, into three parts. These were: 1) support time (t_1), defined as the elapsed time from the starting signal until the feet left the block; 2) flight time (t_2) from block clearance (end of support time) to head entry in the water; and 3) glide time (t_3), which represented the period from head entry until the feet crossed the 5.5-m line.

Table 3 contains the correlation coefficients for these variables and the total start time (efficiency). The results indicate that total time depends most strongly on support and glide times.

The second stage of the analysis focused on the three phases of the start: support, flight, and in-water (glide). Ideally, support time should be as short as possible, while the takeoff conditions should provide for maximum horizontal velocity and optimal vertical velocity.

Results of the correlation analyses are shown in Table 4. Significant relationships are noted between support time and latent time, and motor and initial movement times. Nonsignificant relationships were found for initial starting position variables (knee, hip, ankle, and arm/body angles), takeoff time, height, and body weight. The most important aspects of the time of flight (t_2) were found to be horizontal velocity $(r = -0.47)$; flight distance $(r = 0.85)$, and height of flight $(r = 0.78)$.

Time of glide depends primarily on length of glide $(r = 0.90)$ and glide velocity $(r = -0.74)$. Further, the glide velocity is closely related to horizontal flight velocity $(r = 0.60)$ and is also influenced by the swimmer's movements during water entry and the hydrodynamic features of the body.

To separate and to isolate these effects, a method was used that involved regression residues or deviations from the regression line that depicted horizontal flight velocity and glide velocity (see Figure 3). The

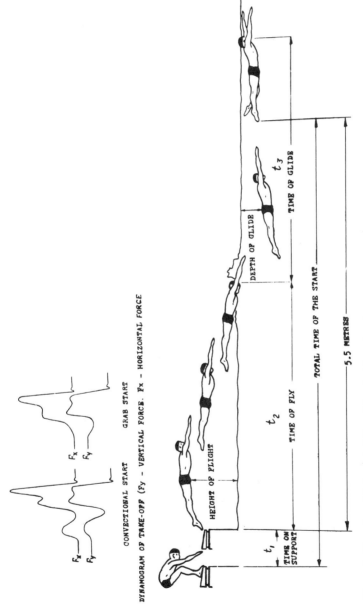

Figure 2. Experimental characteristics of the start in swimming.

Table 3.   Relationships total start time, support, flight and glide times ($N = 60$)

Variable	X (sec)	SD (sec)	Correlation with total time
1. Support time (t_1)	0.930	0.084	0.60
2. Flight time (t_2)	0.387	0.065	0.13
3. Glide time (t_2)	1.680	0.250	0.94

regression residues reflect the variations in glide speed for the same horizontal flight velocity.

It is evident that the magnitude of the deviations depends primarily on the movement of the swimmer in the water and on specific morphological features. Correlation analyses revealed no relationship between the regressive residues and angle of water entry ($r = 0.04$), depth of glide ($r = 0.01$), or height ($r = 0.15$).

This means that these indicators apparently do not influence the decrease in velocity during the transition from air to water. The only factor with which regressive residue values are correlated rather markedly is distance of glide from the moment of entry into the water to the beginning of the first swimming movement ($r = -0.55$). In other words, speed losses in the water were observed to be less for those swimmers who started swimming movements earlier. It is possible that this was typical of our subjects only, because many of them seemed to delay the start of their first swimming movements.

Finally, start efficiency in swimming depends significantly on the swimmer's jumping ability (as measured by the vertical jump), height,

Table 4.   Relationships among support time and selected biomechanical variables ($N = 60$)

Variable	Support time
Initial starting position:	
Knee angle	−0.26
Hip angle	0.16
Ankle angle	−0.13
Arm/body angle	−0.22
Latent time (Premotor)	0.52
Motor time	0.86
Initial movement	0.71
Takeoff	−0.12
Height	−0.18
Weight	0.01

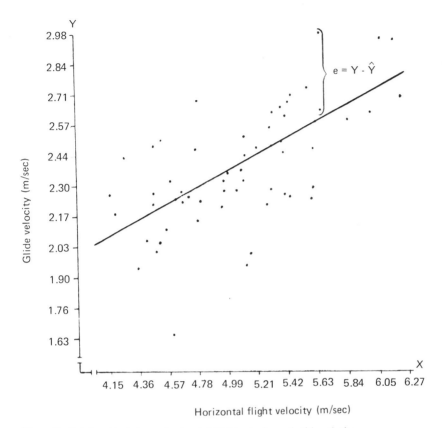

Figure 3. Relationship between horizontal flight velocity and glide velocity.

and body weight (see Table 5). These correlations can be explained entirely by their relationships with flight time and time of movements in the water, while support time was not correlated with body size or the jumping ability of the sportsman.

Table 5. Relationships among time characteristics of the start and height, weight, and jumping ability ($N = 60$)

		Time		
No.	Indicators	Total	Support	Fly and glide
1.	Height	−0.67	0.13	−0.74
2.	Weight	−0.75	−0.01	−0.78
3.	Standing vertical jump	−0.64	0.021	−0.68

CONCLUSIONS

Swimming starts involving a full arm swing, forward arm swing, or grabbing the starting block are equally efficient, while the track-start style is less efficient. Flight time and glide times for the grab start depend mainly on the jumping ability and size of the swimmer; details of technique (body positions, entry angle, and so forth) are less important.

ACKNOWLEDGMENT

The authors acknowledge the technical assistance of A. A. Dianov in the development of the instrumentation systems used in this study

REFERENCES

Fitzgerald, J. 1973. The track start in swimming. Swimming Tech. 10:89–94.
Hanauer, E. 1967. The grab start. Swimming World (June).
Hanauer, E. 1972. Grab start faster than conventional start. Swimming World (April).
Lowell, J. 1975. Analysis of the grab and the conventional start. Swimming Tech. 3:66–69, 76.
Maglischo, Ch. 1969. A comparison of three racing starts used in competitive swimming. Swimming Tech. (October).
Michaels, R. 1973. A time distance comparison of the grab starts. Swimming Tech. 10:16–17.
Nivandi, R. 1963. A method of determining a start jump efficiency and control of timely start of initial swimming movements (in Russian). Ph.D. thesis, Tartu University.
Parfionov, V. 1959. Analysis of a start jump technique and a method of training swimmers of starts in competitive swimming (in Russian). Ph.D. thesis, Institute of Physculture, Kiev.
Roffer, B., and Nelson R. 1972. The grab start is faster. Swimming Tech. 8:4.
Torre, C. 1976. Starting technique. Swimming Times 3:30–31, 56.
Van Slooten, P. 1975. An analysis of two forward swim starts using cinematography. Swimming Tech. 3.

Influence of
Starting-Block Angle
on the Grab Start
in Competitive Swimming

J. R. Stevenson and C. A. Morehouse

The manufacture of starting blocks with a slanted starting surface began in the late 1960s but stimulated little interest on the part of researchers. Elliott and Sinclair (1970) used block angles of 0°, 10°, and 15° in their study, in which the method of starting was the conventional circular arm-swing style. In an earlier study by Tuttle, Morehouse, and Armbruster (1939) block angles of 10°, 20°, and 30° were used, but because of the problem of stability the 30° block angle was eliminated. The results of both studies indicated that the use of a starting block set at an angle was of no advantage in the swimming starts. Theoretically, however, a swimmer should be able to apply a greater horizontal force against a starting block surface that is placed at an angle and, therefore, gain a possible advantage in the start if the problem of instability in the starting position could be overcome.

The grab start was used by many competitors in the 1972 Olympic Games, and since then it has been adopted by many swimmers of all levels of ability. Bowers (1973) and Roffer (1971) conducted investigations in which the grab start was compared with the conventional start. The conclusions of these studies indicate that the grab start provides a faster start off the block and increases stability in the "set" position. For these reasons the grab start seemed to be a feasible technique for studying the effects of starting-block angle on sprint starts in swimming because instability in the starting position would not be as great a problem using this starting technique.

PURPOSE OF THE STUDY

The purpose of this study was to determine, through the use of cinematography and a strain-gauged starting block, the effects of starting-block angles of 0°, 10°, 20°, and 30° above the horizontal on a 22.86-m (25-yard) swimming performance using the grab start. The differences in the grab-start performances from the four block angles were analyzed with respect to 15 selected biomechanical factors, which included the angles of projection at takeoff and incidence at water entry, takeoff and entry velocities, horizontal distance of projection, vertical hand forces on the front edge of the starting block, and time data for various phases of the start.

PROCEDURES

Penn State male competitive swimmers ($N = 10$), with a mean height of 182.8 cm (72 inches) and a mean weight of 74 kg (163 lb.), served as subjects. Each subject performed three trials from each of the four selected block angles. One of the trials from each block angle was filmed. Each trial consisted of a grab start and a freestyle swim at maximal speed to the opposite end of a 22.86-m pool. At least 8 min of rest was provided between trials for each subject. Each subject attended one morning and one afternoon session, during which all the subjects performed six trials from the selected block angles in a random order.

A regulation electronic starting gun was used as the starting stimulus. A 16-mm electrically driven, Locam camera was used to film all starts and was connected to a pulse generator that placed timing marks on the film at the rate of 50/sec. The camera was started as the starter's arm was raised to ensure that the camera was running at the desired speed before the gun was fired. The camera was stopped when the subject's body was completely submerged under the surface of the water after the start. Times for the 22.86-m distance were recorded to the nearest 0.01 sec by an electronic timing system, which was activated at the moment of gun flash and was deactivated by the subject's first contact with an automatic touch-pad apparatus.

The standard 10° inclined starting block surface was replaced by a 2-cm plywood board that was fitted with a milled steel bar, 2.54 cm in diameter, suspended from angle-iron supports at the side of the board. Sensing elements were placed 7.62 cm from each end of the bar, with one edge of the elements firmly fixed to the angle-iron supports (Figure 1). Foil strain gauges were applied to the sensing elements, and a four-active-arm Wheatstone bridge was formed for both vertical and horizontal measurements. Cavanagh, Palmgren, and Kerr (1975) reported that the measured cross-sensitivity values of these devices showed less than 6% error in both directions. Because only hand forces were required, a piece of galvanized sheet steel, 1.6 mm thick, was fitted to cover the bar over a

Figure 1. Sensing element used on special starting block.

30.5-cm region of foot contact. This plate had no physical contact with the bar at any time during the start.

The strain-gauged platform was fitted to cover the entire upper surface of the standard starting block. The platform was elevated by supports at the back of the block, which provided upper surface angles of 0°, 10°, 20°, and 30° above the horizontal (Figure 2).

The outputs from the strain gauges were amplified and then recorded on a Sanborn strip chart recorder. The strip chart recorder traced the horizontal and vertical force components that were produced by the subject's hands while he performed the grab start. Figure 3 illustrates a typical force record. The force records and film data were synchronized by matching gun flash on the film with a simultaneous electrical contact closure in the gun, which was recorded on the chart paper.

All raw data from the film were extracted by a Bendix digital data acquisition system that was equipped with a Vanguard projector. These data were processed in a Fortran-Watfiv computer program and fed into an IBM System 370/model 168 digital computer to calculate the body's center of gravity at takeoff and water entry, horizontal distance covered from block edge to initial entry, angle of projection at takeoff, angle of incidence at initial entry, and horizontal, vertical, and resultant components of velocity at take-off and initial entry.

Analysis of variance with repeated measures was used for statistical

Figure 2. Starting block angle of 30°.

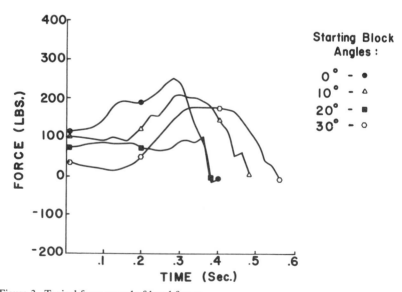

Figure 3. Typical force record of hand forces.

analysis to compare the performances of the grab start from each of the four selected block angles. If a significant difference was found, the Student-Newman-Keuls post-hoc comparison test was used to determine which block angle produced a significant mean difference in the performance variable.

RESULTS

The mean performance of the group was determined for each variable at each of the four selected block angles. Each start was divided into seven temporal categories to allow comparison of any differences among the performance of the grab start from each block angle. Among the seven temporal categories the following differences were found, which are illustrated in Figure 4.

1. The 20° block angle produced a slightly shorter total block time; however, the differences among mean block times were not statistically significant.
2. The 20° block angle produced a significantly ($\rho \leq 0.01$) shorter flight time than both the 0° and 10 block angle but not the 30° block angle.
3. The 20° block angle produced a significantly ($\rho \leq 0.05$) shorter time to initial entry than the 0° block angle, but this time was not significantly less than that of the 10° or 30° block angles.
4. The 0° block angle produced a significantly ($\rho \leq 0.01$) shorter 22.86-m than the 10° and 30° angles, but this time was not significantly less than that of the 20° block angle.
5. The 30° block angle produced a significantly ($\rho \leq 0.05$) shorter time to reach peak hand force than the 10° block angle but not significantly less than both the 0° and 20° angles.

Comparison of the mean velocities and angles of projection at takeoff and the angles of incidence at entry revealed that there were no statistically significant differences among the four block angles. Likewise, no significant differences were found among the horizontal distances covered in flight for the four block angles.

Two of the three force variables studied revealed significant differences among the four block angles. There were no differences among the pregun steady forces; however, the 30° block angle produced a significantly ($\rho \leq 0.05$) lower mean peak vertical hand force than the 0° angle, but this value was not significantly smaller than those produced by the 10° and 20° block angles. The large magnitudes of the standard deviations, ranging from 41.43 to 85.20 lb for the pre-gun steady force and 74.72 to 191.92 lb for the peak force, resulted from the fact that some subjects pushed down on the force-measuring bar, particularly when starting

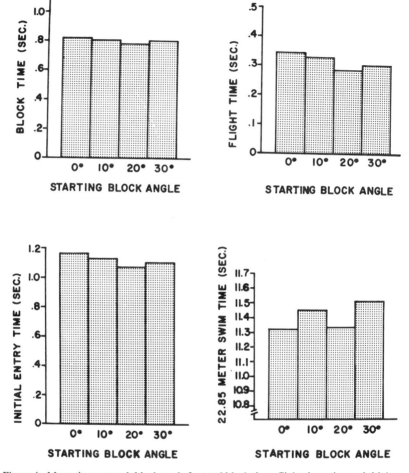

Figure 4. Mean times at each block angle for total block time, flight time, time to initial entry, and 22.85-m swim time.

from the 20° and 30° block angles. This phenomenon concerning the application of the vertical forces by the hands at the higher block angles needs additional investigation.

DISCUSSION

The results indicate that in this group of subjects the performance of the grab start from the block angles of 0°, 10°, 20°, and 30° above the horizontal differed significantly with respect to most of the temporal components involved in the start and subsequent 22.86-m swim. Analysis of the various time measurements revealed that the 20° block angle produced the shortest total block time, flight time, and time from gun flash to initial entry. The 0° and 20° block angles produced a shorter time to 22.86 m than did the 10° and 30° angles. Probably the shorter block time, flight time, and initial entry time when starting from the 20° block angle contributed to a reduction of the 22.86-m swimming time.

The final temporal factor among the four block angles was the time required to reach peak vertical hand force from gun flash, where the 30° block angle produced a significantly shorter time than did the 0° block angle.

The 30° block angle produced a significantly smaller amount of peak vertical force during the performance of the grab start than both the 0° and 10° block angles. These findings suggest that the swimmers used less upward pull on the front edge of the starting block as the starting-block angle increased in degrees above the horizontal.

Although there was a difference in the grab-start performance in terms of vertical hand forces required from the 30° block angle, this did not seem to significantly affect the speed with which the subject was able to get off the block, enter the water, and swim at top speed to the opposite end of the pool. The time variables involved in this swimming act do not seem to be affected by the different vertical hand forces used in the starts from starting blocks that are placed at varied angles from 0° to 30°.

CONCLUSION

The performance of the grab start and subsequent 22.86-m swim is affected by a change in starting-block angle above the horizontal. Further, the 20° block angle provided the most advantages in reducing the time required for the performance of the grab start and subsequent 22.86-m swim.

REFERENCES

Bowers, J. 1973. A biomechanical comparison of the grab and conventional sprint starts in competitive swimming. Master's thesis, The Pennsylvania State University, University Park.

Cavanagh, P., Palmgren, J., and Kerr, B. 1975. A device to measure forces at the hands during the grab start. In: L. Lewille and J. P. Clarys (eds.), Swimming II, pp. 43–50. University Park Press, Baltimore.

Elliot, G., and Sinclair, H. 1970. The influence of block angle on swimming starts. In: L. Lewille and J. P. Clarys (eds.), Proceedings of the First International

Symposium on Biomechanics in Swimming. Universite Libre de Bruxelles, Brussels.

Roffer, B. 1971. A comparison of the grab and conventional racing starts in swimming. Master's problem, The Pennsylvania State University, University Park.

Stevenson, J. 1977. The influence of starting block angle on the grab start in competitive swimming. Master's thesis, The Pennsylvania State University, University Park.

Tuttle, W., Morehouse, L., and Armbruster, D. 1939. Two studies in swimming starts. Res. Q. 10:211-227.

Effects of Weight, Height, and Reach on the Performance of the Conventional and Grab Starts in Swimming

J. G. Disch, W. W. Hosler, and J. A. Bloom

In performances where the criterion for excellence is time, the starting component is one of the primary contributing factors. Also, the shorter the distance of the event, the more important is effect of the start. One of the major areas of research in both track and swimming has been the analysis of starting techniques. At least two types of starts are usually compared.

In swimming, analysis often contrasts the grab start to the conventional start. Examination of much of the current research indicates that there is still controversy as to whether or not the grab start is faster than the conventional start. Michaels (1973) found that the grab start produced faster times on a dive and 25-ft glide. However, only six male varsity swimmers and five trials were involved. No statistical tests were conducted, so these results offer only tentative evidence.

Lowell (1975) analyzed various performance components and found that the results favored the grab start. Using 20 skilled male swimmers, he concluded that the grab start was significantly faster ($P < 0.01$) than the conventional start in time off the block and time of flight. Although he concluded that the grab start produced significantly faster times at 20 ft, the results were tested at the 0.07 level. This suggests that he was "data snooping," and the credence of this finding should be questioned.

On the other hand, Gibson and Holt (1976) found that time from 0 to 25 ft accounted for only 1% of the variance in the different types of dives. They used 22 skilled performers, and although they reported a difference of 0.1 sec in favor of the grab start in terms of response time (time from gun until toes off the blocks), this difference was no longer present at 25 ft. They concluded, on the basis of their study, that no dive is a better

215

starting technique than the others. Coaches should not treat their swimmers collectively but should examine individual variations.

Hosler, Bloom, and Disch (1977) found that significant differences among various components of the grab and conventional swim starts disappeared when age, weight, height, and reach were used as covariants. This indicates that some type of interaction might exist between components of the type of start and certain anthropometric variables.

Therefore, the problem of this study was to examine the effects of weight, height, and reach on the performance of various components of the grab and conventional starts in swimming. The components are: reaction time—time from starting stimulus to first visible movement; movement time—time from first visible movement to toe clearance off the blocks; and flight time—time from toe clearance until entry into the water. The research hypothesis of this study was that weight, height, and reach would be significantly related to these three components of the swim start.

PROCEDURES

The subjects were 30 college women who had not participated in competitive swimming. Untrained subjects were selected primarily to minimize the effects of previous experience on the performance of the two types of starts and also to examine the effects of the experimental variables on initial levels of performance. The average age of the swimmers was 21.3 years, with a range from 19 to 26 years.

The subjects were randomly assigned to either the conventional or grab-start group and were trained for 10 sessions. Two of these sessions involved practicing the starts using an interval timer/bell system with a random foreperiod. The bells and the random foreperiod were used to remove the human element from the start. Therefore, the swimmers could not anticipate the starter's gun.

Testing took place during the spring semester of 1976 at the University of Houston indoor pool. The subject's weight, height, and reach were measured to the nearest 0.25 unit. The subjects then executed 12 starts according to their group assignment. The subjects were allowed four practice trials. Random foreperiods of 1.0, 1.2, and 1.4 sec were used.

The starts were videotaped using a Sony AVC/3200 camera with a 1:2 lens. The camera was positioned perpendicular to the plane of flight and in line with the front edge of the starting block. A swimming clock, accurate to 0.01 sec, and a white mark on the side of the pool 10 ft down the lane were also visible on the videotape. The 10-ft mark was used to measure the flight time component. When the subject's hands reached this point, the flight time measure was recorded.

Table 1. Subjects X trials ANOVAs for swimming start components

	SS	df	MS	F	Rjj
		Reaction time			
Subjects	0.96013	29	0.03311	14.330	
Trials	0.01537	11	0.00140	0.606[a]	0.993
Subjects X trials	0.73664	319	0.00231		
		Movement time			
Subjects	3.18337	29	0.10977	14.146	
Trials	0.05984	11	0.00544	0.701[a]	0.998
Subjects X trials	2.47418	319	0.00776		
		Flight time			
Subjects	0.53607	29	0.01849	9.108	
Trials	0.03218	11	0.00293	1.443[a]	0.996
Subjects X trials	0.64777	319	0.00203		

[a] Trial effect is not statistically significant in all cases. Therefore, all trials are averaged to obtain score.

DATA ANALYSIS AND DISCUSSION

Since multiple trials of the swim starts were administered, the effects of warmup and fatigue were examined by using a subjects-by-trials analysis of variance. The results of these ANOVAs are presented in Table 1. No significant trial effects were reported. Therefore, all 12 trials were averaged to produce the criterion scores. The intraclass reliability estimates for these components of the swim starts were 0.933 (reaction time), 0.998 (movement time), and 0.996 (flight time).

The intercorrelations among the variables measured in this study are presented in Table 2. This table also includes the means and standard deviations. Nine significant correlations were present among the 21 possible coefficients. The three experimental variables (weight, height, and reach) were significantly related to reaction time, whereas height and reach were significantly correlated with flight time. Movement time was not significantly related to any of the three measures; however, it was related to type of start. This would indicate that there was a difference in movement times in the starts. The mean movement time for the grab start was 0.708, whereas the mean conventional start was 0.776. No significant differences between starts were present on the reaction-time or flight-time components. The other significant intercorrelations were among the three experimental variables. The correlations among the starting components were not statistically significant. Since the correlations between type of

Table 2. Means, standard deviations, and correlation coefficients among the experimental variables[a]

Variable	Reaction time	Movement time	Flight time	Weight	Height	Reach	Type of Start	$\overline{X}$	S_x
Reaction time (sec)	1.000							0.294	0.061
Movement time (sec)	−0.204	1.000						0.742	0.096
Flight time (sec)	−0.073	0.088	1.000					0.211	0.040
Weight (lb)	0.543	0.214	−0.261	1.000				129.23	12.460
Height (inches)	0.367	0.257	−0.446	0.787	1.000			65.68	3.00
Reach (inches)	0.366	0.175	−0.533	0.731	0.965	1.000		83.17	4.59
Type of start	0.155	0.362	0.292	0.264	−0.045	−0.144	1.000	—	—

[a] A correlation of 0.361 was needed to be significant at the 0.05 level.

start and the experimental variables were not statistically significant, all subjects were grouped for subsequent analyses.

Multiple correlations were then calculated to examine the research hypotheses that weight, height, and reach would effect performance of various swimming components. For this phase of the study, weight, height, and reach were considered independent variables. The dependent measures were the starting components; type of start was used as a control variable. Type of start was entered first in each analysis, and then the other variables were entered in a stepwise manner.

The summary tables for the multiple regressions on the three dependent variables are presented in Table 3. The full model (type of start, weight, height, and reach) was significant ($P < 0.05$) in each case. A step-down approach was then used to analyze the unique contributions of the various independent measures to the starting components.

For the reaction-time component 31.9% of the variance was accounted for by the full model. Of this percentage only 2.4% was related to type of start. The three independent measures accounted for 29.5% of the variance, with weight being the primary contributor (27.1%). Contributions of height and reach to the reaction time variance were negligible.

Since weight is significantly related to reaction time, coaches should carefully analyze the body composition of their swimmers. A swimmer who is a few pounds overweight is probably losing some precious time during this phase of the start. Further analysis of this component as to body composition factors, such as lean body mass and fat, would allow the coach to make specific decisions about the effects of body weight on reaction time.

The full regression model accounted for 26% of the variance in movement times, however, the independent measures as a group or individually were not significantly related to this component. Type of start was significantly related to movement time and accounted for 13.1% of the variance. As previously mentioned, the mean movement time for the grab start was faster than that for the conventional start. The fact that weight, height, and reach were not significantly related to movement time indicated that these factors do not need to be considered when working with swimmers.

For the flight-time component the full regression model accounted for 36.9% of the variance ($P < 0.05$). Type of start was not significantly related to this component, whereas the independent measures were. As a group the independent measures accounted for 28.4% of the variance in flight time, with reach being the only significant individual contributor (24.6%). This indicates the obvious fact that flight time depends to some extent on reach.

Table 3. Multiple regression summary table

	SS	df	MS	F	r^2
Reaction time					
Regression	0.03473	4	0.00868	2.926[a]	0.319
Type of start	0.00261	1	0.00261	0.879	0.024
Independent measures	0.03208	3	0.01069	3.600[a]	0.295
(weight)	(0.02953)	(1)	(0.02953)	(9.943)[a]	(0.271)
(height)	(0.00110)	(1)	(0.00110)	(0.370)	(0.010)
(reach)	(0.00145)	(1)	(0.00145)	(0.488)	(0.014)
Residual	0.07419	26	0.00297		
Movement time					
Regression	0.06892	4	0.01723	4.222[a]	0.260
Type of start	0.03468	1	0.03468	4.429[a]	0.131
Independent measures	0.03424	3	0.01141	1.457	0.129
(height)	(0.01976)	(1)	(0.01976)	(2.524)	(0.075)
(weight)	(0.00913)	(1)	(0.00913)	(1.166)	(0.034)
(reach)	(0.00535)	(1)	(0.00535)	(0.683)	(0.020)
Residual	0.19576	26	0.00783		
Flight time					
Regression	0.01675	4	0.00419	3.661[a]	0.369
Type of start	0.00385	1	0.00385	2.600	0.085
Independent measures	0.01290	3	0.00430	3.772[a]	0.284
(reach)	(0.01115)	(1)	(0.01115)	(9.781)[a]	(0.246)
(height)	(0.00173)	(1)	(0.00173)	(1.518)	(0.038)
(weight)	(0.00002)	(1)	(0.00002)	(0.018)	(0.000)
Residual	0.02860	26	0.00114		

[a] Significant at the 0.05 level.

CONCLUSIONS

On the basis of these findings two of the three research hypotheses were accepted. It was concluded that the anthropometric measures of weight, height, and reach were related to the components of reaction time and flight time. The hypothesis that the anthropometric measures were related to movement time was rejected. Type of start was found to be significantly related to the movement-time component, which was consistent with the findings of Michaels (1973) and Lowell (1975). This finding also corroborated the finding of Gibson and Holt (1976) that the grab start was significantly faster from the time of the gun until toe clearance.

There are several interesting implications of this study. First, in all components significant portions of the variance were accounted for by either type of start or the independent measures. The fact that weight was significantly related to reaction time could be used in diagnosing starting deficiencies of overweight or out-of-shape swimmers. The finding that reach was significantly related to flight time was informative but of little practical importance.

A second implication is that only 26–36.9% of the variance of the components was related to these predictor variables. Therefore, 63–74% of the variablility in swim start components is related to other factors. These factors could be leg strength, power, technique, and so forth. They can be directly modified through proper coaching. An interesting followup study could involve variables of this nature as predictors.

In conclusion, the analysis of the findings add some information to the knowledge about swimming starts. Controversy still exists, and one major problem may be the fact that tests of statistical significance may not be sensitive to substantial differences in motor performance times. A difference of 0.01 sec may not show up as significant in an F test, yet it may mean the difference between first place and fifth place in a race.

REFERENCES

Gibson, G., and Holt, L. E. 1976. A cinema-computer analysis of selected starting techniques. Swimming Tech. (Fall): 75–76, 79.
Hosler, W. W., Bloom, J. A., and Disch, J. G. 1977. Differences in reaction time, movement time, and flight time between the conventional and grab starts in novice swimmers. Proceedings of the Southern District Association of AAHPER, Atlanta, Ga. (abstract).
Lowell, J. C. 1975. Analysis of the grab start and the conventional start. Swimming Tech. (Fall): 66–69, 76.
Michaels, R. A. 1973. A time:distance comparison of the conventional and grab start. Swimming Tech. (April): 16–17.

Impulses Exerted in Performing Several Kinds of Swimming Turns

K. Nicol and F. Krüger

PURPOSE OF THE STUDY

The purpose of this study was to provide biomechanical descriptions and analyses of the flip turn and the open turn (orthodox freestyle turn) used in freestyle swimming.

DESCRIPTION OF THE MOVEMENTS

The freestyle flip turn, which is executed without touching the wall with the hand, starts with the movement of the body around a nearly horizontal transverse axis. This is followed by a twisting rotation around the longitudinal axis of the body before, during, and after the pushoff. The open turn, which involves touching the wall with the hand, starts with a rotation around the longitudinal axis of the body during the touch, followed by rotations around the transverse and frontal axes until a lateral body position for pushoff is attained. During and after pushoff, rotation is continued until the body is in the prone position.

REVIEW OF THE LITERATURE

The few publications that describe experimental research of freestyle swimming turns indicate the difficult measurement problems involved. Selle (1955), Fox, Bartels, and Bowers (1963), and Scharf and King (1964) used stop watches and tape measures to obtain biokinematic measurements of different turn techniques to separate optimal from less optimal techniques. Up to the present, researchers have not used the potential of force platforms to investigate swimming turns. Likewise, they have not used time and velocity measurements that give greater accuracy than the stop watch.

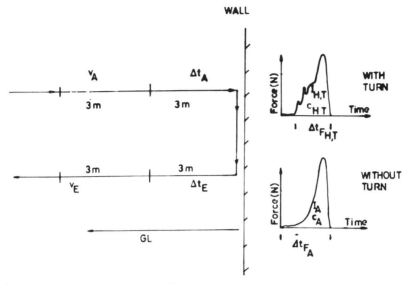

Figure 1. Definitions of measured values.

METHODS

Research Protocol

Five trained university swimmers (four females and one male) were the subjects for a pilot study. The subjects swam three times each, executing the following techniques: 1) pushoff, gliding only, 2) freestyle flip turn, 3) open freestyle turn, and 4) flip turn, gliding only. The measurements taken during these performances included:

1. The mean velocity over 3 m by time measurements taken at 6 and 3 m, respectively, before reaching the wall.
2. The forward and return times of the swimmer, from the measured interval to the wall and from the wall to the measured interval.
3. The horizontal impulse during pushoff from the wall.
4. The length of the glide after pushoff, gliding only.

Force-Measuring Device

To measure the force exerted on the wall, a capacitance-type force platform was used, which has been utilized in several other studies (Nicol and Hennig, 1976; Nicol, 1978). The sizes of the platforms vary widely; normally a 140 × 25 cm size is used for gait analysis, and a 40 × 60 cm or 70 × 70 cm size is used for research and teaching. The platforms are 12 mm thick. As usual, with measuring systems designed for general purposes, the accuracy should be verified by a set of data. Because the limited length

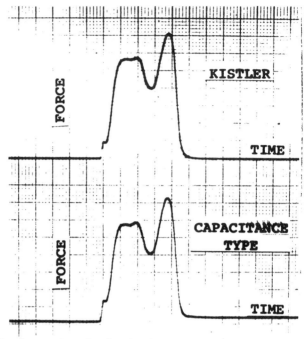

Figure 2. Signal comparison of a piezoelectric and a capacitance-type force platform.

of this article, accuracy was substantiated by comparing the forces measured by the capacitance plate with a piezoelectric force platform. Figure 2 shows the results with respect to the vertical forces of gait, which are similar to the forces measured in water.

The force platform was waterproofed as follows. A 40 × 60-cm force platform was placed in the middle of a 100 × 100-cm waterproof rubber mat, which had a self-adhesive surface on both sides (Figure 3). Another mat of the same type was then glued to both the mat and the force platform. The connecting cable was glued along the edges of both mats by self-adhesive tape, and the gap between the mat, cable, and tape was filled with elastic glue. For the investigation, the waterproofed mat was positioned vertically against the wall with the normally "upper" surface in contact with the water. The other surface was glued to the wall after it had been in contact with the water for 10 sec. The mat position was such that the upper and lower edges were 10 and 70 cm below the water's surface, respectively. Because the water contact time was short, the self-adhesive strength of the glue was sufficient to keep the mat in position. Although the mat had glue on both sides, after an extended period of contact with the water, the surface that the swimmers touched lost its adhesive properties so that the swimmers were not affected.

Figure 3. Self-adhesive rubber mat covering the 40 × 60 cm force platform. The outline of the force platform can be seen. The silver wire electrodes have been placed on the mat. For measurement, the left electrode was fastened to the wall of the pool, and the right electrode and a load were fixed on the lane boundary, forming the gate. The rubber belt, the battery set (center), and the two electrodes are shown at the upper end of the mat. During measurement, the electric field of the belt electrodes passed the gate, and a signal was picked up by the stationary silver electrodes.

Time-Measuring Device

The mean swimming speed was computed from the time interval required by the subjects to swim the timed 3-m distance before touching the wall. This distance was chosen after consideration was given to the nature of the measuring method and the different approaches to the turns by the swimmers. Swimming time was measured without contact or interfering effects. The swimmer wore only a rubber belt over his suit. Two copper electrodes (40 × 100 × 0.1 mm), mounted on the belt near the hips, were connected to a 9-V battery. (They are shown as part of Figure 3). Also two pairs of silver-coated copper electrodes were fixed at the sides of the lane opposite each other, thus forming two "gates," 3 m apart. The vertical positions of the electrodes in the water (ca. 30 cm below surface) were stabilized.

When the swimmer passed by, the electric field caused by the battery voltage influenced the silver electrodes, and a varying voltage was picked up between the first pair of electrodes. Then the amplifier was switched to the second pair of electrodes. Undoubtedly, it will be possible to perform this switching automatically in the future.

A low pass filter limited the frequency range, and the corresponding time delay was considered. With such an arrangement, every signal caused by partial body rotations around the longitudinal axis was suppressed. In addition, the movement of the electrodes caused by waves and the changes in the swimming speed during a single swimming cycle, which are small in freestyle, were also suppressed. The results of the speed measurement gave a sinusoidal graph. Maxima and minima, after a change in the direction of swimming, indicated the time coordinates of passing through one pair of electrodes. The measurement error (± 0.01 m/sec) was determined with photoelectric cells and a floating device.

Data Processing

The differences in the measurements were tested with the Wilcoxon sign ranked test. This nonparametric statistic was used beause the sample was small and the population distribution was unknown. To describe the functional correlations among selected measurements, single linear regression equations were computed. The basic assumptions of regression were not checked because they were used to describe the sample only.

RESULTS AND DISCUSSION

Mean Values

Included as part of Figure 1 are two typical force graphs; the maximum force varied between 600 and 1,100 N. Variables, mean values, and standard deviations are defined in Table 1. When there were no significant differences for different performances, only a single value was listed.

Biokinematic Parameters

The complete time ($\Delta t_A + \Delta t_F + \Delta t_E$) of the freestyle flip turn was significantly shorter than that of the open turn. When the swimming interval was increased by the additional velocity interval, significant differences among the total times of both turns were no longer present. These tendencies were evident even for the better swimmers.

There were no significant differences among the return swimming times for both turns (Δt_{E_H}, Δt_{E_T}) or among the durations of the impulses. Therefore, the existing differences were limited to the different forward swimming times. The analysis of the return swimming times during gliding, after different approaches, showed that the return swimming time, Δt_{E_A}, after pushoff, without forward swimming was significantly shorter. The reason the return swimming times of the turns did not differ

Table 1. Definitions, mean values, and standard deviations[a,b]

		V_A (m/sec)	Δt_A (sec)	I (Ns)	c (m/sec)	Δt_F (sec)	GL (m)	Δt_E (sec)	V_E (m/sec)	V_L (m/sec)
Pushoff, gliding only	A			I_A		$t_{FA,TA}$	GL_A			
	$\bar{x}$			210		0.62	8.20			
	s			26		0.17	0.95			
Flip turn	T		Δt_{AT}	$I_{T,H}$	$c_{T,H}$	$\Delta t_{F_{T,H}}$		$\Delta t_{E_{T,H}}$	V_{ET}	$V_{L_{T,H}}$
	$\bar{x}$		2.56	217	3.49	0.51		1.12	1.26	−0.85
	s		0.34	28	0.43	0.11		0.27	0.07	0.47
		$V_{AT,H}$								
	$\bar{x}$	1.36								
	s	0.11								
Open turn	H		Δt_{AH}						V_{EH}	
	$\bar{x}$		2.83						1.36	
	s		0.18						0.11	
Flip turn, gliding only	TA			I_{TA}			GL_{TA}			
	$\bar{x}$			229			7.00			
	s			35			0.95			

[a]Sympols: V_A = forward swimming velocity; Δt_A = forward swimming time; I = horizontal impulse; c = velocity change; Δt_F = duration of impulse; GL = glide length; Δt_E = return swimming time; V_E = return swimming velocity; V_L = velocity lost; $\bar{x}$ = mean; s = standard deviation.
[b]Subscripts: A = pushoff, gliding only; T = flip turn; H = open turn; TA = flip turn, gliding only.

must lie in the demands of forward swimming and execution of the flip turn without breathing. The mean swimming velocities obtained after pushoff for both turns differed significantly. The velocity after the open turn was greater than after the flip turn. This surprising result can be explained by comparing the forward and return swimming velocities of each turn. For the open turn, there was no significant difference in these velocities. The velocities of the flip turn were significantly different ($V_{AT} > V_{ET}$). The different executions of the techniques of the turns and the lack of motor abilities could be reasons for the differences, although observers could not confirm this.

The horizontal velocity changes computed by the impulse of the flip and open turn did not differ significantly. The loss of velocity:

$$V_{LT,H} = V_{AT,H} + V_{ET,H} - c_{T,H}$$

indicated that the velocity changes c were greater than necessary, without taking hydrodynamic conditions into consideration. The loss of velocity is the amount the body will be slowed to the beginning of the velocity interval. The most striking results shown by the biokinematic parameters were the significant differences in the glide length (about 1 m $\hat{=}$ 15%) after pushoff versus that after pushoff with forward swimming.

Biodynamic Parameters

Comparisons of the impulses relative to both turns showed no significant differences in those of pushoff and flip turn. Therefore, the reason why the length of glide after a flip turn is less than after a pushoff lies in the interval of greater resistance just after pushoff. The initial reason could be the adverse hydrodynamic conditions presented by the twisting body since the necessary rotation in the prone position has not yet been completed. Second, it could be the need for greater motor ability in order to swim forward and to execute the flip turn.

Correlations among Biodynamic and Biokinematic Parameters

Using the gliding length GL_A, as a predictor of velocity change, the linear regression equation:

$$y = 1.3x + 3.8$$

was obtained (see Figure 4). The influence of the velocity change is as follows. An increase in velocity change by 1.0 m/sec causes an increase in gliding length of 1.3 m. Use of the return swimming times, $\Delta t_{ET,H}$, of both turns as a predictor of the horizontal impulse, $I_{T,H}$, yielded the linear regression equation:

$$y = -0.003x + 1.8$$

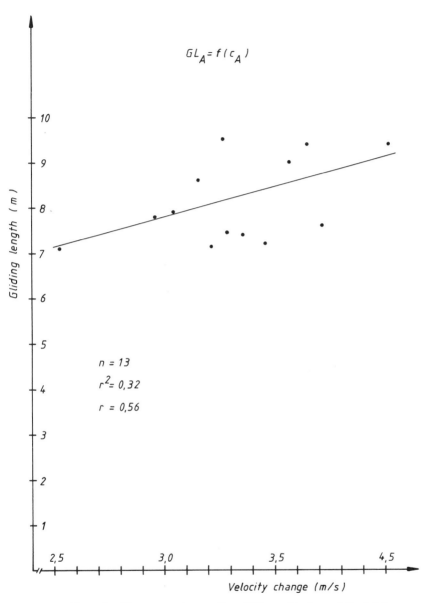

$$GL_A = f(c_A)$$

Figure 4.   Linear regression equation of $GL_A = f(c_A)$: $y = 1.3x + 3.8$.

as shown in Figure 5. An increase in the impulse of 100 Ns shortened the return swimming time by 0.3 sec. Use of the velocity changes, $c_{T,H}$, of each turn as predictors of the forward swimming velocities, $V_{AT,H}$, yielded the linear regression equations:

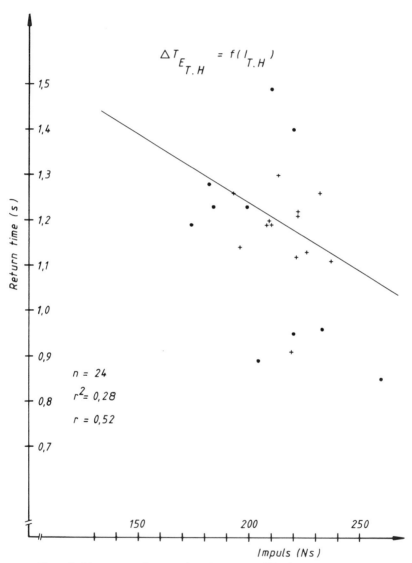

Figure 5. Linear regression equation of $\Delta t_{ET,H} = f(I_{T,H})$: $y = -0.003x + 1.8$.

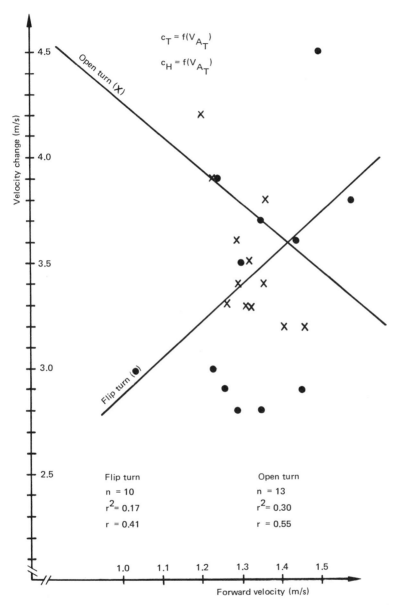

Figure 6.   Linear regression equation of $c_T = f(V_{AF})$: $y = 1.7x + 1.2$; and of $c_H = f(V_{AH})$: $y = -2.5x + 6.9$.

$$y = 1.7x + 1.2 \qquad \text{(flip turn)}$$

$$y = -2.5x + 6.9 \qquad \text{(open turn)}$$

Increase of the forward swimming velocity when executing the flip turn caused a change in velocity. If the forward swimming speed just before the open turn increased, the velocity change was decreased. The swimming velocity must be decreased by the touching arm just before the rotation and pushoff can start. This deceleration lasts longer as the swimming velocity is increased. During the flip turn, velocity is maintained, but the kinetic energy changes. The locomotion of the body changes to rotation before pushoff. Therefore, the flip turn has the advantage over the open turn.

REFERENCES

Fox, E. L., Bartels, R. L., and Bowers, R. W. 1963. Comparison of speed and energy expenditure for swimming turns. Res. Q. 34:322–326.

Hay, J. G. 1973. The Biomechanics of Sports Techniques. Prentice-Hall, Inc., Englewood Cliffs, New Jersey.

Nicol, K. 1978. Pressure distribution over the feet of athletes while jumping. Proceedings of the International Congress of Physical Activity Sciences, Book 6, Biomechanics of Sports and Kinanthropometry, pp. 103–114. Symposium Specialists, Miami.

Nicol, K., and Hennig, E. M. 1976. Time-dependent method for measuring force distribution using a flexible mat as a capacitor. In: P. V. Komi (ed.), Biomechanics V-B, pp. 433–440. University Park Press, Baltimore.

Scharf, R. J., and King, W. H. 1964. Time and motion analysis of competitive freestyle swimming turns. Res. Q. 35:37–44.

Selle, E. 1955. Der Einfluss der Schwimmgeschwindigkeit und der Wendetechnik auf Wendegeschwindigkeit (The influence of swimming velocity and the turning technique on turning velocity). Theor. Prax. Körperkult. 115–122.

Training Methods

Fallacies of "Hypoxic Training" in Swimming

A. B. Craig, Jr.

People who do repetitive breath-hold diving can increase their time underwater with practice (Schaefer, 1955; Hong et al., 1970). It has been assumed that this increased time is related to an individual's responses to repeated hypoxia. It is further reasoned that one of the features of an adaptation to repeated hypoxia might be in increase in one's anaerobic capacity.

These arguments are not new. Most recently Counsilman (1975) and Vasar and Laidre (1975) have suggested that "hypoxic" methods of training swimmers might be useful despite the strong warning that such techniques might be dangerous (Craig, Jr., 1961a; Lanphier and Rahn, 1963a, b; Craig, Jr., 1976). It is interesting that many swimming coaches in the Rochester, N.Y. area have accepted Counsilman's (1975) suggestions and use many variations of so-called "hypoxic training."

The present investigation was designed to simulate the effects of varying the breathing frequency during swimming. The experiments were compared with previous work (Craig, Jr., and Harley, 1968; Craig, Jr., and Medd, 1968a, b), which indicated that the limitations of repetitive breath holds *without* prior hyperventilation were related primarily to the increase of the partial pressure of carbon dioxide (P_{CO_2}), and hypoxia had relatively little influence.

METHODS

The subject for this series of experiments was a 26-year-old male who was an excellent athlete and who was experienced as a participant in studies related to respiratory and exercise physiology. His maximal oxygen consumption that was measured repeatedly while pedaling a bicycle averaged 5.0 liters/min (65 ml/min/kg).

In each experiment the subject pedaled at the desired load for 5 min. During this time he was instructed not to control his respiratory rate. In

235

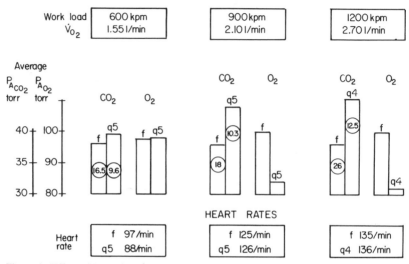

Figure 1. Effect of breathing frequency on alveolar gas composition during exercise. The f and $q4$ and $q5$ above each bar and in the boxes showing heart rate indicate that the subject was breathing at his natural frequency (f) or was instructed to breathe at a controlled frequency of one breath every fourth or fifth revolution of the bicycle pedal. Circled numbers indicate the measured breathing frequency in each experiment.

all experiments the pedaling rate was 50 rpm. He then continued working but breathed at a set ratio of the pedal speed—i.e., every second, third, fourth, or fifth revolution. Usually he required only a few seconds to establish this new breathing frequency, which was continued for at least 1 min before experimental observations were made.

Oxygen consumption ($\dot{V}_{O_2}$) and carbon dioxide production ($\dot{V}_{CO_2}$) were calculated from the volumes of timed collections of expired air and the concentrations of O_2 and CO_2 in these samples. Alveolar gas composition was assessed from the P_{CO_2} and P_{O_2} of the end-tidal air. The subject breathed continuously through a low resistance, one-way breathing valve, and an aliquot of air from the mouthpiece was withdrawn at a constant rate through meters that monitered and recorded the CO_2 and O_2 concentrations. Pulse rate was measured during these periods of gas collection from recordings of the output of a photoelectric finger plethysmograph.

Three different workloads (600, 900, and 1,200 kpm/min) were used, and these were associated with $\dot{V}_{O_2}$ values of 1.55, 2.10, and 2.70 liters/min, respectively.

RESULTS

As shown in Figure 1, the breathing frequency when the respiratory rate was not controlled averaged 16.5, 18, and 26 breaths/min for the 600,

900, and 1,200 kpm/min loads, respectively. The end-tidal P_{CO_2} (P_{ACO_2}) was 38 torr, and the end-tidal P_{O_2} (P_{AO_2}) was 97 torr. These values did not differ for the three workloads and were not different from those when the subject was at rest.

In all the controlled breathing experiments, P_{ACO_2} increased and P_{AO_2} decreased progressively as the frequency of breathing was decreased. When the subject was breathing every fifth revolution at the lightest workload, P_{ACO_2} increased to 40 torr, but there was no measurable change in P_{AO_2}. When breathing at this frequency with the intermediate load, P_{ACO_2} was 44 torr and P_{AO_2} was 83 torr. During the heaviest workload the minimum respiratory rate which the subject could tolerate was 12.5 breaths/min or once every four revolutions of the pedals. Under these conditions P_{ACO_2} was 45 torr and P_{AO_2} was 81.5 torr.

The subject found that breathing every fifth breath during the intermediate load or every fourth breath during the heaviest load created the most unpleasant sensations, characterized by an "urge to breath more."

$\dot{V}_{O_2}$ and $\dot{V}_{CO_2}$ during controlled breathing were not different from their values during periods of breathing at the subject's natural frequency. The exchanges ratios (R) were also not different, indicating that after the initial rise in P_{ACO_2}, there was no further retention of CO_2 in the body's stores. Pulse rates varied with the workloads, and $\dot{V}_{O_2}$, and $\dot{V}_{CO_2}$ were not significantly influenced by any of the breathing patterns.

DISCUSSION

Although laboratory experiments using a bicycle ergometer may seem remote from swimming, there are no essential differences in terms of gas exchange (Craig, Jr., and Dvorak, 1969; McArdle et al., 1976). Using a pedaling rate of 50 rpm and adjusting the breathing frequency in rhythm with the pedaling movements is analogous to swimming at 50 strokes/min and breathing with various patterns in relationship to the arm movements.

It was apparent that the subject's ability to slow his respirations was limited by the increase in P_{CO_2} in the alveoli and arterial blood and not by the decrease in P_{O_2}. In fact the lowest P_{AO_2} observed in these studies was 80 torr, which is about the value of P_{AO_2} at an altitude of 1220 m (4000 ft). It could hardly be called "hypoxic."

In another study of breath holding and exercise in air and in water (Craig, Jr., and Medd, 1968b) subjects held their breath for 30 sec and breathed for 30 sec and continued this cycle for 12 min after a 5-min period of exercise with normal breathing. Under these conditions P_{ACO_2} of the first breath after each breath hold averaged 61.7 torr and P_{AO_2} was 73.6 torr. Again this value for P_{AO_2} is not low enough to be considered as a sign of arterial hypoxia.

During repetitive breath-hold diving it is certainly possible to develop various decreases in $P_{A_{O_2}}$ including those that are considered hypoxic (Schaefer and Carey, 1962; Lanphier and Rahn, 1963a; Craig, Jr., and Harley, 1968; Craig, Jr., and Medd, 1968a.) However, the changes in P_{CO_2} and P_{O_2} are influenced by the depth of the dive, and the conditions are not comparable with swimming at the surface.

Another way a swimmer can become hypoxic is to hyperventilate and thus to lower his $P_{A_{CO_2}}$ before swimming with the respiratory frequency demanded by the coach. Under these conditions it is quite possible to incur such hypoxia that the swimmer loses consciousness (Craig, Jr., 1961a; Craig, Jr., 1976). This is certainly an undesirable but not unlikely result. Most experienced swimmers learn quickly that they can hold their breath or breathe less frequently by vigorous hyperventilation before the swim (Craig, Jr., 1961a; Craig, Jr., 1976). The greater the persuasion of the coach, the more chance one takes that this will be the swimmer's response. Such situations should certainly be avoided.

However, if the guidelines for "hypoxic training" are followed (Counsilman, 1975), it is apparent that the limiting factor to decreasing the number of breaths taken is the increase of P_{CO_2} or hypercapnia. Therefore, "hypoxic training" is really hypercapnic "training."

Studies of breath-holding divers indicate that there is a "training" effect that results in longer dives. The "training" seems to be an increase in the tolerance to P_{CO_2} (Schaefer, 1955; Hong et al., 1967, 1970). However, it is difficult to see how such an adaptation to increased P_{CO_2} could benefit the swimmer. Even during maximal swimming the calculated $P_{A_{CO_2}}$ from the data of Magle and Faulkner (1967) did not increase to the degree noted during exercise and intermittant breathing in our studies.

Theoretically, it is possible that the initial retention of CO_2 results in a slightly greater decrease in the pH in the muscles during exercise than one might have with normal breathing. This change would imply a slightly greater respiratory acidosis. However, the same result can be achieved if the subject swims a little faster while breathing normally and avoids the risks.

The results of our studies do not suggest that short, fast, repetitive swims are not useful in training competitive swimmers. The specific adaptations of this type of repetitive stress are unknown. In humans there is little information to decide if a person's anaerobic capacity can be increased, or if more work can be performed, because of an increased tolerance to the consequences of anaerobic metabolism. In either case breathing less frequently probably doesn't accomplish anything that cannot be done by swimming faster.

REFERENCES

Counsilman, J. E. 1975. Hypoxic and other methods of training evaluated. Swimming Tech. 12(1):19–26.

Craig, A. B., Jr. 1961a. Underwater swimming and loss of consciousness. JAMA 176:255–258.

Craig, A. B., Jr. 1961b. Causes of loss of consciousness during underwater swimming. J. Appl. Physiol. 16:583–586.

Craig, A. B., Jr. 1976. Summary of 58 cases of loss of consciousness during underwater swimming and diving. Med. Sci. Sports 8:171–175.

Craig, A. B., Jr., and Dvorak, M. 1969. Comparison of exercise in air and in water of different temperatures. Med. Sci. Sports 1:124–130.

Craig, A. B., Jr., and Harley, A. D. 1968. Alveolar gas exchanges during breath-hold diving. J. Appl. Physiol. 24:182–189.

Craig, A. B., Jr., and Medd, W. L. 1968a. Oxygen consumption and carbon dioxide production during breath-hold diving. J. Appl. Physiol. 24:190–202.

Craig, A. B., Jr., and Medd, W. L. 1968b. Man's responses to breath-hold exercise in air and in water. J. Appl. Physiol. 24:773–777.

Hong, S. K., Song, S. H., Kim, P. K., and Suh, C. S. 1967. Seasonal observations on the cardiac rhythm during diving in the Korean Ama. J. Appl. Physiol. 23:18–22.

Hong, S. K., Moore, T. O., Seto, G., Park, H. K., Hiatt, W. R., and Bernauer, E. M. 1970. Lung volumes and apneic bradycardia in divers. J. Appl. Physiol. 29:171–176.

Lanphier, E. D., and Rahn, H. 1963a. Alveolar gas exchange during breath-hold diving. J. Appl. Physiol. 18:471–477.

Lanphier, E. D., and Rahn, H. 1963b. Alveolar gas exchange during breath holding in air. J. Appl. Physiol. 18:478–482.

McArdle, W. D., Magel, J. R., Lesmes, G. R., and Pechar, G. S. 1976. Metabolic and cardiovascular adjustments to work in air and water at 18, 25, and 33 degrees C. J. Appl. Physiol. 40:85–90.

Magel, J. R., and Faulkner, J. A. 1967. Maximum oxygen uptakes of college swimmers. J. Appl. Physiol. 22:929–933.

Schaefer, K. E. 1955. The role of carbon dioxide in the physiology of human diving. In: Loyal G. Goff (ed.), Proceedings of the Underwater Physiology Symposium. Natl. Acad. Sci.-Nat. Res. Council (U.S.A.) Publ. No. 377, pp. 131–139.

Schaefer, K. E., and Carey, C. R. 1962. Alveolar pathways during 90 foot, breath-hold dives. Science 137:1051–1052.

Vasar, E., and Laidre, H. 1975. Usage of apnea technique in endurance training. Swimming Tech. 12(1):8–9.

Interval Training and
The Progressive Load Principle
in Novice Child Swimmers

P. J. Smit, H.-O. Daehne, G. Van Wyk, and E. S. Steyn

Children who have just learned to swim and who still lack the ability to race are often forced to participate in competitions for which they are not suited. In the post-beginner phase, a program of training must be followed that will lead the novice up to a competitive standard in the most effective way. Two methods—long distance training (L) and interval training (I)—hold promise for bridging this gap. By applying either method following the progressive principle, children will learn to swim farther and better. The aim of this study was to determine which method was the more suitable for advancing the swimming of prepubertal children; based on: 1) improvement in swimming times and 2) physiological and biomechanical variables measured before and after a winter training season.

METHOD

During the summer, swimming instruction was given to prepubertal Caucasian children, aged 7-12 years, who had volunteered for the program. It turned out that only a few—8L, 8I, and 4C (C = controls)—achieved a level of skill where they could swim 400 m. Swimming times over 100 and 400 m were taken as the main criteria for evaluating progress. These times were measured during private competitions held at the start and at the end of the training season. Could any improvements be explained physiologically?

Somatotypes were determined by the Health-Carter method (Hebbelinck, Duquet, and Ross, 1972), using anthropometry only, and the percentage body fat (Siri and Donner, 1956) and body density (Durnin and Rahaman, 1967) were calculated.

Investigation supported in part by research grants from the Department of Sport and Recreation and the University of Pretoria, South Africa.

Vital capacity (VC) and forced expiratory volume ($FEV_{1.0}$) were determined on a Godart expirograph. $\dot{V}_{O_2}^{max}$ was determined on a cycle ergometer (Secher and Oddershede, 1974) with the subjects' being permitted to pedal standing up for the last 3–5 min. Gas analyses from these tests and of the total oxygen uptake (active plus oxygen debt) during a 3-min burst of tethered swimming ($V_{O_2}^{teth}$) were made after all expired gas was collected in Douglas bags and the contents were analyzed by Rapox (F_{O_2}) and Uras (F_{CO_2}), with frequent checks by a Haldane analyzer to ensure stability of the electronic instruments. Maximal heart rates (MHR) either during cycling or swimming were determined telemetrically.

Force (F), measured separately (best of three trials) for the left and right upper limbs in a simulated swimming position, and continuous swimming force (SF) were determined by strain gauges. The force required to keep the tethered swimming body afloat was added to SF. This was calculated from each subject's body density as estimated from skin folds (Durnin and Rahaman, 1967). The sum of these forces was designated total force (TF). Thus, TF = SF + SiF (sinking force) (Holmér, 1974).

Swimming tests took place in a small circular pool kept at 30°–32°C, but training took place in a swimming bath held at 25°C. Training was done in winter and involved 30–40 sessions; there was no interaction among groups. Swimming times were extended progressively from 10 min to 1 hr per session. Although the aim was to swim three sessions per week, lack of facilities sometimes dictated fewer training sessions.

The precise method of training was to make group L swim as fast as they could for a predetermined period, executing turns but never stopping. Group I dove in at one end, swam 25 m, climbed out at the other side (not using a ladder), ran around to their starting point, and dove in again. Motivation was a prize for the winners; group I was required to show a total of at least two-thirds of the total distance covered by group L daily.

Statistical analyses on data derived before and after the winter training program by one-tailed tests were aimed at finding differences and correlations that were significant at the 5% level. Group C did not take part in any swimming during the times the others were trained. No statistical analyses were performed on group C, but no initial values differed significantly among the groups.

RESULTS

The distances swum by the two groups are illustrated graphically in Figure 1, which includes 40 sessions of training. The total distance swum by group L was 209.058 km, and by group I it was 144.815 km; the difference resulted from the two programs that were used. Since the running

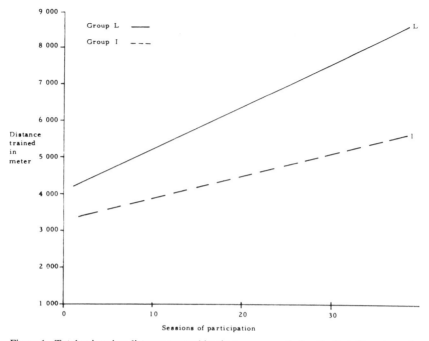

Figure 1. Total swimming distance covered by the two groups during the first 40 sessions of winter training.

distance for Group I more or less equalled their swimming distance, this group also ran at least 144 km during the program. When calculated on an individual basis, the L group subjects each had covered 26.132 km, and the I group subjects had covered 18.102 km. Initially, daily distances were swum at mean speeds of 0.54 m/sec by group L and 0.58 m/sec by group I, but toward the end of the program, these speeds had increased to 0.59 and 0.75 m/sec ($P \leq 0.01$ for I), respectively.

Table 1 shows the improvement in swimming times over 100 and 400 m for the groups. For group I, the mean swimming time over 100 and 400 m improved significantly, but not for group L. (Group L did, however, also improve in mean swimming time, but not Group C.) However, the mean swimming times at the end of the season hardly differed among the three groups.

As could be expected, there were significant increases in stature and gross body mass in all groups, but somatotype, body fat, and $FEV_{1.0}$ did not change significantly. These findings are presented in Table 2.

Force (F) on dry land, exerted while lying prone and simulating a swim arm pull (left and right), mean swimming force (SF), and mean total force (TF) were compared, but no significant differences were found in any of these variables measured before and after the season. However,

Table 1. Mean swimming times in 100- and 400-m before and after training season[a]

		L	I	C
100 m	(before)	2:29.7	2:30.4	2:11.9
	(after)	2:19.2	2:11.1	2:17.0
			$P < 0.05$	
400 m	(before)	11:40.5	13:03.9	12:09.3
	(after)	10:45.3	10:51.4	12:02.1
			$P < 0.01$	

[a]Only where P values are shown have changes been found to be statistically significant.

these measures constituted a useful reference point for calculating other variables.

Oxygen uptake during a 3-min burst of tethered swimming and oxygen debt were added to obtain the total oxygen cost ($V_{O_2}^{teth}$) of exerting SF and TF over 3 min. As shown in Table 3, correlations between $V_{O_2}^{teth}$ and TF were better than those between $V_{O_2}^{teth}$ and SF. Correlations were better in the final test than in the first test. A highly significant correlation ($r = 0.90$) was found between $V_{O_2}^{teth}$ and TF in group I at the end of the program.

Table 4 lists the physiological parameters studied before and after the winter program. $\dot{V}_{O_2}$, taken as the mean total oxygen in liters used by the subjects during the swimming burst and divided by 3, did not change appreciably in any of the groups. However, the total oxygen cost ($V_{O_2}^{teth}$) of the activity, which included the oxygen debt, dropped by 0.36 liters in group L, 1.98 liters in group I ($P \le 0.01$), and 1.41 liters in group C at the end of the season. The standard deviations in $V_{O_2}^{teth}$ by this time had dropped to 0.83, 0.64, and 0.80 in the three groups, with coefficients of variation (v) of 0.29, 0.26, and 0.21, respectively.

The economy of tethered swimming (which was interpreted as oxygen required to maintain a swimming force (SF) of 1 kp improved significantly in group I (48.8%); group C, however, also showed a consistent improvement (38.2%).

$\dot{V}_{O_2}^{max}$ cycling improved in all three groups, but when expressed as ml/kg·min, only groups I and C improved. The improvements in group I were highly significant ($P \le 0.01$).

Peak heart rate during swimming decreased significantly (from 177 to 166) in group I but not in group L.

DISCUSSION

The swimming speed maintained during training by group I increased significantly ($P \le 0.01$), whereas the increase in group L was not signifi-

Table 2. Mean age, mean stature, gross body mass (GBM), somatotype, percentage body fat (% BF), and forced expiratory volume in 1 sec (FEV$_1$) before and after training season[a]

Group	Mean age (years)	Stature (cm) B	Stature (cm) A	GBM B	GBM A	Somatotype B	Somatotype A	% BF B	% BF A	FEV$_1$ (% of VC) B	FEV$_1$ (% of VC) A
L (n = 8)	9.928 (±1.463)	141.0 (±8.2) $P < 0.01$ Increase: 1.49%	143.1 (±8.1)	32.9 (±5.4) $P < 0,01$	34.2 (±5.9)	3 4 3½	3½ 4½ 4	21.1 (±4.8)	20.4 (±4.8)	88 (±4.8)	90 (±5.3)
I (n = 8)	9.649 (±1.686)	137.9 (± 10.4) $P < 0.01$ Increase: 1.52%	140.0 (±10.1)	31.9 (±3.1) $P < 0.01$	33.2 (±4.0)	3½ 4½ 3	3½ 4 3	19.6 (±4.2)	20.4 (±5.1)	84 (±5.3)	83 (±7.3)
C (n = 4)	9.880 (±0.467)	143.1 (±5.1)	145.7 (±5.1) Increase: 1.82%	32.8 (±3.9)	34.5 (±4.5)	2½ 3½ 4	2½ 4 4	16.8 (±5.3)	17.2 (±4.7)	85 (±6.0)	87 (±5.7)

[a]Only where P values are shown have changes been found to be statistically significant.

Table 3. Relationship (r = Spearman's rank correlation coefficient) between total oxygen cost of tethered swimming ($\dot{V}_{O_2}{}^{teth}$) and swimming force (SF) and total swimming force (TF) before and after winter training program[a]

	$\dot{V}_{O_2}{}^{teth}$:SF		$\dot{V}_{O_2}{}^{teth}$:TF	
Group	Before	After	Before	After
L	0.48	0.60	0.55	0.69
I	−0.17	0.76	−0.17	0.90
		($P < 0.05$)		($P < 0.01$)
C	−0.80	0.20	−0.80	0.20

[a] Only where P values are shown have correlations been found to be significant.

cant. Although group I covered a shorter total swimming distance in training, they trained by swimming faster while engaged in their intermittent program. Using the arms to climb out of the water and then running back to the start as fast as they could, combined with the swimming, provided a training program that required speed, strength, and cardiorespiratory endurance. It seems that this combination resulted in a greater improvement in the 100- and 400-m swimming times in group I than the greater distances covered by group L during training could produce. Therefore, the unqualified slogan of many trainers, "distance for speed," seems to be questionable, particularly with reference to prepubertal children in the intermediary phase of training.

Our results suggest that, in tethered swimming, one must take account of the force that is required for a swimmer to stay afloat in addition to the pull exerted by his swimming movements. More of the oxygen uptake is accounted for in the correlations between $V_{O_2}{}^{teth}$ and TF than between $V_{O_2}{}^{teth}$ and SF alone. Therefore, every subject's specific gravity should be calculated, and TF is preferred to SF. Since there is no upward movement, no work (W) can be calculated; one would like to think of the mean TF as a useful W substitute because it holds promise of indicating how much the subjects exerted themselves. It appears from these results that there had been a considerable amount of wasted splashing during the first test, even though all subjects stayed afloat for the full 3 min and performed the test absolutely correctly. As compared with the initial tests, there were increases in TF in all three groups, but none was significant. During the last test, when the greatest correlation ($r = 0.90$) between $V_{O_2}{}^{teth}$ and TF was demonstrated, the subjects must have swum far more economically, performing fewer undirected movements than at first. This is corroborated by the instructor's observation that, while training in the swimming bath, the children swam better toward the end of the season despite an intentional absence of systematic style correction once the

Table 4. Physiological reactions to winter training programs in prepubertal Caucasian children[a]

Group		$\overline{V}_{O_2}$ (swimming)		$V_{O_2}^{teth}$ (liters)			Economy (liters/kg)		
		B	A	B	A	Improvement	B	A	Improvement
L	M	1.10	1.19	3.22	2.86	0.36	0.29	0.25	0.04
	σ	0.30	0.24	1.27	0.83		0.10	0.14	
I,	M	1.18	1.14	4.45	2.47	1.98	0.41	0.21	0.20
	σ	0.15	0.24	1.38	0.64		0.25	0.09	
					$P < 0.01$			$P < 0.05$	
C	M	1.39	1.45	5.14	3.73	1.41	0.34	0.21	0.13
	σ	0.09	0.27	1.29	0.80		0.23	0.10	

[a]Only where P values are shown have changes been found to be statistically significant

Table 4. (continued)

| Group | | $\dot{V}O_2^{max}$ (cycling) | | | | | Maximal heart rate | | | |
| | | (liters) | | (ml/kg·min) | | | Swimming | | Cycling | |
		B	A	B	A	Improvement	B	A	B	A
L	M	1.46	1.60	47.14	46.73	-0.41	167	170	192	197
	σ	0.42	0.32	14.57	6.22		22	18	8	7
		$P < 0.01$								
I	M	1.33	1.60	41.60	48.34	6.74	177	166	198	201
	σ	0.25	0.23	5.46	6.76		24	19	8	4
		$P < 0.01$		$P < 0.01$			$P < 0.01$			
C	M	1.57	1.78	48.37	52.04	3.67	186	184	196	201
	σ	0.11	0.11	7.66	7.00		6	7	10	8

winter season had started. One may conclude that there had been an improvement in test swimming economy toward the end of the season and that this improvement was highly significant in group I, not necessarily but possibly related to real swimming. Exercise specificity has been dealt with by Magel et al. (1975).

$\dot{V}_{O_2}$ did not show any remarkable or significant change at the end of the program, but when the oxygen debt was added to the total swimming V_{O_2} for $V_{O_2}^{teth}$, a highly significant change was observed in group I (1.98 liters). This value and the 48.8% swimming economy improvement, must be tempered by the similar trend witnessed in the control group (1.41 liters and 38.2%). In $\dot{V}_{O_2}^{max}$ (ml/kg·min) studied during cycling, the improvement in group I was 16.2%, and that in group C was 7.6%; in group L there was no improvement. It is possible that the improvement in the children including the controls bore some relation to growth factors. The controls grew the fastest and added 2.6 cm (1.82%) to their mean stature as compared with 2.1 cm in both of the test groups (1.49% in group L and 1.52% in group I). (This indicates that the two test groups were quite comparable in growth.) Assuming that group C's improvement in swimming economy and $\dot{V}_{O_2}^{max}$ in ml/kg·min resulted from a combination of growth factors and previous test experience, and that group I's values also improved as a result of these two considerations, one may argue that there is still about 10% (48.8 minus 38.2) of group I's improvement in tethered swimming economy and about 8% of their improvement in $\dot{V}_{O_2}^{max}$ (16.2 minus 7.6%) that are unaccounted for by growth factors and test experience. Group L is ignored for this part of the discussion for want of significant improvements. If the children in group I had grown as fast as those in the control group, these percentages might have been slightly higher, but any deduction in this regard is complicated by the group I's lack of $\dot{V}_{O_2}$ improvement but similarity in growth. It is concluded that approximately 10% and 8% of the observed improvements were likely to have resulted purely from the interval training. In the 100- and 400-m swims, group I's improvements were statistically significant, amounting to 12.83 and 16.90% respectively. Swimming time improvements may be explained partly by improvements in swimming economy and $\dot{V}_{O_2}^{max}$.

The significant drop in peak heart rate during tethered swimming matches group I's decrease in $\dot{V}_{O_2}^{teth}$ despite an increase in both SF and TF. This group had most probably become significantly more fit for swimming by the end of the winter season. From the present findings, it is strongly suggested that interval training is superior as an intermediary program.

REFERENCES

Durnin, J. V. G. A., and Rahaman, M. M. 1967. The assessment of the amount of fat in the human body from measurements of skinfold thickness. Br. J. Nutr. 21:681–689.

Hebbelinck, M., Duquet, W., and Ross, W. 1972. A practical outline for the Heath-Carter somatotyping method applied to children. In: O. Bar-Or (ed.), Pediatric Work Physiology, Proceedings of the Fourth International Symposium. Wingate Institute.

Holmér, I. 1974. Physiology of swimming man. Acta Physiol. Scand. 407(suppl.): 1–55.

Magel, J. R., Foglia, G. F., McArdle, W. D., Gutin, B., Pechar, G. S., and Kasch, F. I. 1975. Specificity of swim training on maximal oxygen uptake. J. Appl. Physiol. 39:1, 151–155.

Secher, N. H., and Oddershede, I. 1974. Maximal oxygen uptake rate during swimming and bicycling. In: J. P. Clarys and L. Lewille (eds.), Swimming II, pp. 137–142. University Park Press, Baltimore.

Siri, W., and Donner, E. 1956. Laboratory of Biophysics and Medical Physics (University of California) Report.

A Mathematical Model of Swimming Performance Improvement for Goal Setting And Program Evaluation

J. D. McClements and W. H. Laverty

This study was done to develop a mathematical model to be used to measure objectively performance improvement in swimming. The basis of this analysis was developmental change over a 12-year period. Performance improvement is the basic goal of all coaches, athletes, and sport administrators. Setting goals and evaluating performance improvement have been based on relative comparisons with peer athletes or "personal bests." The basic question is, "how much improvement is meaningful?" Research on goal setting and self-directed behavior change by Kolb and Boyatzis (1970) concluded that the goal-setting process is crucial for success. A mathematical model of improvement should make this process more objective.

Historically, research on improvement of athletic performance has focused on two issues: 1) the development of performance scoring tables and, 2) the prediction of world records and/or the theoretical limits of man. Although there has been debate on the nature of scoring tables in track and field, there has been consensus (Mueller, 1965; Herr, 1966; Witt, 1966; Jahnel, 1966; Purdy, 1974) that running events should be scored on a progressive rating scale. A progressive rating scale allows more points for a unit of improvement as performance maximizes. The study of man's limitations and the prediction of world records have used two research models. Henry (1955) predicted world record track performances by using an exponential velocity formula that is based on a theoretical model. This model included the physiological factors of alactate oxygen debt, lactate oxygen debt and the depletion of glycogen

Project supported by SASK SPORT research grant S-21.

reserves, and an acceleration factor. The second method of predicting performance used the relationship between world records and chronological times. Fruct and Jokl (1964), Jokl and Jokl (1968), and Jokl (1974) used an exponential model, while Ryder, Carr, and Herget (1976) used a linear model. These studies concluded that future performance can be predicted using a mathematical model.

More recently, McClements and Laverty (1979) analyzed changes in speed skating performance using the exponential progressive model. They also identified a 4-year cyclic trend linked to the Olympics and recommended smoothing the curves using moving averages over a 4-year period to allow for this trend.

Fruct and Jokl (1964) identified four periods of development in track and field; the last of these periods is a post-World War II era. McClements and Laverty (1979) studied performance improvement in speed skating and identified a fifth period of change in the mid-1960s. They concluded that performance analysis should avoid the use of pre-1965 data whenever possible.

Purdy (1975) developed a series of principles that became the basis for developing scoring tables. Many of these principles dealt with absolute and comparative value of points; however, those that apply to objective performance evaluation have been paraphrased appropriately:

1. Diminishing Returns Principle. It is more difficult to achieve a unit of performance improvement as performance approaches the theoretical limits of man.
2. Constant Conditions Principle. The rules defining an event, the manner in which it is conducted and the equipment used must remain constant during the period studied.
3. Regularity of Change Principle. Improvement in performance occurs in a regular and orderly fashion.
4. Equivalence principle. Each unit of an index of improvement represents a constant magnitude of difficulty of improvement.

METHODS AND RESULTS

Independent Variable

Based on the findings of McClements and Laverty (1979), the study was limited to the years from 1964-65 to 1975-76. It was assumed that historical developmental trends in world class performance of each event represented the difficulty of improvement. Therefore, annual best performance can be considered to be the independent variable.

The study was also restricted to events regularly reported. The events were 100-, 200-, 400-, 800-, and 1,500-m freestyle, 100- and 200-m backstroke, 100- and 200-m breaststroke, 100- and 200-m butterfly, and 200- and 400-m individual medley. Because data were not reported in some years for the male 800-m freestyle and the female 1,500-m freestyle, data from 1960–61 to 1963–64 were also used for those events.

Dependent Variable

The best five performances by different individuals for each year, each event, and each sex were collected from Swimming World's (1966–1977) annual lists of top world times. It was assumed that the average of the top five individuals' performances would represent world class performance for each event for each year. The average of five performances was selected instead of the best performance or a series of world records because the aim of the study was to predict competitive world class performance, not winning or world records. The choice of the number five was consistent with the studies of Jahnel (1966) and McClements and Laverty (1979).

Descriptive Analysis

The means of the five best individuals' performances are reported in Tables 1 and 2. Because of the 4-year cyclic trend attributed to the Olympic Games, the data were smoothed using moving averages over a 4-year period. For the males, a median value of 3.95% of the variance was attributed to the Olympic cycle, and for the females a median value of 3.35% of the variance was attributed to this trend (see Table 3).

Curve Fitting

The work of Henry (1955), Fruct and Jokl (1964), Jokl and Jokl (1968), Purdy (1972), Jokl (1974), and McClements and Laverty (1979) suggests an exponential model, with the most appropriate equation being:

$$Y = Ae^{Bx} + C$$

where: Y = predicted performance, A = a constant representing the discrepancy between performance and C at $X = 0$, B = a constant representing the relative rate of improvement per year, C = projected limit of performance, and X = chronological years minus a starting year. The data were analyzed using an unconstrained, nonlinear least squares, iterative curve-fitting technique developed by Marquardt (1963). The computer program used was NONLS2, published by Westley (1970). Because many of the B values approached zero (as B approaches zero the exponential curve essentially becomes linear), a linear regression analysis was also calculated between chronological years and observed values, using a Hewlett-Packard 55 calculator. The results of both analyses are reported in Tables 4 and 5.

Table 1. Means of the best five performance times (sec) for male swimming events for the years 1964-65 through 1975-76

Year	Freestyle					Backstroke		Breaststroke		Butterfly		Individual medley	
	100 m	200 m	400 m	800 m	1,500 m	100 m	200 m	100 m	200 m	100 m	200 m	200 m	400 m
1964-65	53.91	119.36	255.17	539.94	1023.17	61.17	133.36	68.19	150.67	58.27	129.55	136.72	293.36
1965-66	53.47	117.60	251.46	536.04	1015.56	61.02	132.52	68.38	149.89	58.33	130.44	134.82	289.37
1966-67	53.13	117.25	249.82	—	1007.97	59.77	130.89	67.44	149.44	57.08	127.02	133.05	289.04
1967-68	52.69	115.67	247.39	523.22	988.62	59.82	128.86	66.94	148.30	56.88	126.91	132.38	281.12
1968-69	53.00	116.33	246.67	521.94	986.08	59.82	128.32	66.89	146.61	56.97	127.60	132.33	281.58
1969-70	52.38	115.33	243.58	513.74	971.26	58.46	126.88	66.67	145.13	56.88	125.58	130.96	276.52
1970-71	52.69	115.30	244.61	511.38	969.33	58.75	127.13	66.49	145.60	56.13	124.85	130.61	276.79
1971-72	51.80	113.75	240.53	—	955.87	57.86	124.91	65.52	143.22	55.50	123.11	128.42	272.47
1972-73	51.89	113.94	240.44	—	945.82	58.58	125.32	65.13	141.83	56.14	127.74	128.77	273.97
1973-74	51.77	112.75	238.13	—	944.52	57.86	124.55	65.21	141.60	55.71	122.49	127.38	270.58
1974-75	51.13	111.85	235.99	—	930.95	57.67	124.42	65.11	141.33	54.47	121.11	127.11	271.35
1975-76	50.50	110.63	233.27	485.02	908.10	56.75	121.50	63.78	138.36	54.67	119.71	127.08	265.66

Table 2. Means of the best five performance times (sec) for female swimming events for the years 1964-65 through 1975-76

Year	Freestyle					Backstroke		Breaststroke		Butterfly		Individual medley	
	100 m	200 m	400 m	800 m	1,500 m	100 m	200 m	100 m	200 m	100 m	200 m	200 m	400 m
1964-65	61.10	134.11	282.23	585.32	1125.96	68.41	149.11	77.60	167.89	66.38	146.66	152.08	323.02
1965-66	60.82	131.82	278.87	582.54	1106.34	68.13	148.36	76.72	164.24	66.16	147.67	150.52	320.13
1966-67	60.24	131.11	274.76	574.58	—	67.89	147.58	75.94	163.61	65.60	144.13	148.00	315.73
1967-68	59.50	127.77	268.43	558.69	1077.22	66.96	144.67	75.41	162.61	64.88	142.47	145.60	311.50
1968-69	59.89	129.00	269.45	559.30	1060.12	66.83	145.03	76.91	165.77	65.91	142.50	147.67	312.86
1969-70	60.16	129.66	268.15	556.78	1062.80	66.88	143.75	76.17	163.44	64.82	139.77	146.69	309.17
1970-71	59.74	127.82	263.90	544.40	1041.35	66.92	143.91	75.82	162.99	64.63	140.05	147.00	308.78
1971-72	58.78	124.91	261.98	535.79	—	66.17	141.66	75.32	162.42	63.72	137.05	143.96	304.14
1972-73	58.61	125.44	260.75	535.47	1016.18	65.71	141.85	75.11	161.28	63.22	137.71	142.77	302.97
1973-74	57.66	123.27	257.32	530.66	1006.99	64.58	139.22	73.55	158.55	62.50	136.22	141.25	298.61
1974-75	57.27	122.86	256.28	527.28	1013.42	64.02	137.11	73.77	158.16	62.13	135.44	140.28	294.77
1975-76	56.30	120.47	252.27	520.43	1008.63	62.61	134.22	72.38	155.66	60.97	132.33	138.89	288.35

Table 3.   Percentage variance[a] attributed to the Olympic phenomena for 1964-65 data

	Male			Female		
	Coefficient of determination			Coefficient of determination		
Event	Smoothed data	Averaged data	Percent variance	Smoothed data	Averaged data	Percent variance
Freestyle						
100 m	0.986	0.927	5.9	0.918	0.893	2.5
200 m	0.992	0.956	3.6	0.983	0.931	5.2
400 m	0.997	0.979	1.8	0.998	0.977	2.1
800 m		[b]		0.999	0.979	2.0
1,500 m	0.998	0.982	1.6		[b]	
Backstroke						
100 m	0.994	0.916	7.8	0.934	0.901	3.3
200 m	0.998	0.960	3.8	0.979	0.941	3.8
Breaststroke						
100 m	0.998	0.948	5.0	0.994[c]	0.947	4.7
200 m	0.999	0.975	2.4	0.993[c]	0.959	3.4
Butterfly						
100 m	0.999	0.907	9.2	0.954	0.922	3.2
200 m	0.997	0.945	5.2	0.997	0.956	4.1
Individual medley						
200 m	0.997	0.969	2.8	0.958	0.921	3.7
400 m	0.999	0.958	4.1	0.986	0.964	2.2
Median	0.997	0.957	3.95	0.983	0.945	3.35

[a] Percent variance attributed to the Olympic phenomena = (coefficient of determination of the smoothed data with calculated − coefficient of determination of the averaged data with calculated) × 100.

[b] Because of the missing data, curve smoothing was not possible.

[c] Because the 1964-65 data did not satisfy the selection criteria, the 1968-69 data that did satisfy the selection criteria were used.

Analysis of Curves

The adequacy of the curves was established by three minimum requirements: 1) the coefficient of determination must be at least 0.90, 2) the projected value for the year 2000 must be less than the current world record and, 3) the curve must be progressive. The coefficient of determination (r^2) is the proportion of variability of observed performance times that is related to variation in predicted performance time. This was used to estimate the quality of the curves' predictability. The projections

Table 4. Values of exponential and linear curve-fitting analysis of smoothed data, 1964-65 through 1975-76, for male swimming events

Event	Exponential: $Y = Ae^{Bx} + C$			Linear: $Y = A + Bx$	
	A	B	C	A	B
Freestyle					
100 m	804.0150	-0.000295	-750.4384	53.58	-0.2375
200 m	1588.8444	-0.000390	-1470.7437	118.10	-0.6188
400 m	4140.2462	-0.000408	-3887.9037	252.33	-1.6890
800 m[a]	21221.3840	-0.000214	-20661.3720	559.99	-4.5293
1,500 m	19798.5880	-0.000472	-18781.1240	1017.42	-9.3198
Backstroke					
100 m	5.0047	-0.121781	56.0675	60.63	-0.3408
200 m	13.1717	-0.122942	119.7552	131.75	-0.9025
Breaststroke					
100 m	316.7305	-0.001155	-248.5902	68.13	-0.3637
200 m	404.7181	-0.002754	-253.9899	150.69	-1.0990
Butterfly					
100 m	4.9483	-0.080044	53.0819	57.81	-0.2690
200 m	609.9022	-0.001414	-480.3857	129.50	-0.8560
Individual medley					
200 m	23.8463	-0.044267	111.3974	134.87*	-0.8495
400 m	30.2360	-0.143307	262.2307	289.04	-2.2025

[a] Data for the 800-m freestyle were not smoothed because of missing data.

Table 5. Values of exponential and linear curve-fitting analysis of smoothed data, 1964-65 through 1975-76, for female swimming events

Event	Exponential: $Y = Ae^{Bx} + C$			Linear: $Y = A + Bx$	
	A	B	C	A	B
Freestyle					
100 m	1655.3370	−0.000211	−1594.3156	61.02	−0.3488
200 m	2957.5067	−0.000338	−2825.1430	132.39	−0.9983
400 m	69.3371	−0.041678	209.2594	277.65	−2.3543
800 m	132.4221	−0.061022	451.2614	580.07	−5.9995
1,500 m[a]	315.2680	−0.064475	888.6561	1172.77	−11.2431
Backstroke					
100 m	1527.5940	−0.000268	−1459.1424	68.44	−0.4088
200 m	4119.6485	−0.000265	−3970.9133	148.72	−1.0898
Breaststroke					
100 m[b]	1440.3573	−0.000408	−1363.6448	76.71	−0.5870
200 m[b]	3274.4906	−0.000350	3109.4120	165.07	−1.2910
Butterfly					
100 m	1697.9104	−0.000265	−1631.3026	66.60	−0.4495
200 m	29.6671	−0.053670	117.2208	146.32	−1.2357
Individual medley					
200 m	3472.5485	−0.000282	−3322.2291	150.31	−0.9792
400 m	8755.6209	−0.000290	−8435.1044	320.52	−2.5377

[a] Data for the 1,500-m freestyle were not smoothed because of missing data.
[b] Because the 1964-65 data did not satisfy the selection criteria, the 1968-69 data that did satisfy the selection criteria were used.

for the year 2000 were that year's projected value minus a correction factor. The correction factor for each event was the correction of the mean performance times with the best performance times for each year. The relationship of the projection for the year 2000 to the 1975 world record was considered to ensure that the curves were not too consecutive. The curves must be progressive to satisfy the principle of diminishing returns. The constant A must be positive, and the constant B must be negative for these curves to be progressive. The data for evaluating these criteria are in Tables 6 and 7.

All of the curves except those for 100- and 200-m breaststroke of the females satisfied these criteria. The coefficients of determination for both curves were less than 0.90 (100 m: $r^2 = 0.856$, and 200 m: $r^2 = 0.876$). These curves were reanalyzed using the 1968–69 through 1975–76 data base.

To facilitate the comparison of the exponential and linear curves, the coefficient of determination of linear projections with observed performances was also calculated. Further, projected values for the year 1988 were calculated using both the linear and exponential equations. These results are in Tables 6 and 7. The year 1988 was selected because 12 years was assumed to be the maximum time that these tables could be considered usable.

DISCUSSION

Curves

Theoretical exponential equations that satisfied the basic criteria and principles were found for the 26 events studied. The exponential progressive model agreed with the earlier work of Henry (1955), Fruct and Jokl (1964), Mueller (1965), Jahnel (1966), Herr (1966), Witt (1966), Jokl and Jokl (1968), Purdy (1972), Jokl (1974), and McClements and Laverty (1979). All of the previous analyses except those of McClements and Laverty (1979) were done on world records, scoring tables, and theoretical models of running. However, many of these curves had very small B values. As B approaches zero, the exponential curve essentially becomes linear. The linear and exponential coefficients of determination were equal (i.e., within 0.001) for eight of the male events and nine of the female events. This suggested that most of the swimming events were improving in a linear manner. This result violates the principle of diminishing returns. There are three possible explanations for this apparent linearity: 1) the training techniques being developed in swimming offset the effect of the principle of diminishing returns, 2) rapid developments in swimming caused by developmental factors, such as increased participation, longer participation, or older participation, offset the effect of

Table 6. Exponential projections for the year 2000, 1977 world records, coefficients of determination, and year 1988 projections for linear and exponential curve-fitting analysis for male swimming events

Event	Year 2000 projection	1977 World record	Coef. determination		Year 1988 projections	
			Exponential	Linear	Exponential	Linear
Freestyle						
100 m	44.96	49.44	0.986	0.986	48.10	47.93
200 m	95.68	110.29	0.992	0.992	103.65	103.62
400 m	192.59	231.56	0.997	0.997	214.27	214.26
800 m[a]	382.50	481.54	0.986	0.986	428.83	426.40
1,500 m	686.12	902.40	0.998	0.998	806.72	805.35
Backstroke						
100 m	54.78	55.49	0.994	0.976	55.07	51.60
200 m	118.13	119.89	0.998	0.980	118.88	110.53
Breaststroke						
100 m	55.01	62.86	0.998	0.998	59.65	59.65
200 m	112.26	135.11	0.999	0.999	125.70	125.27
Butterfly						
100 m	52.55	54.18	0.999	0.990	53.13	51.19
200 m	99.43	119.23	0.997	0.997	110.25	110.05
Individual medley						
200 m	115.11	125.31	0.997	0.994	119.55	115.15
400 m	259.37	263.68	0.998	0.980	260.54	238.61

[a]Data for the 800-m freestyle were not smoothed because of missing data.

Table 7.   Exponential projections for the year 2000, 1977 world records, coefficients of determination, and year 1988 projections for linear and exponential curve-fitting analysis for male swimming events

Event	Year 2000 projection	1977 World record	Coef. determination		Year 1988 projections	
			Exponential	Linear	Exponential	Linear
Freestyle						
100 m	48.59	55.65	0.926	0.926	53.13	53.09
200 m	96.88	119.26	0.983	0.983	109.74	109.71
400 m	223.27	248.91	0.998	0.996	235.11	224.58
800 m	461.26	515.04	0.999	0.994	480.79	444.95
1,500 m	912.57	984.60	0.982	0.969	952.54	916.11
Backstroke						
100 m	53.06	61.51	0.934	0.933	58.88	58.86
200 m	109.28	132.47	0.979	0.979	123.81	123.32
Breaststroke						
100 m[b]	57.66	70.86	0.994	0.994	62.90	62.86
200 m[b]	123.48	153.35	0.993	0.994	135.35	134.92
Butterfly						
100 m	50.48	59.78	0.954	0.954	56.28	56.25
200 m	120.26	131.22	0.997	0.994	124.96	118.13
Individual medley						
200 m	114.90	135.85	0.958	0.957	127.74	127.52
400 m	229.12	282.77	0.986	0.986	261.89	261.76

[a] Data for the 1,500-m freestyle were not smoothed because of missing data.
[b] Because the 1964–65 data did not satisfy the selection criteria, the 1968–69 data that did satisfy the selection criteria were used.

diminishing returns, and 3) swimming performance is so far below man's limits that the principle of diminishing returns does not apply.

In five male events and four female events, the exponential curve accounted for more variance than the linear curves. After smoothing the data using moving averages over a 4-year period, an average of 99.7% (median $r^2 = 0.997$) for males, and an average of 98.3% (median $r^2 = 0.983$) for females of the variability of observed performance was related to the predicted values. Further, for every event, the 1988 exponential projection was slower than the 1988 linear projection; this result satisfies the principle of diminishing returns.

It was concluded that the exponential progressive model was most appropriate for swimming events. This was based on the evidence that the model was not violated, some curves definitely were progressive, and the fact that the progressive exponential model can become essentially linear.

APPLICATIONS

Objective Individual Goal Setting and Evaluation

It is difficult to set a reasonable objective performance goal for an athlete for a training year. It is equally difficult to evaluate objectively last year's training. If the curve-fitting strategy described above can be accepted as an index of improvement *and* if the individual can determine a long term performance goal, than reasonable short term goals can be set and evaluated.

For example, the curve can be used to determine how many index-of-improvement units the performer is from his long term goal (see Figure 1a). These units are divided by the number of years available. This quotient is added to the index units associated with the current performance level (see Figure 1b), and the sum is used to extrapolate the short term performance goal (see Figure 1c). This goal can be used to evaluate the performance and training at the end of the short term period. Of course, evaluation of the success should consider the effort of the athlete, the appropriateness of the training program, and the time available for training as well as the effort and ability of the athlete.

Evaluation of Training Programs on Successive Years

The classical problems in evaluation programs, which involve behavioral change, are the questions of whom to place in which training program, the effect of different coaches or the preference of a coach for one method, and the specificity of the training program. The research paradigm of using the same coach and the same athletes in successive years has not been utilized because of the principle of diminishing returns. However, this is

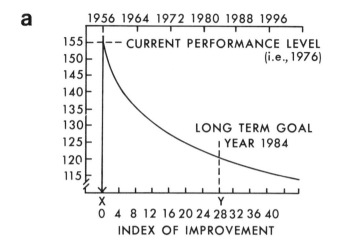

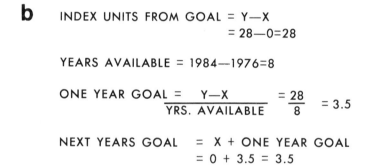

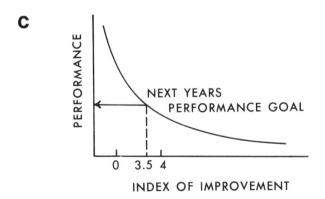

Figure 1. Example of individual, short-term goal setting.

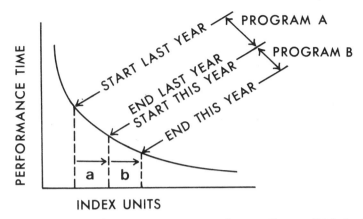

Figure 2. Evaluation of training programs over successive years. Program B is better if a/b < 1; program A is better if a/b > 1.

how real training programs are conducted. In fact, most coaches evaluate the effect of training by a subjective evaluation of performance or ranking.

The concept of the index-of-difficulty curves can make this evaluation more objective. This is illustrated in Figure 2. Quite simply, the performance changes of programs A and B are converted to index units, and these units are set in a ratio. If the ratio is less than 1, the numerator program is more effective; if the ratio is greater than 1, the denominator program is more effective. For this to be true, one must assume that there was the same amount of talent and interest in both programs or years. Perhaps it would be better to consider each individual on the two training programs and to base the general decision on the trend of individual change.

Evaluation of Total Program

Another possible application concerns the evaluation of a total program, such as a national program. Traditional political evaluation of programs is unfortunately based on the number of medals that are won. It is theoretically possible for a program to be causing dramatic changes without reaping any more medals being won by the participants. If a program curve were calculated and compared with international curves, one could estimate when a program would become internationally competitive. This same method might be used to direct emphasis in funding, coaching, and/or promotion.

SUMMARY

This paper suggests that performance changes in swimming can be represented mathematically. Using recent trends in changes allows one to predict for the near future. The mathematical model of change can then be used as the basis for objective goal setting and evaluation of individual training and total program as well as the evaluation of training programs in successive years. However, this form of analysis should be only part of an evaluation process. The usefulness of this approach depends on its common-sense application.

REFERENCES

Fruct, A. H., and Jokl, E. 1964. The future of athletic records. In: E. Jokl and E. Simon (eds.), International Research in Sport and Physical Education. Charles C Thomas, Publisher, Springfield, Ill.

Henry, F. M. 1955. Prediction of world records in running sixty yards to twenty-six miles. Res. Q. 26:147–58.

Herr, E. 1966. Is the IAAF scoring table justified after all? Leichtathletic 36:1105.

Jahnel, F. 1966. The IAFF multiple discipline scoring system in light of critics. Leichtathletik 16:463.

Jokl, E. 1974. The physiological basis of athletic records and superior performance. In: L. Percival (ed.), International Symposium on the Art and Science of Coaching, Vol. 2. FI Productions, Willowdale, New York.

Jokl, E., and Jokl, P. 1968. The Physiological Basis of Athletic Records. Charles C Thomas, Publisher, Springfield, Ill.

Kolb, D. A., and Boyatzis, R. E. 1970. Goal setting and self-directed behaviour change. Hum. Relat. 23:439–457.

Marquardt, D. W. 1963. An algorithm for least-squares estimation of nonlinear parameters. J. Soc. Appl. Math. 11:431–441.

McClements, J. D., and Laverty, W. H. 1979. Mathematical model of speed-skating performance improvement for goal setting and program evaluation. Can. J. Appl. Sport Sci., Vol. 4. In press.

Mueller, H. 1965. Principle error in the IAAF scoring tables. Leichathletik 51/52:1481.

Purdy, J. G. 1972. The application of computers to model physiological effort in scoring tables. Ph. D. thesis, Stanford University, Stanford.

Purdy, J. G. 1974. Computer-generated track and field scoring tables. I. Historical development. Med. Sci. Sports 6:287–294.

Purdy, J. G. 1975. Computer-generated track and field scoring tables. II. Theoretical foundation and development of a model. Med. Sci. Sports 7:111–115.

Ryder, H. W., Carr, H. J., and Herget, P. 1976. Future performance in foot-racing. Sci. Am. 234:109–116.

Swimming World. 1966-1977. Swimming world's top 25 world times. Swimming World 7(3), 8(1), 9(6), 10(1), 11(1), 12(1), 13(1), 14(1), 15(1), 16(1), 17(1).

Westley, G. W. 1970. NONLS 2—Marquardt nonlinear least squares. In: G. W. Westley and J. A. Watts (eds.), The Computing Technology Center Numerical Analysis Library. National Technical Information Service, Springfield, Va.

Witt, D. 1966. Measured with the wrong scale. Leichtathletik 3:84.

Use of Stroke Rate, Distance per Stroke, and Velocity Relationships During Training for Competitive Swimming

A. B. Craig, Jr., W. L. Boomer, and J. F. Gibbons

The locomotion of all animals can be characterized by the intermittant application of force that moves the body. Applying this principle to swimming, velocity (V) is the product of stroke rate (Ṡ) and the distance moved through water with each complete stroke cycle (d/S). These relationships of Ṡ, d/S, and V were described for competitive swimmers with varying skills, and the results were compared with those observed during the 1976 U.S. Olympic Trials (Craig and Pendergast, 1978). In general, increased V was achieved by increasing Ṡ and decreasing d/S (Figure 1). The front crawl swimmers who had the greatest maximal V also had the longest d/S at Ṡ of 20–25 S/min. For the males there was a direct relationship between the maximal V and the proportional decrease in d/S.

The relationships of Ṡ and V during the freestyle events at the Olympic Trials are shown in Figure 2. The faster V of the 100-m versus the 200-m race for men was accounted for by an increase in S from 46 to 54 Ṡ/min and a decrease in d/S from 2.27 to 2.03 m/Ṡ. Similar changes for both the men and women were noted in the 100- and 200-m backstroke and breaststroke events. In effect, these points represent a short section of a stroke rate–velocity curve (Ṡ–V) for very skilled swimmers.

The Ṡ used by the men in both the 400- and 1,500-m freestyle distances was 44 Ṡ/min, and the slower V of the 1,500-m race was accounted for by a shorter d/S. Theoretically, each race could have been swum at a slower Ṡ and a longer d/S. However, to achieve the same V at a slower Ṡ, a greater force for each stroke would be needed, and greater local muscle fatigue would result. Such considerations might also account for the observation that the 100-m butterfly races for both men and women were swum with a longer d/S and a faster Ṡ than was used in the 200-m events.

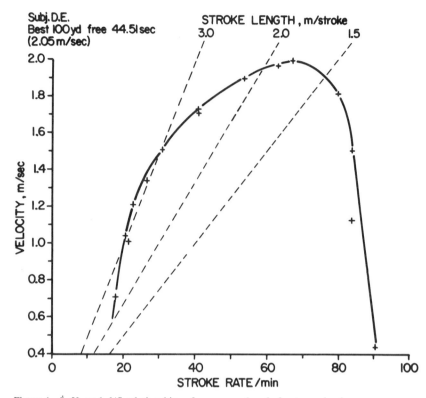

Figure 1. Ṡ, V, and d/S relationships of a very good male front crawl swimmer.

Freestyle races for women were quite different from those for men. In the 400-, 200-, and 100-m events the increase in V was accounted for entirely by the increase in Ṡ, from 52 to 55 to 58 S/min, respectively, and the d/S values were not different (1.76 m/S). The Ṡ used in the 800-m race was the same as in the 400-m race, but d/S decreased to 1.73 m/S. These differences between men and women who swam the front crawl may be related in some way to the energetics of swimming (di Prampero et al., 1974; Holmer, 1975).

These observations have implications for swimming coaches. We wish to indicate how relationships of Ṡ, d/S, and V can be useful in practice. As much as possible, programs for competitive swimmers should be based on experimental evidence related to the sport rather than speculation and extrapolation from generalities.

METHODS

In most of our studies we used a "swim meter" to measure the distance and time swum for a given number of strokes. The swimmer wears a light

RELATIONSHIPS OF STROKE RATE AND VELOCITY IN THE FRONT CRAWL

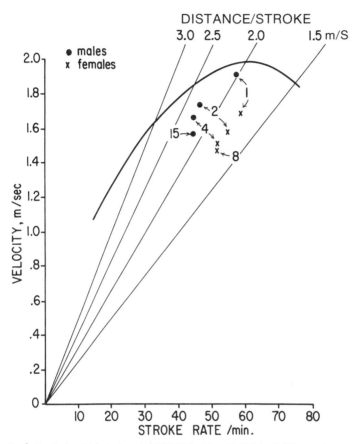

Figure 2. Ṡ-V relationships during the 1976 U.S. Olympic Trials. Solid curve is part of the Ṡ-V curve shown in Figure 2. The numbers which label the data points indicate that the results were from the 100-, 200-, 400-, 800-, and 1,500 freestyle events. Solid circles indicate the men's events, and the crosses indicate the women's events. Data were collected during the preliminary events, and the points indicate the averages. The number of swimmers observed ranged between 18 to 27 for the different events.

collar, to which is attached a fine, nonelastic, malleable, stainless steel wire. As the swimmer goes down the pool, the wire is pulled from the swim meter, which is attached to the end of the pool. The meter measures the distance traveled and emits an electrical signal that is directly proportional to the velocity.

The swimmer is instructed to push off from the side and to swim one pool length at a constant speed. After two or three strokes, an observer at the side of the pool presses a hand-held switch at a precise point in the stroke pattern. This first signal starts the measurement of distance and time. The observer continues to press the switch at the same point in the stroke cycle, and after a predetermined number of strokes, the measurements of time and distance are automatically stopped and displayed as a digital readout. From these data, $\dot{S}$, V, and d/S are calculated. Repeated swims from very slow to maximal V are made. At very high speeds it is necessary for the subject to swim only part of a 23-m (75-yd) pool.

The major aim of the swim meter is to ensure that time and distance measurements begin and end at a constant point in the stroke pattern. This is necessary to obtain a true mean velocity. It is also useful to have a record of the instantaneous velocity during each stroke to detect the effects of defective swimming techniques.

We have also obtained good results by measuring the time it takes a swimmer to go between two marks on the side of the pool, which are set 10 m (32.8 ft) apart. At the same time, another observer measures the time it takes the swimmer to complete five strokes during approximately the same time that velocity is being measured. In counting strokes, the count starts with zero, not 1. These two times are used to calculate $\dot{S}$, V, and d/S, using a hand-held computer or the nomogram shown in Figure 3.

RESULTS AND DISCUSSION

The relationships of $\dot{S}$, V, and d/S for one very good swimmer using the front crawl stroke are shown in Figure 1. The dashed lines indicate d/S. At about 22 S/min this subject achieved his maximal d/S of 3.2 m/S. Increases in V were related to increasing $\dot{S}$ and decreasing d/S. At his maximal V of 2.0 m/sec, $\dot{S}$ was 65 S/min and d/S was 1.85 m/S. This represents about a 40% decrease in his d/S. Further increases in $\dot{S}$ resulted in a decrease in V, which indicates that the maximal V had actually been measured.

$\dot{S}$-V curves were obtained on many other swimmers of varying skill. In general, we found that those who had the longest S.L. at 20-25 S/min had the greatest maximal V. There was also a positive correlation between the degree of shortening and the maximal V. These two observations suggest that practice for competitive swimming should probably involve considerable swimming with slow $\dot{S}$ (20-30 S/min) to achieve a greater d/S. If a swimmer does not have a long d/S, there is less latitude for shortening and a greater dependence on $\dot{S}$ to swim fast.

Another worthwhile feature of the $\dot{S}$-V curve is the relationship of $\dot{S}$ to d/S at a given V. At any point on the curve, the indicated $\dot{S}$ for a particular V is the minimal $\dot{S}$ and the maximal d/S that the swimmer can use for that speed. On the other hand, he could swim that V with a faster $\dot{S}$

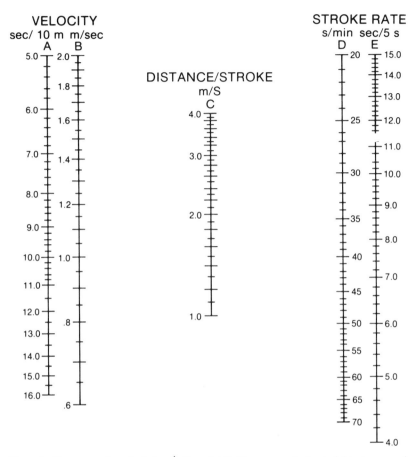

Figure 3. Nomogram for calculating Ś, V, and d/S. Place one end of a straight edge on scale A at a point indicating the observed time to swim 10 m. Place the other end on scale E at a point indicating the observed time to swim five complete strokes. In counting five strokes, the count must begin with zero, not 1. The point at which the straight edge crosses scale C indicates d/S. V can be calculated by drawing a horizontal line from scale A at a point indicating the observed time to swim 10 m to scale B, from which V can be read. Ś can be calculated by drawing a horizontal line from scale E at a point indicating the observed time to swim five complete strokes to scale D, from which Ś can be read. Note that scales A and D are inverted.

and shorter d/S. As the V increases, there is less and less choice of Ś and d/S, and maximal V represents a unique combination of Ś and d/S. All the competitive swimmers we have studied have been able to develop such curves, but even good recreational swimmers are not able to "swim on a curve." This negative result suggests that part of the early learning process for competition is knowing how to adjust Ś and d/S.

The results from observations at the Olympic Trials discussed above also have implications for competitive swimming. Maximal V can be sustained for only 8–10 sec. Therefore, all races must be swum at some submaximal V. In races involving 200 m or less, swimmers seem to select a combination of Ṡ and d/S that falls on the Ṡ–V curve. In very short sprints, Ṡ and V are quite near maximal, and longer races are swum farther "down the curve."

Because swimming a race in competition is a learned technique, the swimmer must practice specifically for an event. By knowing an individual's Ṡ–V relationships, it is possible to have some idea of how a particular race should be swum. We have found that if Ṡ is measured frequently during practice and if the information is given to the swimmer, he learns to swim at a precise Ṡ. Acquiring the ability to swim at a given V by consciously controlling Ṡ seems to be easier than trying to swim a certain length in a certain time.

During competition we also measured the Ṡ during each length of the race. Although the time of the race is the desired measure of performance, the comparison of the Ṡ used with the individual's Ṡ–V curve gives another evaluation of how well the race was swum.

Another use of Ṡ–V relationships as a coaching tool is illustrated in Figure 4. This male swimmer was in his first year of college and was new to the swimming team. This study was conducted to evaluate his swimming ability at the beginning of the season. The curve shown by the solid line was developed, and the point marked A indicated a maximal d/S of 2.39 m/S at an Ṡ of 30 S/min. Repeated swims using faster Ṡ resulted in the expected increase of V to point B.

At this point the coach suggested that the swimmer correct the pattern of his arm movement. The next swim, point C, represented an increase in V of from 1.50 to 1.73 m/sec, with a small increase in Ṡ of from 51 to 55 S/min. It was obvious that the change in the stroke pattern meant that the swimmer was on a completely different Ṡ–V curve, represented by the dashed line. This was partially confirmed by having the swimmer use an Ṡ of 20 S/min as a set by a pacing device, which provided the subject with an audible signal. The change in stroke pattern increased his d/S from 2.39 to 3.18 m/S (point D). Studies such as this document the effects of changing stroke mechanics.

A somewhat different use of the Ṡ–V relationship is shown in Figure 5. This female swimmer was in her last year of competitive swimming. She had joined the team 3 years earlier and had improved significantly in her times for the 50- and 100-yd freestyle events, but during the second year her times changed very little. The initial Ṡ–V curve was developed after about 2 months of practice in the third year. The swimmer's times in competition during the first half of this season equaled those of the previous season, but there was no indication that she was improving. A careful examination of the Ṡ–V curve suggested that it was somewhat "flattened" in

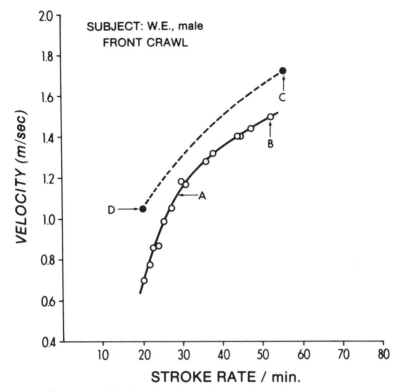

Figure 4. Ṡ-V relationships for one swimmer. See text for explanation.

the Ṡ range of 30-55 S/min. Measurement of her Ṡ during competition revealed that she swam the 100-yd freestyle event with an average Ṡ of 59 S/min.

The coach carefully examined her stroke pattern from below the surface and found that she was not effectively maintaining arm force in the latter part of the pulling phase. She was able to correct this fault. As shown in Figure 4, her Ṡ-V curve was also improved, and the maximal V increased by about 4%. Her time for the 100-yd race immediately improved by 1.7 sec (3%), which correlated well with the increase in maximal V. Although her best time in the 50-yd race was not improved, she swam that distance in 26.1-26.9 sec rather than in the 26.9-27.2 sec she had done before the change.

Figure 6 shows another problem that was defined by observing the Ṡ-V relationship. This swimmer was also new to the team. Her previous experience was limited to interclub swimming competition during the summer. From direct observation it was apparent that she had a long and smooth front crawl stroke. The first Ṡ-V curve done at the beginning of

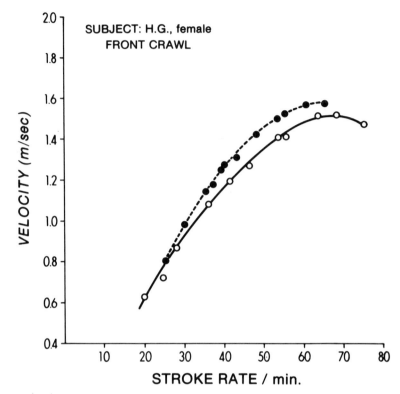

Figure 5. Ŝ–V relationships for one swimmer. Solid curve indicates the relationships before and the dashed line indicate the relationships after a change in stroke pattern.

the season confirmed this impression. Her maximal d/S was 2.4 m/S and her maximal V was 1.64 m/sec. Average values for other women swimmers on the team were: maximal d/S, 2.1 m/S and maximal V, 1.43 m/sec. During the season her best times for the 50-yd freestyle event averaged 27.6 sec and for the 100-yd distance, 1:00.2. Four other swimmers on the team had better times for these distances but had slower maximal values.

Two weeks before the final championship meet she was studied again. The results are shown by the dashed line in Figure 5. Although her maximal d/S had not changed, her maximal V had decreased to 1.51 m/sec. The d/S at the maximal V had decreased from 1.9 to 1.65 m/S. After talking with this swimmer it was apparent that she had "shortened" her stroke in response to the stresses of daily practice. Workouts produced considerable local fatigue of her shoulder girdle muscles, which she could minimize only by decreasing the force during the pulling phase and decreasing d/S. Unfortunately, she showed no improvement in the final meet. These results suggest that this swimmer might benefit from a pro-

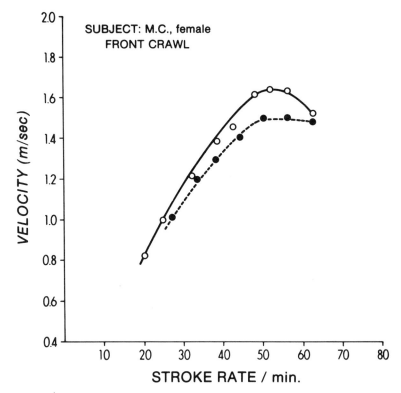

Figure 6. Ṡ-V relationships for one swimmer during the first part of the season (solid line) and during the last two weeks (dashed line).

gram of weight lifting, designed to increase the strength and power of the shoulder girdle. Although she can achieve a fast maximal V for a short distance, she cannot maintain the speed long enough to swim well for the 50- or 100-yd events.

These examples indicate that measurements of Ṡ, d/S, and V relationships can provide data that are useful to the individual swimmer. The general principles have also been useful to the coaches who must plan practices during the season. During the past three seasons at our university, distances swum each day have been decreased, and there has been an increasing emphasis on "quality" rather than "quantity." Stroke mechanics are continuously emphasized. Tethered swimming against known retarding forces has also been an important tool. During such practice Ṡ is measured, and this information helps the swimmer to minimize Ṡ and maximize the force of each pull.

Studies of the energetics and biomechanics of swimming (di Prampero et al., 1974; Holmér, 1975; Pendergast et al., 1977; Craig, Jr., and Pendergast, 1978) strongly suggest that swimmers can improve by increasing their efficiency and decreasing their active body drag. Although optimizing maximal aerobic capacity is important, most races do not last long enough to make this a major concern.

The ability of a swimmer to improve his technique will probably determine success more than increasing his capacity to tolerate 3-4-hr workouts. In one study (Pendergast et al., 1977) the oxygen costs of swimming the front crawl, which is a measure of a swimmer's proficiency, varied between 35 and 60 liters O_2/km for male competitive swimmers and between 40 and 100 liters O_2/km for noncompetitors. These results can be compared with a similar study of running, where the oxygen cost for the untrained person was only 5% greater than for skilled distance runners (Margaria et al., 1963).

Although the variability of proficiency in world class competitors is probably not great, most coaches deal with swimmers who are less skilled and for whom considerations of drag and efficiency are very important. It is now possible to design swimming programs for this latter group, based at least in part on the growing body of scientific information about this sport, rather than by empirically copying methods used to coach the current champions.

REFERENCES

Craig, A. B., Jr., and Pendergast, D. R. 1978. Relationships of stroke rate, distance per stroke and velocity in competitive swimming. Submitted for publication.

di Prampero, P. E., Pendergast, D. R., Wilson, D. W., and Rennie, D. W. 1974. Energetics of swimming in man. J. Appl. Physiol. 37:1-4.

Holmér, I. 1975. Physiology of swimming man. Acta Physiol. Scand. 407(suppl.): 1-53.

Margaria, R., Cerretelli, P., Aghemo, P., and Sassi, G. 1963. Energy cost of running. J. Appl. Physiol. 18:367-370.

Pendergast, D. R., di Prampero, P. E., Craig, Jr., A. B., Wilson, D. W., and Rennie, D. W. 1977. Quantitative analysis of the front crawl in men and women. J. Appl. Physiol., Respirat. Environ. Exercise Physiol. 43:475-479.

Use of a Heart Rate Meter in Swimming and Athletic Performance Measurement

R. J. Treffene, J. Alloway, and J. Jull

Swimming efficiency has been investigated by many researchers, including Holmér (1974) and di Prampero et al. (1974). di Prampero and his associates deduced a relationship between swimming efficiency (E), body drag (Db), swimming speed (V), and net oxygen uptake (V_{O_2}).

Using two submaximal speeds (0.55 and 0.90 m/sec) di Prampero et al. (1974) showed that E/Db remained relatively constant in this range. Treffene (1975) investigated the relationship between the velocity of swimming and heart rate (HR) for swimmers and suggested that a linear relationship existed and yielded a constant value for E/Db.

The use of heart rates to evaluate swimming performance requires a technique to measure heart rate. The technique described here requires a test in a swimming pool that is similar to a bicycle ergometer test. If a subject swims for more than 2 min at a constant pace, his heart rate will become steady after about 40 sec. This steady rate is characteristic of the use of oxygen at that speed. Therefore, if the heart rate is measured either during the swim or "immediately" after the swim, that rate is an indirect measure of the oxygen consumption at that speed. It is important to determine the heart rate immediately after the swim or within 5 sec of cessation of the exercise because the heart rates of elite swimmers decrease very rapidly.

This study was directed at using a heart rate meter constructed for pool heart rate measurement to determine the velocity–heart rate curves for swimmers.

METHODS AND APPARATUS

A heart rate meter was specially designed for use with swimmers. It is now commercially available from Heart Rate Industries (48 Goldieslie Rd., Indooroopilly, Brisbane, Australia).

275

Heart rate can be measured instantaneously by applying two electrodes to the body. The insulated electrodes can be applied by an assistant or by the subject if they are simply pressed against the subject's skin. Alternatively, the electrodes can be connected permanently by using a rubber belt, or 3M red dot disposable electrodes can be used for more vigorous activity.

To record a swimmer's heart rate, a stable heart beat can be obtained within two heart beats by touching an electrode while at the side of the pool. The instrument can be facing the swimmer, or it can be held by a coach. The digital readout indicates the time interval between heart pulses (using the ECG). A table for direct conversion to heart rate is attached permanently to the small, light, plastic heart rate meter container (4.75 × 2.5 inches; weight, 200 g [7 oz]). It is small enough to be carried in a shirt pocket.

Heart rate can be measured: 1) during activity—e.g., in squash, track and field, bicycle ergometry, 2) after an activity such as swimming or track and field by immediately touching the electrodes or, except in the case of swimming, by carrying the meter on one's person, 3) in hospital situations where pulse is difficult to take (3M electrodes applied at two sites on opposite sides of the body will normally register a pulse), and 4) from any commercial ECG (special lead is needed).

The electrical signal activity in the heart that causes the ventricles to contract spreads throughout the body. Thus, if two suitable electrodes are placed on two parts of the body, a voltage will be generated between them, which is repeated with every heart beat.

The QRS signal of the ECG is used to trigger a counter, and the time between QRS spikes is read digitally in milliseconds. If this time is divided into 60, a heart rate count in beats per minute can be obtained—e.g., 400 msec is a heart rate of $60/400 \times 10^{-3} = 150$ beats/min. A chart is provided for easy conversion, and some conversion values are included on the face of the meter. The sensitivity knob, which can be rotated with two fingers, controls the gain of the amplifiers. The gain should be turned down so that the heart beat light indicator only blinks once per heart rate cycle. This can be checked by having the subject feel the carotid pulse in his neck with two fingers while he leans his head slightly to one side. Each carotid pulse will coincide with the red flashing light. The number that appears will vary from beat to beat, and at rest it will be quite variable in most athletes. For example, the pulse interval for an athlete could be 1200, 1040, 923, 950, 1010, in five beats. This is a natural respiratory control phenomenon called sinus arrhythmia. It is recommended that the highest and lowest readings of 10 beats be taken for a resting pulse rate count and recorded as resting HR, 60–82 beats/min.

On exercise, the heart rate will increase, and if it exceeds 120 beats/min, the marked difference in pulse intervals in consecutive beats cease. For example, 450, 453, 452, 454, would by typical values over four consecutive beats. If values twice as great as those expected occur every few beats, the sensitivity is set too low and should be increased slightly so that every beat is counted.

Best results are obtained by attaching or holding (using the plastic insulating cups) one electrode to the sternum and the other electrode at a position 3 or 4 inches below the nipple (or the subject may hold one electrode in his left hand). Position of attachment is not important as long as the two electrodes occupy two distinct positions relative to the left and right sides of the heart—e.g., forehead and stomach, left and right hand, left and right feet, carotid and left hand.

In the swimming pool one of the electrodes is immersed in the pool water and kept still, and the other is touched by the swimmer (who stands with his chest out of water) or held by him on his chest. The full chest should be out of the water. Readings should appear within two beats if the sensitivity setting is adjusted correctly. Some subjects with higher skin resistance may need to have the sensitivity increased to give stable readings.

The electrode pads should be applied with gel only rarely and the pad may be washed and reused. Normal tap water can be used to wet the pads, but this should be done only sparingly. Pool water is a good conductor and is excellent for use on the pads.

The electrodes can be used for bicycle ergometry by inserting them in holes in a rubber belt so that they are held in place on the subject. Best results will be obtained by standard preparation procedures for ECG electrodes, although direct application is normally successful. The rubber belt attachment is satisfactory for recovery work for runners, where movement is fairly limited, and also for bicycle ergometer work. For more vigorous sports or improved readings, 3M red dots or any fixed attached electrodes similar to type 650418 Beckman electrodes can be used.

The efficiency of swimmers can be determined by having the subject swim: 1) six laps at 50 sec (constant lap time) (measure HR by hand touch at end of swim), then 2) six laps at 45 sec, 3) eight laps at 40 sec, and finally 4) eight laps at 35 sec. If a swimmer is unable to hold a steady velocity in 35-sec laps because of lack of skill, he should rest and swim six laps at 55 sec.

Plot velocity (length of pool/time) (abscissa) against heart rate (ordinate); the gradient is a measure of the ratio of swimmer's efficiency to body drag in beats per min/m per sec. Four swimmers can be measured simultaneously by having them swim two laps apart.

Now request the subject to swim 200 m all-out and measure the heart rate immediately upon finishing. Extrapolate the curve to find the speed

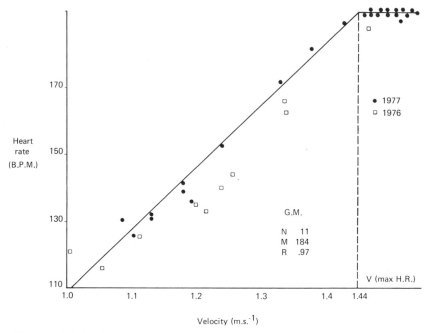

Figure 1. Relationship between heart rate and freestyle swimming velocity for subject G. M. in 1976 and 1977.

at which the swimmer would first reach maximal heart rate. The swimmer is not always able to swim at the required speeds, but he is allowed to continue swimming as long as a steady velocity is maintained.

Previous work using both the heart rate meter and a hand-touch radiotelemetry electrocardiogram has been reported (Treffene, 1977). Velocity–heart rate curves were linear at submaximal speeds for 20 subjects. By extrapolating the plotted lines to the maximal heart rate of the swimmer, which was obtained by using the heart rate for a maximum 200-m freestyle, the speed (V_{HR}^{max}) at which maximal heart rate is first reached is determined. Four subjects were chosen from the original sample of 20 for extensive testing for 1 week. Heart rates were measured at rest in the water and after two or three controlled speeds and after maximum 200-m swim.

RESULTS

Typical results are illustrated in Figure 1 for subject G. M. Linear regression gave a line, HR = 184 V = 78, with a regression coefficient of 0.97. For comparison, values obtained at the end of the previous training season are also plotted. Values for gradient (m), V_{HR}^{max}, regression coefficient

Table 1. Gradient (m), maximum heart rate velocity, and recent best time in 100 m for four subjects

Subject	Trials (n)	HR$_{max}$ (beats/min)	r	m(beats/ min/m-sec	V$_{HR}$^{max} (m/sec)	100 m (sec)
GM	11	190	0.97	184	1.44	56.5
SB	9	187	0.95	154	1.06	85
TH	9	178	0.95	177	1.225	74
JG	11	186	0.94	202	1.32	67

(R), sample number (N), maximum HR, and recent best 100-m times for all four subjects are given in Table 1.

DISCUSSION

The results for HR/velocity curves for all subjects show good linearity ($r \geq 0.94$) at high velocities. The gradients of these curves are calculated to give an index of ability; the lower the gradient, the more efficient the swimmer. Subject G. M. experienced a definite shift to a higher gradient compared with gradients obtained at the end of the previous season. This was probably caused by a lower V_{O_2}^{max} at this early stage of the swimming season. The change in gradient means that the speed at which G. M. first swims at maximum heart rate has decreased over the winter months. In lap times this has altered from 32-sec laps to 34-sec laps. This lowest velocity at maximum HR can be calculated by extrapolating the linear plot to the maximum heart rate of the swimmer. This information can be used to determine the training load for that particular swimmer. Endurance events are swum at a speed just slightly higher than V_{HR}^{max}.

The speed at which the oxygen uptake first reached a maximum was suggested as the best endurance training speed by Kipke (1978), an East German researcher. He indicated that elite swimmers showed a decrease in oxygen use at speeds higher than the lowest speeds eliciting a maximum V_{O_2} uptake.

The heart rate meter has also been used to determine heart rates during interval training, so that a better understanding of the physiology of training routines can be obtained. Recovery from maximal heart rates to 150–170 beats/min during 15-sec rests is normal.

All 100-m intervals brought the heart rate to a maximum if the pace was above V_{HR}^{max}. When the pace fell below this value, the heart rate recorded was below maximum swimming heart rate.

In the next series of experiments, an attempt will be made to formulate a prediction table for optimal pool length times for best performance over various distances.

REFERENCES

di Prampero, P. E., Pendergast, D. R., Wilson, D. W., and Pennie, D. W. 1974. Energetics of swimming in man. J. Appl. Physiol. 37:1-5.

Holmér, I. 1974. Physiology of swimming man. Acta Physiol. Scand. 407(suppl.): 1-53.

Kipke, L. 1978. Dynamics of oxygen uptake during step-by-step loading in a swimming flume. In: B. Eriksson and B. Furberg (eds.), Swimming Medicine IV, pp. 137-142. University Park Press, Baltimore.

Treffene, R. J. 1975. Investigation of the ECG in sports and sports medicine using radiotelemetry. Master's thesis, University of London, London.

Treffene, R. J., Frampton, C., Tunstall, P. D., and Idle, M. 1977. Energetics of swimming using heart rate telemetry. Proceedings of the 13th Annual Conference of the Australian Sports Medicine Federation, August, 1976.

Variations in the Front Crawl and Back Crawl Arm Strokes of Varsity Swimmers Using Hand Paddles

L. J. Stoner and D. L. Luedtke

Increased use of hand paddles as a training device for competitive swimmers has led to a diversity of opinion regarding the value of such training. It has been claimed that hand paddles increase strength and improve stroke patterns, although at least one author (Anderson, 1976) questions the use of hand paddles for development of speed. Anderson suggests further that hand paddles may be of greater value to the beginner than the skilled swimmer. This study was done to determine arm pattern differences in varsity swimmers as they executed both the front crawl stroke and the back crawl stroke with and without hand paddles.

PROCEDURES

Subjects were eight college varsity swimmers (four males and four females) who had used hand paddles for training purposes for at least one season before this study. At least half of the subjects were national contenders in the small college championships in the United States. Each subject performed three trials of each stroke using hand paddles and three trials of back crawl without hand paddles at a practice pace. Male subjects used large paddles (195 × 128 × 2.5 mm), and female subjects used medium paddles (187 × 119 × 2.5 mm), which were anchored to the hand by a single strap over the middle finger. Modern Swimming Concepts hand paddles were used by all swimmers. Black and white quadrant targets, 50 mm in diameter, were placed on the joint centers of the wrist, elbow, and shoulder of each arm. Subjects were filmed as they swam directly toward an underwater camera; a second camera filmed the side view above the water.

A 16-mm Photo Sonics 1PL motor-driven camera was located at an underwater window, and a 16-mm Bell and Howell model 70DL spring-driven camera was located on the pool deck to film an above-water side view. Both cameras operated at 50 frames/sec. The start of the event was identified synchronously on the two cameras using the strobe flash units and a slave unit to trigger the second flash, as established by Ben-Sira, Stoner, and Luedtke (1978). One flash unit was located at a second underwater window directly opposite the window that housed the underwater camera. This flash was positioned to direct the flash toward the water surface at a 45° angle with the horizontal. The second flash unit, triggered by a slave unit, was placed above water at the pool's edge and directed toward the above-water camera (Figure 1).

Data reduction was done with a 16-mm Lafayette motion analyzer model 0100 that was projected against a vertical wall. A t-test for dependent means was used to contrast the hand paddle and normal performance for all variables. Measurements were taken from the underwater film for all variables except forward hand travel, which utilized the above-water film. For the front crawl the variables were: elbow angle at the deepest point, elbow angle at the narrowest point, time of underwater hand travel, distance of forward hand travel, and the pattern width of the two hands at the deepest and narrowest positions. Variables for the back crawl included: angle of shoulder roll, elbow angle, wrist angle, shoulder-humerus angle, elbow depth, hand depth, width of pull, and pulling time.

RESULTS AND DISCUSSION

Front Crawl

Results are presented for the right hand in Table 1 and for the left hand in Table 2. During the pulling phase the elbow angle of the left arm at the deepest position was significantly smaller when the swimmers used hand paddles. Elbow angles for the right arm were not significantly different at either the deepest or narrowest points of the pull. At both the deepest and narrowest points of the pull for each arm the mean elbow angle was greater than the 90°–100° suggested by Counsilman (1968, 1977).

For both right and left arms, more time was spent in the underwater phase of the front crawl when the subjects used hand paddles. This probably was the result of the increased surface area provided by the paddle. Schleihauf (1974) demonstrated that the hand tends to exit forward of the entry point in the front crawl, so this distance was also measured. Because some subjects traveled out of the camera view, fewer subjects were used to determine t ratios. Mean differences for the right hand were not significant; however, left-forward hand travel was significantly greater when hand paddles were used ($N = 6$; $t = 2.59$ for $P < 0.05$).

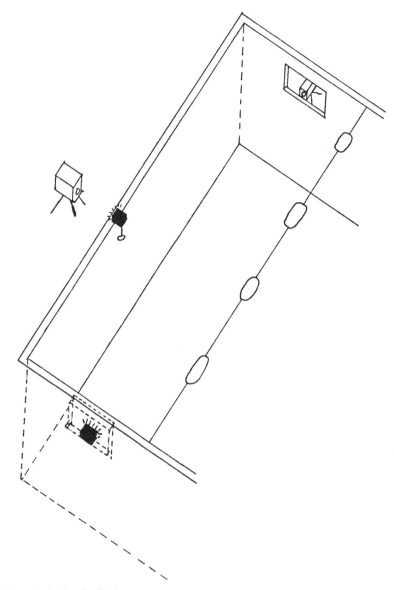

Figure 1. Setting for filming.

The width of the pull at the deepest and narrowest points of the stroke pattern was taken as the distance of lateral excursion between left and right arms. At the deepest point of the pull, the mean pattern width was 20.2 cm without paddles and 26.0 cm with paddles; these values were not significantly different. The width of the pull at the narrowest point

Table 1. Means, standard deviations, and t ratios for front crawl right arm ($N = 8$)

		No hand paddle	Hand paddle	t Ratio
Elbow angle (deepest point)	$\overline{X}$	124.63°	124.13°	0.19
	SD	17.67	20.18	
Elbow angle narrow	$\overline{X}$	114.00°	110.75°	0.66
(greatest medial position)	SD	15.67	22.95	
Distance (cm) of hand travel	$\overline{X}$	68.4	92.6	2.25
(entry to exit)	SD	27.4	30.5	($N = 7$)
Time (sec) of total underwater	$\overline{X}$	1.40	1.55	4.05[a]
hand travel	SD	0.22	0.22	

[a]The t ratio is significant at the 0.05 level for $N = 8$; $t = 2.36$ for $P < 0.05$.

was significantly greater (t $= -4.16$) when hand paddles were used. Thus, it seems that the swimmer maintains a similar width pattern with hand paddles at the deepest point of the stroke but pulls wider at the point below the body when the stroke pattern is at the narrowest point.

Back Crawl

Angle measurements are presented for the right hand in Table 3 and the left hand in Table 4. In all subjects the angle formed by the line connecting right and left shoulder targets and the horizontal consistently reached a maximum just before or simultaneously with the deepest elbow position of the pull pattern. This maximum angle and the shoulder angle at lowest elbow position were not significantly different when hand paddles were used. The angle of this shoulder line with the horizontal at the point of lowest hand position was also not significant and tended to be negative,

Table 2. Means, standard deviations, and t ratios for front crawl left arm ($N = 8$)

		No hand paddle	Hand paddle	t Ratio
Elbow angle (deepest point)	$\overline{X}$	132.38°	126.50°	2.37[a]
	SD	12.73	12.29	
Elbow angle narrow	$\overline{X}$	111.75°	113.25°	0.63
(greatest medial position)	SD	13.30	7.83	
Distance (cm) of hand travel	$\overline{X}$	80.8	102.1	3.41[a]
(entry to exit)	SD	35.7	35.6	($N = 6$)
Time (sec) of total underwater	$\overline{X}$	1.42	1.54	2.60[a]
hand travel	SD	0.17	0.22	

[a]The t ratio is significant at the 0.05 level for $N = 8$; $t = 2.36$ for $P < 0.05$.

Table 3. Means, standard deviations, and t ratios for pattern angles of back crawl, right arm ($N = 8$)

		No hand paddle	Hand paddle	t Ratio[a]
Maximum shoulder	$\overline{X}$	40.0°	38.8°	0.40
roll	SD	7.0	9.2	
Midway shoulder				
roll (deepest	$\overline{X}$	29.0°	35.1°	0.88
elbow position)	SD	6.8	14.0	
Shoulder roll				
(deepest hand	$\overline{X}$	−3.8[ob]	−2.3[ob]	0.45
position)	SD	9.6	13.0	
Elbow angle				
(deepest elbow	$\overline{X}$	125.4°	126.7°	0.20
position)	SD	14.6	16.3	
Wrist angle				
(deepest elbow	$\overline{X}$	166.2°	167.6°	0.33
position)	SD	11.7	6.8	
Shoulder-humerus,				
angle (deepest	$\overline{X}$	161.2°	163.1°	0.33
elbow position)	SD	15.5	16.2	
Shoulder-humerus				
angle (lowest	$\overline{X}$	96.9°	91.0°	1.55
hand position)	SD	16.5	12.6	

[a]The t ratio is significant at the $P < 0.05$ ($t = 2.36$) for $N = 8$.
[b]Negative value indicates roll toward nonpulling side.

demonstrating that the pulling shoulder was higher than the nonpulling shoulder before the pulling hand left the water. The shoulder joint angle, formed by the shoulder line and the humerus of the pulling arm, was significantly greater at the low elbow position of the stroke for the left-hand paddle condition. The shoulder joint angle that was formed at the end of the pull (at the lowest hand position), however, was not significantly different for either hand.

Counsilman (1977) indicated that the elbow angle for the deepest elbow position should not exceed 90°-110° and that a more extended elbow was a common error in back stroke performance. Varsity swimmers in this study clearly exceeded this elbow angle in both the paddle and no-paddle conditions, demonstrating elbow angle means of ca. 132° for the left hand and 125° for the right hand. The use of hand paddles did not alter this angle significantly. Wrist angles at this stroke position of deepest elbow angle were also not significantly different when hand paddles were used.

One might expect that the width of pull or depth of pull would be affected by the use of hand paddles; however, the width of pull as measured

Table 4. Means, standard deviations, and t ratios for pattern angles of back crawl, left arm ($N = 8$)

		No hand paddle	Hand paddle	t Ratio
Maximum shoulder roll	$\overline{X}$	37.9°	36.7°	0.63
	SD	8.4	8.8	
Shoulder roll (midway)	$\overline{X}$	28.9°	29.9°	0.45
	SD	7.8	9.3	
Shoulder roll (deepest	$\overline{X}$	−5.4[o,b]	−7.0[o,b]	0.49
hand position)	SD	8.9	8.5	
Elbow angle (deepest	$\overline{X}$	132.7°	130.8°	0.41
elbow position)	SD	16.7	15.4	
Wrist angle (deepest	$\overline{X}$	164.8°	170.8°	1.27
elbow position)	SD	16.7	9.2	
Shoulder-humerus angle	$\overline{X}$	166.6°	163.2°	2.83[a]
(deepest elbow position)	SD	9.1	8.0	
Shoulder-humerus angle	$\overline{X}$	102.8°	104.0°	0.31
(lowest hand position)	SD	7.8	12.7	

[a]The t ratio is significant at the $P < 0.05$ ($t = 2.36$) for $N = 8$.
[b]Negative value indicates roll toward nonpulling side.

from the wrist target was not significantly changed by the use of hand paddles. The depth of the pattern, however, changed significantly when hand paddles were used. Subjects pulled with a deeper elbow position and finished with a higher (less deep) hand position at the end of the final elbow extension for the pulling arm on the left. The authors suggest that the information presented thus far seems to indicate that very few changes occur in the back crawl stroke pattern when hand paddles are used. For these eight varsity swimmers the adjustments were such that the left arm

Table 5. Means, standard deviations, and t ratios for width, depth, and time of pull for back crawl, right arm ($N = 8$)

		No hand paddle	Hand paddle	t Ratio
Elbow depth (cm)	$\overline{X}$	25.6	27.2	1.02
(at deepest point)	SD	6.9	6.0	
Lowest hand depth (cm)	$\overline{X}$	44.5	41.7	0.86
	SD	13.7	11.6	
Width of pull (cm) (at	$\overline{X}$	55.6	54.8	0.65
deepest elbow position)	SD	1.2	1.4	
Time (sec) of pull	$\overline{X}$	1.27	1.43	4.89[a]
	SD	0.17	0.15	

[a]The t ratio is significant at the $P < 0.05$ ($t = 2.36$) for $N = 8$.

Table 6. Means, standard deviations, and t ratios for width, depth, and time of pull for back crawl, left arm ($N = 8$)

		No hand paddle	Hand paddle	t Ratio
Elbow depth (cm)	$\overline{X}$	22.3	26.7	2.74[a]
(at deepest point)	SD	6.1	5.1	
Lowest hand depth (cm)	$\overline{X}$	47.9	43.6	2.40[a]
	SD	7.9	7.6	
Width of pull (cm) (at	$\overline{X}$	63.3	57.7	0.42
deepest elbow position)	SD	11.6	6.9	
Time (sec) of pull	$\overline{X}$	1.31	1.45	4.03[a]
	SD	0.15	0.76	

[a]The t ratio is significant at the $P < 0.05$ ($t = 2.36$) for $N = 8$.

had a deeper elbow position and a smaller shoulder joint angle at the point of greatest elbow depth and a higher left-hand position at stroke completion when hand paddles were used. This alteration seems to be consistent with the concept of a symmetrical pulling action of the right and left arms for the back crawl, indicating that the adjustment that was made because hand paddles were used really moves the subject toward a more symmetrical use of the left and right arms.

Temporal aspects of the pulling pattern are presented in Table 5 for the right hand and Table 6 for the left hand. As reported for the front crawl, significantly more time was spent in the pulling phase of the back crawl when hand paddles were used. This was true for both left and right hands. Of the total time spent in pulling, ca. 60% was spent from the initial catch of the hand to the point of lowest elbow position, and the remaining 40% of the pull occurred in the final downward pushing action both for hand paddle and no-hand paddle conditions. The additional time spent in pulling was expected because of the additional surface area for pulling that the hand paddle provides.

SUMMARY AND CONCLUSION

Varsity swimmers who use hand paddles do not seem to make major alterations in either front or back crawl stroke patterns, although the amount of time spent in pulling is increased. In the front crawl, although the elbow angle for the left hand was smaller at the deepest position when paddles were used, the stroke pattern was similar through the deepest position and slightly wider at the narrowest position directly under the body. In performing the back crawl there was evidence that swimmers made adjustments that resulted in greater symmetry of their right- and left-arm pulls. The authors conclude that hand paddles do not greatly alter the front or back crawl stroke patterns for varsity swimmers and thus may not be useful as a device for stroke development in proficient swimmers. However, this does not rule out their use for stroke development in the beginner, as suggested by Anderson (1976).

REFERENCES

Anderson, P. 1976. The use of hand paddles, overload training and after effects. Swimming Tech. 13(2):60–62.

Ben-Sira, D., Stoner, L. J., and Luedtke, D. L. 1978. A simple procedure for event marking when filming with one or two cameras. Res. Q. 49(3):381–384.

Counsilman, J. E. 1968. The Science of Swimming. Prentice-Hall, Inc., Englewood Cliffs, New Jersey.

Counsilman, J. E. 1977. Competitive Swimming Manual for Coaches and Swimmers. Counsilman Company, Inc., Bloomington.

Schleihauf, R. D. 1974. A biomechanical analysis of freestyle. Swimming Tech. 11(3):91–96.

Swim Fin Design Utilizing Principles of Marine Animal Locomotion

E. R. Lewis and D. Lorch

Man has been active in the sea for as long as he has walked on the earth, but only in the past 100 years has technology been used to develop better devices for underwater exploration and mobility. However, we have not advanced very far in the area of underwater self-propulsion; even small fishes can easily outswim man.

Scuba divers rely on their legs for propulsion; they use swim fins to increase kicking forces and to help resolve the sideways motion into thrust that is directed parallel to the diver's body. To improve underwater locomotion, it is necessary to design better swim fins. To accomplish this, it is first desirable to learn as much as possible about the swim dynamics of fishes and the dynamics of underwater locomotion.

PURPOSE

The purposes of this investigation were: 1) to determine the mechanical efficiency of commercially available swim fins in order to evaluate the feasibility of design improvements, and 2) to make several design changes to fins, utilizing principles of marine animal locomotion, and to compare swimming performances with these new fins with performances with commercial fins.

Studies of Fish Locomotion

Studies by Lang and Daybell (1960) have shown that the swimming power of dolphins, as indicated by hydrodynamic theory, is five to ten times greater than the capabilities of their muscle. Researchers have discovered that salmon use far less fat and protein than required by known drag data (Bret, 1965). Navy tests have shown that sea animals can move through water with great efficiency because they can maintain laminar flow over most of their body (Rosen, 1959; Lang and Daybell, 1960). It is now known how this is accomplished. Experiments conducted on the Pacific barracuda (Rosen and Cornford, 1972) indicate that its capabilities for high speed swimming may depend a great deal on the thin layer of slime solution on its skin, which suppresses turbulence and lowers water friction.

Another possible explanation for the efficient propulsion of a fish is that the sideways motion of its head sets up alternate vortex centers against which the fish's sides and tail can push with very little slippage (Rosen, 1959). The motion of this vortex system is such that the fluid flow next to the fish's skin may be very low; this would significantly reduce skin friction, and it may be the reason why a fish can maintain laminar flow over most of its body. When this author dissected a bluefish, unusual tail characteristics were noted. The two main branches of the tail are pivoted at right angles to the plane of the tail oscillations. The water loads on these two main branches, and on the center membrane, spread the tail wide apart during the stroke. Perhaps this is why the fin has been observed to bend less at midstroke, where the thrust forces are greatest, than at the ends of the stroke. When the fin is spread, the tension field on the stretched fin membrane offers additional strength to the fin, thus minimizing bending strain. The bony rays of the tail fin do not seem to follow Hook's Law after a small deflection. This may result from the action of the gelatinous material within the fin rays that acts as a hydraulic lock. No such measurements were made on the fin, so that this is a fertile area for further investigation.

Studies done on living fishes to photograph the surrounding flow patterns have always been difficult to conduct (Rosen, 1959; Kent, 1961). Attempts were made to perform similar tests using a water tunnel but were unsuccessful because good pictures could not be obtained. At present, no one knows the amount of thrust developed by a fish's tail fin or body or the nature of the interaction between them. It is not certain that the fish's V tail is the most efficient oscillating propulsion system or whether or not it must be considered in combination with the head motion.

Factors in Designing Underwater Propulsion Systems   Swim fins have not changed in shape drastically from those first produced in the early 1940s. The only significant improvements have been the increase in fin stiffness and surface area. Preliminary experiments and studies were done to determine the problems of underwater propulsion for the scuba diver and to investigate possible solutions to these problems. Before designing new swim fins, several commercial fins were evaluated for their efficiency. Figure 1 shows three types of commercial fins, types A, B, and C. Then several types of fins were designed, using information on marine animal locomotion, and the performances with the new fins were com-

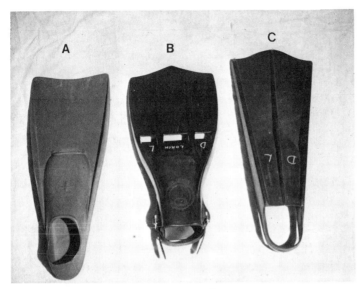

Figure 1. Commercial swim fins, types A, B, and C.

pared with the commercial fins. In designing the new fins, consideration was given to the fact that stiff fins should be used for high speeds, and flexible fins should be used for low speeds. The fish's tail seems to have this ideal self-adjusting stiffness. However, it was recognized that it would be most difficult to design a fin to function in this manner, even though it is the most efficient.

SWIM FIN DESIGN

Figure 2 shows an experimental type D swim fin. Its base plate was designed with two things in mind: 1) to enable several types of fin blades to be tested with a minimum of reworking, and 2) to provide as large a separation of the two attachment straps as possible, so that the fin forces transmitted to the ankle would be minimized and the swimmer would not get leg cramps.

The aluminum fish blade could flex only at the attachment to the base plate; otherwise it was rigid over its entire length. The blade was made as wide as possible without permitting the fins to strike each other when the swimmer's legs crossed. Since the fins did not flex much, the swimmer had to adjust the fin's angle of attack by allowing his ankle to bend just enough to get maximum thrust. The angle extrusions along the side provided stiffness and acted as end plates, which would reduce turbulence near the edges of the fin and, therefore, improve the thrust effi-

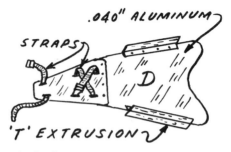

Figure 2. Experimental swim fin, type D.

ciency. The V cutout was made to resemble the tail of a fin, so that enough water would move toward this cutout to reduce the tip turbulence further.

The fin blade of type E (Figure 3) was designed to approximate the shape of a fish's tail. The two fiberglass rods on both sides of the blade provided stiffness for the vinyl plastic sheet. Because the rods were mounted rigidly, they did not perfectly simulate the action of the bony rays in a fish's tail, which spread under load. The fins were also made as wide as possible without permitting them to interfere when the swimmer's legs crossed.

These fins were constructed to test whether or not it would be possible to improve efficiency by reducing fin-tip vortices (induced drag) by allowing water to flow through the center of the V. Squared-off fins, with no V cutout, have a low aspect ratio and, therefore, a large induced drag. The resultant force on these fin blades is developed near the base rather than at the ends. Likewise, the resultant thrust of a fish's tail would also be close to the base of the tail, enabling the fish to get maximum thrust, but the bending moment arm would be small. When this principle is applied to swim fins, a small moment arm results in minimum ankle-bending loads and, therefore, less chance of leg cramps.

The type F leg fin shown in Figure 4 was designed to enable the swimmer to handle very high fin loads without concern for ankle flexing. These fins were attached to the calf of the swimmer rather than to his foot.

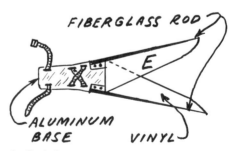

Figure 3. Type E swim fin design.

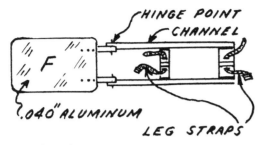

Figure 4. Type F swim fin design.

Because alternate kicking was used, the width of the fin blades was limited to avoid interference, but the length and stiffness of the blade were unrestricted. If the rectangular blade had functioned successfully, other blade shapes using this support system would have been tried.

PROCEDURES

Drag Test

A spring scale was calibrated and then connected to a 5-m long rope. One end of the rope was attached to the back pack of the scuba diver, and the other end, with the spring scale attached, was pulled by an assistant. A distance of 4 m was provided to enable the assistant who pulled the tow line to stabilize the force applied. The assistant maintained this force while he towed the subject 10 m. The plot of drag force versus speed[2] is shown in Figure 5.

Leg Forces

To measure the leg forces during swimming, the same spring scale used for towing was attached to the diver's ankle at 90° with his leg. The test subject lay on his side and applied leg forces similar to what he thought he applied while swimming at 0.86 m/sec. A plot of fin force versus leg distance is given in Figure 6.

To obtain a meaningful comparison of the overall performance of the various fins, it was necessary to devise a fin performance factor, P, where:

$$P = \frac{\text{distance/kick cycle}}{(\text{change of tank pressure)(time})}$$

The distance/kick cycle was determined by having the subject swim 15m with skin diving equipment (no scuba tank) while an assistant counted the kick cycles. Air consumption and time were determined for the subject who used scuba equipment while swimming underwater 229

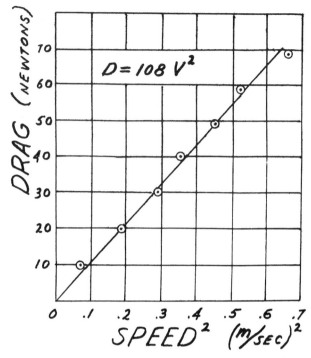

Figure 5. Drag versus speed². Subject, 160 lb, 5 ft, 10 inches tall, with 72 ft³ scuba rocket jet fins, wet suit top, and 6-lb weight belt.

m. The air consumed was proportional to the change of pressure in the tank. Before the initial pressure was measured, the tank was placed in the pool for 30 min to permit the air temperature inside the tank to reach water temperature. The test subject maintained an uncomfortable water speed to keep from holding his breath and going into oxygen debt. This technique provided a reasonably accurate measurement of air consumption.

RESULTS

Mechanical Efficiency of Commercial Fins (Type B)

The conditions were 0.82 leg cycle/sec with a water speed of 0.86 m/sec. The Leg power input (see Figure 6) was:

$$\text{Total work for one leg cycle} = 88 \text{ J/cycle}$$

$$\text{Work for both legs} = 2 \times 88 = 176 \text{ J/cycle}$$

The power input was 176 J/cycle × 0.82 cycle/sec = 144 W.

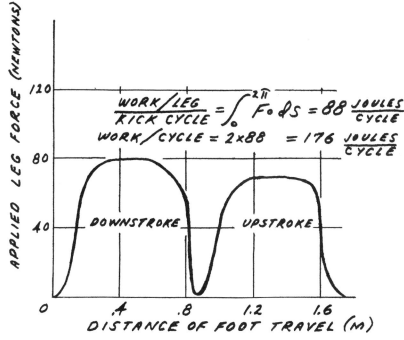

Figure 6. Applied leg force versus distance of foot travel.

The fin performance factors and the mechanical efficiency were calculated. The mechanical efficiencies were determined by assuming a direct relationship between fin performance factor and mechanical efficiency. These computations were based on one of the three commercial fins evaluated, fin B, shown in Figure 1. This fin had an efficiency of 48% and a performance factor of 1.86. The tabulations of results for six types of fins are shown in Table 1.

Table 1.   Performance factors and efficiencies for six fin types

Fin type	Change in tank pressure (lb/inches^2)	Time (sec)	Distance/ kick cycle (m/cycle)	Performance factor (m/ cycle/psi-sec)	Efficiency (%)
A	250	265	1.30	1.96×10^{-5}	50
B	285	270	1.43	1.86	48
C	275	255	1.50	2.14	55
D	275	285	1.15	1.47	38
E	280	280	1.50	1.91	49
F	—	—	1.15	—	—

These tests and calculations indicate that commercial swim fins are much more efficient mechanically than anyone had suspected (48-55%). However, if the determination of the power input is incorrect by 10% or 20%, the efficiency is far greater than the 3% physiological efficiency reported by Goff, Brubach, and Specht (1957). This would indicate that there must be some physiological reason why an underwater swimmer utilizes so much oxygen. Perhaps it has something to do with the body's utilizing oxygen to maintain body temperature through increased oxidation of fats and protein. Even if a diver wears a wet suit, he will still lose a great deal of heat through his head. It would be easy to conduct tests to verify this point.

Also, if swim fins were 100% mechanically efficient and the diver maintained a comfortable 0.82 kick cycle/sec, he would be able to attain a speed of only 1.1 m/sec. This is not very encouraging. In fact, when the maximum possible speed was calculated using the maximum possible mean thrust, 178 N, it was determined that a diver could reach the top speed of 1.28 m/sec.

The drag data (Figure 5) and the empirical equation for drag as a function of swim speed can be used for future studies of underwater swimmers.

Performance of New Fins

The base plate functioned well, and the swimmer experienced small ankle loads with both fin blades, D and E. Actually, much larger fin forces could have been handled with this base plate, but it was not possible to make the fins wider without having them interfere during swimming, and if the length were increased, ankle loads would be too large. The rigid blade did not seem to offer any advantage over a flexible rubber one.

The type E fin performed well at low ankle forces. Much larger forces could have been handled, but interference of the fins with alternate kicking prevented this. Because it seems that the tail of a fish is shaped to operate with a vortex system generated by the fish's head and because no such vortex system is generated by the swimmer, the V fin offers no advantage other than to shift the forces closer to the ankle.

The type F leg fins allowed large loads to be applied without ankle fatigue, but they were so awkward to use that the disadvantages outweighed any possible advantages.

The fin performance factor seems to be a very good measure of overall fin performance; a fin that is large and stiff will enable a diver to travel farther per kick cycle, but he will consume more oxygen in the process. If it is assumed that there is a direct relationship between fin performance factor and mechanical efficiency, the mechanical efficiencies of the fins tested vary from 38 to 55%.

CONCLUSIONS

The following conclusions are based on the results of this study.

1. The mechanical efficiency of most commercial swim fins is between 48% and 55%.
2. If underwater swimmers continue to use foot fins in the present manner, sustained underwater speeds will not exceed 1.5 m/sec. If higher speeds and greater ranges are to be attained, radically different types of fins will have to be used.
3. The fin with the best performance characteristics is type C. This type is presently being used by U. S. Navy underwater swimmers.

REFERENCES

Bret, J. R. 1965. The swimming energetics of salmon. Sci. Am. 213(2).

Goff, L. G., Brubach, H. F., and Specht, H. 1957. Measurement of respiratory responses and work efficiency of underwater swimmers utilizing improved instrumentation. J. Appl. Physiol. 10.

Kent, J. C. 1961. Flow visualization and drag about a swimming fish. NOTS Contract 123(60530)20579A. Fisheries Research Institution, College of Fisheries, University of Washington.

Lang, T. G., and Daybell, D. A. 1960. Results of performance tests conducted on a porpoise in a salt water tank. Technical Note P 508-13. U.S. Naval Ordnance Test Station, Pasadena Annex.

Rosen, M. 1959. Water flow about a swimming fish. NOTS TP 2298-ASTIA 238395. U.S. Naval Ordnance Test Station, China Lake, Cal.

Rosen, M., and Cornford, N. 1972. Pacific barracuda. Sea Frontiers 18(4).

Multiple-Victim
Body Contact Water Rescues

D. I. Miller and A. M. Dahl

Water accidents remain one of the leading causes of accidental death in Canada and the United States. Although reasonable volumes of literature have been accumulated on drowning statistics, physiological effects of drowning, and treatment of near-drowning (Modell, 1978), little is known of the details of successful water rescues (Miller and McQueen, 1978). Although lifesaving organizations, such as the American Red Cross, the Royal Life Saving Society, and the YMCA, teach methods of rescue, there is a lack of data to indicate whether or not the techniques taught are being used in actual emergency situations and whether or not they are effective.

In a recent survey of approximately 500 trained lifesavers, Dahl and Miller (1979) found that over 50% of the respondents had performed one or more swimming rescues involving direct body contact with the victim before reaching safety. The incidence of these "body contact rescues" (BCR) of conscious victims was much higher than expected because such techniques are categorized as "last resort—high risk" procedures by most lifesaving organizations.

More than 7% of the BCR incidents reported dealt with the rescue of more than one individual. Clearly, these multiple-victim accidents present the lifesaver with difficulties over and above those encountered in single-victim rescues. Because of the dearth of information on these situations, it was felt that it was important to analyze them separately in an attempt to identify probable causes of the emergencies, problems faced by the lifesavers, and rescue methods used. Descriptive information based on actual cases should be valuable in providing realistic situations for simulation and analysis in the initial and continuing education of lifesavers.

Supported in part by grants from the Council for National Cooperation in Aquatics and the Royal Life Saving Society Canada.

METHOD

The survey that was conducted to gather data on BCRs involved the use of two forms. The first was one page long and was intended to identify lifesaving experience and personal characteristics of the respondents. If the individuals had performed BCRs, they also completed a four-page questionnaire for each rescue that involved a single victim and/or a six-page questionnaire for each multiple-victim incident. These forms requested data on the rescuer, victim, water accident, rescue procedures, and outcome. Although most of the items required only a simple check response, provision was made for comments on the details of the rescue.

The questionnaires were administered to groups of trained lifesavers, lifeguards, and water safety instructors primarily in the Canadian provinces of British Columbia and Saskatchewan and in the state of Washington (U.S.). The general information portion of the survey was returned by 482 individuals. Of this group, 249 also completed a total of 372 forms describing the circumstances of BCRs of single victims (Dahl and Miller, 1979) and 29 forms containing information on water accidents involving two or more victims. Only the latter are the subject of this discussion. Because of the relatively few multiple-victim reports, a combined case study and descriptive approach was taken in the data analysis.

RESULTS AND DISCUSSION

At least 6% (29 of 482) of the respondents had been involved in multiple-victim body contact rescues (MVBCR). These rescues represented over 7% (29 of 401) of the total BCRs reported. At the time of the emergency, almost all the respondents were lifeguards and had previously received advanced lifesaving training (Table 1). Nine of the rescues occurred in lakes, seventeen in swimming pools, one in the ocean, and two in rivers (Table 2).

Nature of the Incident

Although two of the lake situations resulted from attempted rescues by weak swimmers, most (seven of nine) occurred when companions or family members were swimming or playing together. In two of these instances, the swimmer urged his companion to attempt something beyond his ability; a 10–14 year old boy who was "helping" his younger friend to swim to a raft 15–20 m distant and a young man who was persuading another to jump off a diving board into deep water. In the latter case, the individual, although a nonswimmer, claimed he knew how to swim, apparently to impress a young lady on shore. Even after the rescue, he maintained that he could swim at one time but had just forgotten how. These are concrete examples of peer pressure as a causal factor in water accidents.

Table 1. Characteristics of the rescuers ($N = 29$)

	N
Age (years)	
14–16	3
17–19	10
20–24	11
>24	5
Sex	
male	19
female	6
missing data	4
Lifesaving training	
none	1
advanced[a]	27
missing data	1
Activity at the time of the accident	
lifeguarding	26
bystander	2
boating	1

[a] Lifesaving or lifeguard training in addition to Bronze Medallion or Senior Life Saving.

Almost 30% of the cases in pools were related to one individual's supporting another in "piggy-back" fashion. An equivalent number of cases ($N = 5$) were precipitated by one swimmer's attempting to rescue another. In the latter incidents, it is significant that these persons took matters into their own hands rather than (or perhaps in addition to) sum-

Table 2. Location of multiple-victim accidents ($N = 29$)

	N
State/Province	
Washington	15
Georgia	1
British Columbia	7
Ontario	2
Saskatchewan	3
Quebec	1
Distance from Safety (m)	
<3	10
3–25	15
>25	3
missing data	1

Table 3.   Characteristics of the victims[a]

	N		N
Number involved			
Two	27	Sex	
Three	2	male (all)	11
Age (years)		female (all)	11
5-9 (all)	9	male and female	6
10-14 (all)	3	missing data	1
15-19 (all)	4	Swimming ability	
20-29 (all)	2	none (all)	5
0-4 and 5-9	2	weak (<25 m) (all)	10
5-9 and 10-14	4	none and weak	7
10-14 and 15-19	3	none and average	3
0-4 and 30-39	1	weak and average	3
10-14 and 40-59	1	average and good (>200 m)	1

[a]Grouped on a per-incident basis ($N = 29$) rather than individually ($N = 60$).

moning aid from a lifeguard. The remaining 41% ($N = 7$) involved companions of a similar age who were swimming together.

The ocean rescue dealt with two children who were taking a swimming test. One of the river incidents was caused by a canoe that capsized, throwing three adult males into the water. All were weak swimmers. The second river MVBCR involved two teenaged girls who were nonswimmers and were caught in a current. One subsequently required artificial respiration to revive her.

MVBCR Victims

Of the 60 victims, one was classified as a "good" swimmer, and three others were judged to be "average" (Table 3). The remaining 95% either could not swim at all or were not able to swim a distance of 25 m. It is also important that 42% of the victims were between 5 and 9 years old, a period of development when many children do not accurately know their abilities and tend to be somewhat overconfident.

Although it is common for children and beginning swimmers to be taught reaching assists for the safe rescue of others, the results of this study suggest that self-rescue techniques, termed "defense methods" by the Royal Life Saving Society Canada and "escapes" by the American Red Cross, should be included at the initial levels of swimming instruction. A simple straight arm block or push-away would probably suffice. There must also be continued emphasis that nonswimmers and weak swimmers stay within their depth. Evidently, many of the persons involved in MVBCRs have heeded the traditional advice of using the buddy system.

Attempts to Grab Rescuers

In 38% ($N = 11$) of all the MVBCR incidents, attempts were made to grab the lifesavers. These attempts seemed to occur at all stages of the rescue: during the approach, while the victims were being separated, and during the tow. In the pool rescues, five of the six grasps were made from the front and were around the lifesaver's wrist or arm. The four rescues in lakes that involved holds included two instances in which both victims simultaneously grasped the rescuer. Equal numbers ($N = 3$) of holds were applied from behind as from in front; they were around the head/neck ($N = 3$) and the body ($N = 3$). In the one ocean rescue, the lifesaver was grasped around the head from the side when he attempted to separate the victims. He noted that they made little or no noise when they were in distress but seemed "stronger than normal," making it difficult to break their grip.

Data from this portion of the survey dealing with multiple victims as well as those from the single-victim analysis indicated that a person can expect to be grasped in at least one out of every three body contact rescues. The victim's attempt to grasp the rescuer seems to be a natural self-preservation response, which may or may not jeopardize the rescuer's safety. In single-victim incidents, there were positive relationships ($P < 0.01$) between the perceived threat to the rescuer and the size of the victim as well as the distance from safety (Dahl and Miller, 1979).

In the multiple-victim situations, four of the rescuers, all adult male lifeguards, felt endangered by the hold of the victim(s), three minimally and one severely. In the first three instances, the victims were two 10–14-year-old females (pool, 3–25 m from edge), two 5–9-year-old boys (lake, 3–25 m from shore), and two 20–24-year-old adult males (lake, 2 m from shore). The one severe threat was reported during the rescue of two 10–14-year-old girls who were more than 25 m from shore in a lake under cold and choppy conditions. One girl, an average swimmer, got into difficulty, and her friend, a good swimmer, tried to keep her afloat and called for help. The rescuer used a tired-swimmer's carry on the original victim, but on the way back to shore, the second girl tired and panicked. She grabbed the rescuer around the neck from behind. The lifesaver struck her and then used a double tired-swimmer's carry. Unlike most of the holds in single-victim rescues, which were made during the approach, from the front, and around the rescuer's head/neck or wrists/arms (Dahl and Miller, 1979), those in MVBCRs seemed to be more diverse and thus required a greater repertoire of skills from the lifesaver.

Methods of Rescue

Because various rescue methods were used, it was difficult to categorize them succinctly. Almost half of the lifesavers ($N = 13$) towed both victims at the same time for at least some portion of the rescue. This reflects the many cases involving two weak swimmers or nonswimmers, both of whom required assistance simultaneously. In other cases, the lifesaver rescued one person and then went back for the second or received help from other lifeguards.

Five of the six rescuers in pools (83%) and two of the four in lakes who were grasped by the victim(s) permitted them to retain their holds while being towed to safety. This finding was similar to the 71% in pools and 50% in lakes who followed the same course when rescuing a single victim (Dahl and Miller, 1979). Thus, it seems advisable to ensure that lifesaving candidates are given adequate practice in swimming while being grasped by one or more persons. If such holds do not threaten the safety of the rescuer, it may be more effective to execute the rescue in this manner rather than to force the victim to release the hold so that the lifesaver can grasp the victim. This does not mean that the victim should be encouraged to grasp the lifesaver or that body contact methods should be the methods of choice. Clearly these situations pose the greatest potential danger to both rescuer and victims. Thus, whenever possible, rescue techniques that avoid direct contact between the lifesaver and victim(s) should be used.

REFERENCES

Dahl, A. M., and Miller, D. I. 1979. Body contact rescues—what are the risks? Am. J. Publ. Health 69:150–152.

Miller, D. I., and McQueen, A. M. 1978. An analysis of body contact lifesaving rescues. In: F. Landry and W. A. R. Orban (eds.), Motor Learning, Sport Psychology, Pedagogy and Didactics of Physical Activity, pp. 485–492. Symposia Specialists, Miami.

Modell, J. H. 1978. Biology of drowning. Annu. Rev. Med. 29:1–8.

Somatotype
and
Morphology

Body Measurements and Heart Morphology of Water Polo Players

L. Vertommen, J. P. Clarys, and W. Welch

Many studies have shown that, for different sports, a certain physical type suits the specific demands of the discipline. At a low level of ability, the body types of athletes vary widely, and this variation decreases as achievement level increases.

The greater the level of ability of any athlete who specializes in a sport, the more the morphology of the athlete conforms to the typical physical characteristics for that sport. However, very few studies have determined the exact influence of selected physical types on performances. For swimmers, it has been shown that body form does not influence swimming resistance (Clarys, 1976).

It is accepted that long, hard physical exercise can lead to a change in the shape as well as an enlargement of the heart. Roentgenological research has broadened our knowledge in this field.

PURPOSE OF STUDY

This study was done to describe the mean body build and heart morphology of a group of Belgian water polo players and to study any possible relationship between external morphology and heart size.

METHODS

Water polo players ($N = 29$) of the First National League were used for this study. The average amount of training involved was 5 hr/week, spread over 3 days. This training level was maintained for at least 5 years. The average age of the sample group was 23 years.

Anthropometric measurements were taken according to the internationally accepted techniques of Martin and Saller (1957). This study included the 10 measurements needed to determine the anthropometric somatotype. These are: height, weight, four skin folds (triceps, subscapular, suprailiac, and calf), bi-epicondylar widths (humerus and calf), and upper arm and calf girth. Thorax circumferences were measured at three positions: axillary level, nipple level, and height of the xyphoid process. These circumferences were measured at rest and at maximal inspiration and expiration. The transversal thorax diameter was measured at the fourth rib. The sagittal thorax diameter was also measured at three positions: the incissura jugularis, the angulus ludovicus, and the xyphoid process, each time at rest.

The anthropometric somatotype was determined according to the Heath-Carter method (1967). This anthropometric method of defining somatotype is based on a precise line of approach and standardized measurements. The photometric method, although based on the reciprocal ponderal index tables, is susceptible to subjective interpretation and depends strongly on the experience of the investigator. To estimate the heart dimensions, the transverse diameter of the heart and the heart/lung quotient were determined (Figure 1) for each subject. These are measured easily and directly. X-rays of standing subjects were taken during inspiration with a Siemens apparatus with moveable grid. The focus distance was 1.5 m. At this distance the divergence of the ray gun is negligible. The heart variable was measured directly from the full-scale negatives.

The relationships of the 13 anthropometric measurements to the anthropometric somatotype data and to the heart variables were quantified by Pearson's product-moment correlation coefficients. For this purpose the S.P.S.S. programming technique (Nie et al., 1975) was used.

RESULTS

Anthropometric Measurements

The measurements needed to define the somatotype were considered. Table 1 compares our results with Dutch water polo players (Willemze and Van Waning, 1971), Belgian water polo players (Clarys and Borms, 1971) and a group of Belgian physical education (PE) students (Carter, Stepnicka, and Clarys, 1973). The PE students served as a reference sample because of their more heterogeneous sport activities. The heights of the group members were approximately the same (1.76 m); only the members of the Dutch group were markedly taller (1.85 m). The average weight of the sample group (74 kg) in this study was about 4 kg heavier than the PE students and ±7 kg lighter than the two other groups of water polo players. The sum of the skin fold measurements of this study's

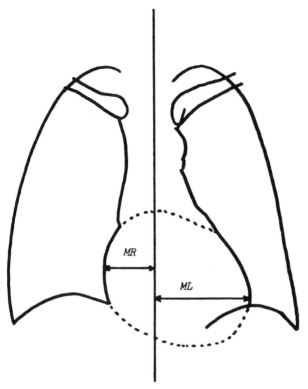

Figure 1. Transverse diameter of the heart. MR = right midline distance. ML = left midline distance. MR + ML = TRH = transverse heart diameter.

group differed little from that of the PE students but was considerably less than that of the Dutch and Belgian water polo players. The upper arm and calf girth and the bi-epicondylar humerus width showed very little differences.

SOMATOTYPE

Figures 2 through 5 present the somatotype distributions of Olympic water polo players (Hebbelinck, Carter, and De Garay, 1975), Belgian water polo players (Clarys and Borms, 1971), PE students (Carter, Stepnicka, and Clarys, 1973), and the sample group. The mean somatotype of the sample group in this study was 2.2-4.7-2.2, a dominant mesomorph. Except for one subject, all the somatotypes were located in the muscular sector of the somatotype chart (Figure 5). The majority of the water polo players (58.65%) were dominant muscular, 24.15% were endomesomorph, 13.80% were ectomesomorph, and 3.45% belonged to the central type (Table 2).

Table 1.   Anthropometric mean values of physical education students and water polo players

	PE students (Carter, Stepnicka, and Clarys, 1973)	WP players (Clarys and Borms, 1971)	WP players (Willemze and Van Waning, 1971)	WP players (Vertommen, 1976)
Height (cm)	176.07	178.20	185.7	175.87
Weight (kg)	69.41	80.20	80.7	73.91
Biceps skin fold (mm)	7.50	10.63	9.39	8.26
Subscapular skin fold (mm)	9.20	13.13	11.27	9.03
Suprailiac skin fold (mm)	7.78	10.10	8.75	5.18
Calf skin fold (mm)	8.18	13.30	—	6.65
Upper arm girth (cm)	32.76	34.13	33.6	32.43
Calf girth (cm)	37.26	37.43	36.9	36.49
Biepicondylar humerus width (cm)	7.08	7.28	7.4	6.98
Biepicondylar femur width (cm)	9.91	9.91	10.0	9.33

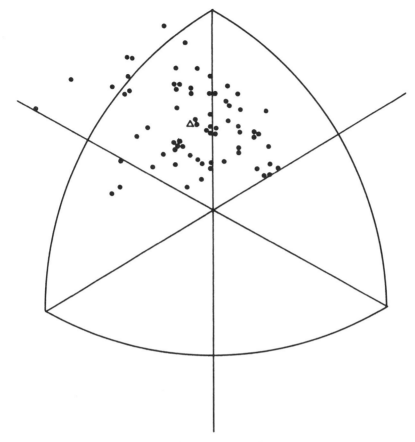

Figure 2. Somatotype distribution of Olympic water polo players. Mean somatotype: Δ = 3.0-5.3-2.3. Number of subjects: N = 70 (Hebbelinck, Carter, and De Garay, 1975).

This study group had a lower relative subcutaneous fat factor and less muscular-skeletal development than the comparison groups. The linearity component of the sample group was almost equal to that of the other water polo players, while the PE students were more linear.

Approximately half of our water polo players were of a dominant muscular body build, and half showed predominant muscular tendencies. This percentage distribution was similar to that of the PE students, whereas two-thirds of the Olympic and Belgian water polo players showed predominant muscular tendencies and only one-third were dominant muscular. Central types were present to the same extent in all groups studied.

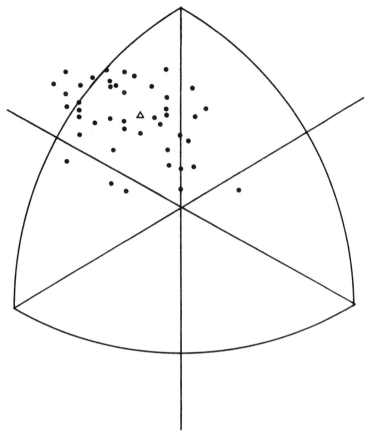

Figure 3. Somatotype distribution of Belgian water polo players. Mean somatotype: $\Delta =$ 3.4-5.3-1.8. Number of subjects: $N = 44$ (Clarys and Borms, 1971).

THE HEART

Although many authors have studied this subject in sportsmen in a number of other sport disciplines, a study of existing literature showed no research results concerning the transverse heart diameter and the heart/lung quotient in water polo players. Most data were derived before 1930 (Kienboĕk, Selig, and Beck, 1907; Herxheimer, 1923). Very often important factors (weight and height) were ignored, so that it was practically impossible to form an overall picture of the groups that were studied. In addition, the continuing changes in body development and the evolution of sports and training methods make it impossible to interpret these data. Therefore, we preferred not to refer to the results of these studies. However, the results of this study were compared with those of

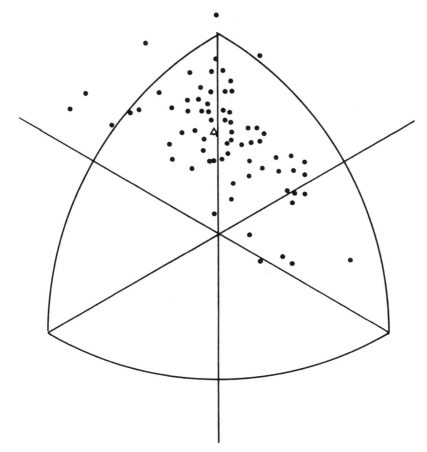

Figure 4. Somatotype distribution of PE students. Mean somatotype: Δ = 2.4-5.4-2.7. Number of subjects: N = 70 (Carter, Stepnicka, and Clarys, 1973).

Hodges and Eyster (1926), Rautmann (1928), and with the nomogram of Ungerleider and Gubner (1958), which allowed us to calculate the theoretically ideal heart diameter for any given person. In this manner, the true heart variables of this sample group were compared with the "normal" heart dimensions.

In this investigation the mean experimental result (TRH (transverse heart diameter) 14.5 cm) was 0.3 cm higher than Rautmann's theoretical value (14.2 cm), 1.4 cm higher than that of Ungerleider and Gubner (13.1 cm), and 2.1 cm higher than that of Hodges (12.4 cm) (see Table 3). The mean heart/lung quotient of this sample group, 45.2%, was similar to the mean of 45% that Danzer calculated in 1919.

In light of this, these results agreed with those of Medved and

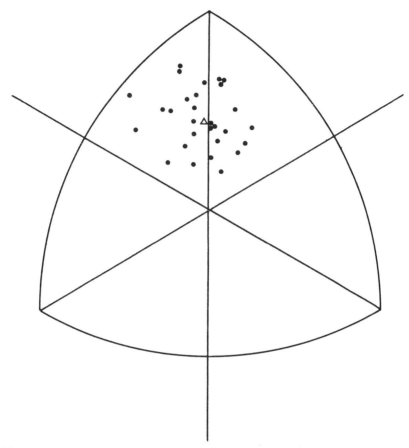

Figure 5. Somatotype distribution of Belgian water polo players. Mean somatotype: Δ = 2.2-4.7-2.2. Number of subjects: N = 29 (Vertommen, 1976).

Friedrich (1966). They studied heart volumes of athletes and found that rowers and water polo players had the largest hearts.

Table 4 presents the significant correlations among the anthropometric variables and the heart variables. Six anthropometric variables showed a statistically significant correlation with the left midline distance and the transverse heart and lung diameters. This permits one to hypothesize that an increase in one of the anthropometric measurements would mean an increase in the left midline distance (see Figure 1) and the transverse heart and lung diameters. These measurements are: 1) weight, 2) thorax girth (at nipple level) at rest at maximum inspiration and maximum expiration, and 3) thorax girth (at the xyphoid level) at rest and at maximum inspiration. The thorax girth (at the xyphoid level) at maximum expiration showed a significant positive correlation with the

Table 2.   Mean somatotype and percent distribution of PE students and water polo players

	PE students (Carter, Stepnicka, and Clarys, 1973)	WP players (Hebbelinck, Carter, and De Garay, 1975)	WP players (Clarys and Borms, 1971)	WP players (Vertommen, 1976)
First component	2.4	2.9	3.4	2.2
Second component	5.4	5.3	5.3	4.7
Third component	2.7	2.3	1.8	2.2
Dominant mesomorph (%)	40.04	28.40	27.3	58.65
Endomesomorph (%)	21.45	38.34	61.4	24.15
Ectomesomorph (%)	27.17	22.72	2.3	13.80
Central	7.15	8.52	9.1	3.45
Endomorph	—	1.42	—	—
Ectomorph	4.29	—	—	—

Table 3.   Comparative table for the transverse heart diameter

Reference	TRH
Ungerleider and Gubner (1958)	13.1[a]
Hodges and Eyster (1926)	12.4[a]
Rautmann (1928)	14.2[a]
Vertommen (1976)	14.495

[a] TRH was calculated for the mean water polo player of the sample group according to the method of the author cited.

Table 4.   Significant correlation coefficients[a]

	ML[b]	TRH[c]	TRL[d]	HLQ[e]
Weight	0.42	0.44	0.65	
Thorax circumference, axillary (rest)			0.70	
Thorax circumference, axillary (max)			0.76	
Thorax circumference, axillary (min)			0.60	
Thorax circumference, nipple (rest)	0.45	0.46	0.72	
Thorax circumference, nipple (max)	0.45	0.49	0.81	
Thorax circumference, nipple (min)	0.44	0.54	0.77	
Thorax circumference, xifoideus (rest)	0.50	0.63	0.72	
Thorax circumference, xifoideus (max)	0.47	0.45	0.65	
Thorax circumference, xifoideus (min)		0.53	0.72	
Upper arm circumference			0.60	
Calf circumference	0.42	0.50		
Thorax breadth			0.63	−0.42
Thorax depth (a. ludovicus)			0.50	
Thorax depth (xifoideus)			0.41	
Bi-epicondylar femur width			0.56	

[a] The correlation coefficient is significant for $r \geq 0.4125$.

[b] ML = left midline distance.

[c] TRH = transverse heart diameter.

[d] TRL = transverse lung diameter.

[e] HLQ = heart/lung quotient.

transverse heart and lung diameters. Significant positive correlations were also observed among the calf girth and the left midline distance and the transverse heart diameter. The thorax width (fourth rib) correlated significantly and positively with the transverse lung diameter and significantly and negatively with the heart/lung quotient. The thorax girth at the axillary level (at rest at maximum inspiration and expiration), the upper arm girth, the thorax depth at the angulus ludovicus and at the xyphoid process level, and the bi-epicondylar femur width showed a significant positive correlation with the transverse lung diameter.

DISCUSSION, FINDINGS, AND CONCLUSIONS

The water polo players studied resembled the PE students more than the water polo players featured in the previous reports, not only with respect to somatotype, but also with respect to basic anthropometric features. There are two possible explanations for these observed differences between the groups of water polo players: 1) the average age of the sample group (23 years) was lower than that of the Belgian water polo players (26.5 years) studied by Clarys and Borms (1971), and 2) the lower competitive level of these players compared with that of the Dutch water polo players studied by Willemze and Van Waning (1971).

The mean transverse heart diameter indicated a possible heart enlargement within the sample group. The mean heart/lung quotient fell within the normal 39–50% limits established by Danzer (1919) except for one subject. A significant relationship was found between 15 anthropometric measurements and the transverse lung diameter (Table 4); of these, 12 were thorax measurements (nine girth, one width, and two depth). The correlations between the thorax measurements and the left midline distance and the transverse heart diameter were lower than those between the thorax measurements and the transverse lung diameter. In the last case, there were weak significant correlations, whereas the correlations with the transverse lung diameter were higher.

From the difference in significance of the correlation coefficients, on the one hand between the thorax measurements and the transverse lung diameter and, on the other hand between the thorax measurements and the transverse heart diameter, it was observed that the lungs were more susceptible to enlargement than the heart as a result of thorax expansion caused by intensive training.

Two facts support these observations: lung tissue is more elastic than heart muscle, and normal heart enlargement is first caused by hypertrophy of the muscular walls. Lengthy and heavy exercise can cause the heart to stretch. Consequently, enlargement of the heart muscle seems to be limited in comparison with that of the lung.

The correlations between body weight and chest girth are confirmed in the literature. Hodges and Eyster (1926) noticed a smaller but significant correlation between body weight and transverse heart diameter. According to Rautmann (1928) the right and left midline distances showed a significant correlation with weight and chest girth (measured at the nipple).

REFERENCES

Carter, J. E. L. 1970. The somatotypes of athletes. Human Biol. 24:534–569.

Carter, J. E. L. 1972. The Heath-Carter Somatotype Method. San Diego State University, San Diego.

Carter, J. E. L., and Heath, B. H. 1971. Somatotype methodology and kinesiology research. Kinesiol. Rev. 10–19.

Carter, J. E. L., Stepnicka, J., and Clarys, J. P. 1973. Somatotypes of male physical education majors in four countries. Res. Q. 44:361–371.

Clarys, J. P. 1976. Onderzoek naar de hydordynamische en morfologische aspekten van het menselijk kichaam (Hydrodynamic and morphological aspects of the human body). Ph.D. thesis, Vrije Universiteit Brussels, Brussels.

Clarys, J. P., and Borms, J. 1971. Typologische studie van water polo spelers en gymnasten (Typological study of water polo players and gymnasts). Geneeskunde Sport 4:2–8.

Danzer, C. S. 1919. The cardiothoracic ratio: an index of cardiac enlargement. Am. J. Med. Sci. 157:513–521.

Heath, B. H. 1966. Need for modification of somatotype methodology. Am. J. Phys. Anthrop. 21:227–233.

Heath, B. H., and Carter, J. E. L. 1966. A comparison of somatotype methods. Am. J. Phys. Anthrop. 24:87–100.

Heath, B. H., and Carter, J. E. L. 1967. A modified somatotype method. Am. J. Phys. Anthrop. 27:57–74.

Hebbelinck, M., Carter, J. E. L., and De Garay, A. 1975. Body build and somatotype of Olympic swimmers, divers and water polo players. In: J. P. Clarys and L. Lewillie (eds.), Swimming II, pp. 285–305. University Park Press, Baltimore.

Herxheimer, G. 1923. Zur grösse, form und leistungsfähigkeit des herzens bei sportsleuten (Form and performance of the heart of sportsmen). Z. Klin. Med. 96:218–235.

Hodges, P. C., and Eyster, J. A. E. 1926. Estimation of transverse cardiac diameter in man. Arch. Intern. Med. 37:707–714.

Kienboćk, R., Selig, A., and Beck, R. 1907. Untersuchungen am suhweimmen (Investigation of swimmers). Münch Med. Wschr. 54:1427–1431, 1486–1488.

Martin, R., and Saller, K. 1957. Lehrbuch der Anthropologie, pp. 323–343. Fischer Verlag, Stuttgart.

Medved, R., and Friedrich, V. 1966. Oarsmen and water polo player sportmen with the largest hearts. XVI Weltkongress für Sportmedizin, Hannover, Kongresbericht, pp. 639–643.

Nie, N. H., Hull, C. H., Jenkins, J. G., Steinbrenner, K., and Bent, D. H. 1975. Statistical Package for the Social Sciences, pp. 181–286. McGraw-Hill Book Company, New York.

Rautmann, M. 1928. Tabellar arrangement of the transverse cardial diameter.

In: E. Zdansky (ed.), Roentgen Diagnosis of the Heart and Great Vessels. Grune and Stratton, London.

Rautmann, M., and Heiss, F. 1927. Zur kenntnis der korrelativen variabilität der orthodiografischen herzagrösse (For the knowledge of correlation variability of orthographical heart dimensions). Z. Konstit. Forsch. 13:567–574.

Ungerleider, and Gubner. 1958. In: G. A. Rose and H. Blackburn (eds.), Heart size measurements. Picker X-Ray Corporation, White Plains, N. Y.

Willemze, R., and Van Waning, E. E. 1971. Een antropologisch onderzoek bij vier takken van sport (tennis, zwemmen, water polo en ski) (An anthropological study of four sport disciplines: tennis, swimming, water polo and skiing). Verslag keuzepraktikum anatomisch embryologisch laboratorium, Universiteit Leiden.

Zdansky, E. 1965. Roentgen Diagnosis of the Heart and Great Vessels, pp. 42–110. Grune and Stratton, London.

Effectiveness of the Breaststroke Leg Movement in Relation to Selected Time-Space, Anthropometric, Flexibility, and Force Data

H. U. B. Vervaecke and U. J. J. Persyn

Most practitioners believe that a good breaststroke kick ensures good propulsion in the total competitive stroke as well as in lifesaving. Velocity fluctuation curves of a breaststroke cycle of some top swimmers (Persyn, 1974; Persyn, De Maeyer, and Vervaecke, 1975) show that the most important acceleration occurs during the kick. The action of the arms that follows keeps the velocity constant or causes a slight acceleration. Within this kick, the greatest acceleration occurs during leg extension. Because the path described by the feet in relation to the water is directed partly backward, we deduced that a paddle wheel propulsion principle was being used. Also during the squeezing action of the legs, in which there is no backward displacement of the feet, acceleration continues. This can be explained only on the basis of a propeller propulsion principle. Among the best swimmers, the ability to perform these propulsion techniques apparently results from a particular flexibility of the ankles and from some anthropometric characteristics of the feet, e.g., shape and surface. Therefore, in this stroke, in which the velocity fluctuates strongly, the kick is important to acceleration of the body and thus to the performance of champion swimmers.

Even among PE freshmen ($N = 370$) there is a high correlation ($r = 0.76$) between the maximum speed of the total stroke and that attained with kicking alone. However, in observing swimmers of this proficiency with only the naked eye, one finds that the ankles are usually extended too early in the kick and seldom remain sufficiently flexed during the squeezing action of the legs. Thus, it is difficult to apply either the paddle wheel or the propeller propulsion principle to its best advantage. In this stroke one or two feet can be oriented so that the sole cannot press the water back at all, yet there seems to be no anthropometric or motor insufficiency. Thus, the combination of knee extension with ankle flexion does not occur automatically. This inability to apply the propulsion principles effectively may lie in the skill of the swimmer.

Using only cinematographic data (time-space) of top swimmers, where one can assume "optimal" anthropometric and motor abilities and "optimal" skill, "optimal" propulsion principles still have been deduced. This study was done to determine (with ordinary swimmers) how much the propulsion possibilities of the legs in the breaststroke are influenced by certain anthropometric and motor abilities, especially flexibility. Most of the anthropometric aspects have been studied separately (Kohlrausch, 1929; Saller, 1929; Cureton, 1951; Kopf, 1957; Kukushkin, 1963; Correnti and Zauli, 1964; Wutscherk, 1966; Carter, 1966, 1970; Stroup, Harris, and McCormick, 1967; Szabö and Szabö, 1969; Tittel and Wutscherk, 1972; Maas, 1974; Hebbelinck, Carter, and De Garay, 1975; De Garay, Levine, and Carter, 1974; Clarys, 1976). Cureton (1930) correlated anthropometric data (and some motor data) with swimming velocity. A cinematographic record of the skill has usually been neglected in such studies.

METHOD

In a pilot study ($N = 469$ PE students) the relationship of a few current anthropometric measurements (using the accepted techniques of Martin and Saller, 1957) with swimming velocity and with lifting force when kicking were studied in the breaststroke. Speed was measured by timing a 12-m swim, using the breaststroke, legs alone, in the back and prone positions. Lifting force was determined by measuring the maximum weight that a swimmer could hold above the water with both hands while swimming 10 m on his back. No high correlation was found between these anthropometric data and the swimming tests. However, the group was not divided into performance levels, and no cinematographic control was used.

To obtain more relevant data, another group of 178 freshmen was studied. In addition to the previously mentioned anthropometric measurements (e.g., height, weight, biacromial width), more "specific" anthropometric measurements (e.g., body volume, length and surface of the sole of the foot) and flexibility measurements of the ankles were taken. These data were selected on the basis of observations of extreme ankle positions among top swimmers who use a whip kick (e.g., considerable flexion, supination, and external rotation). Basically the same swimming tests as those used in the pilot study were administered. However, considering the high correlation ($r = 0.89$) between the velocity of breaststroke kicking in the prone and back positions, the safety kicking test on the back was selected and complemented the whole breaststroke test. Because of the necessity of a movement control and because it was impossible in our swimming pool to observe and to film a bottom view of the leg movement during the lifting force test, a horizontal pulling force test was choosen. This test quantifies the kick by measuring the weight a person could hold on a horizontal cable attached through a pulley to a weight. During this test the leg movements of the subjects were always observed by the naked eye for technical control. The best and the poorest subjects for the horizontal pulling force ($N = 21$) test were filmed from the rear. A Bolex 16-mm motion picture camera was placed in a fixed underwater aquarium, and each performance was filmed at 32 frames/sec. The camera was 8 m from the subject. The angle of the foot in relation to the path of its movement, the backward projection of the sole during the kick, and the timing of the leg movement are presented in Figure 1. To quantify the orientation of the sole, a long length and width axis was fixed to its surface. The collected anthropometric, flexibility, and swimming data were computed, and the performances of the different groups were compared.

RESULTS AND DISCUSSION

The reliability of the swimming tests (three chronometers per subject), anthropometric measurements (Martin and Saller, 1957), and the cinematographic data (Persyn, 1974) studied previously were not examined in this work. For the flexibility data, the reliability was controlled and appeared high. Flexion was the least satisfactory parameter (see Table 1).

In the pulling force test, body weight seemed to be more relevant than height. In addition, the surface of the sole seemed to be relatively important in this type of tethered swimming. Calf girth and bi-iliocristal width seemed to be unimportant in all of the tests for this group of noncompetitive swimmers. Biacromial width was relevant only at higher speeds during normal breaststroke swimming (see Table 2).

The most relevant flexibility measurements were supination and external rotation of the foot. Their importance increases in proportion to swimming speed. Flexion seems to be unimportant, but, paradoxically, extension seems to be relevant. This can be explained partly by the significant correlation between supination and extension ($r = 0.36$).

It was assumed that skill would have a considerable effect on flexion. Among the 25% better and poorer subjects, the best ones ($N = 9$) and the poorest ones ($N = 12$) showed totally different foot angles (ankles) in relation to the outward path of movement ($+65°$ for the best and $-43°$ for

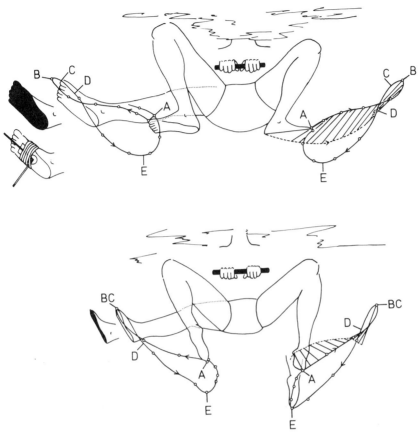

Figure 1. Time and space data of two breaststroke kicks from the rear view. Top: better subject (21 kg pulling force). Bottom: poorer subject (6 kg pulling force). A, outward thrust of the leg starts. B, spreading of the kick is at maximum width. C, the legs are at their most extended point. D, beginning of knee flexion. E, deepest point of the toe. O, path described by the big toe. ——, line between heel and toe. - - -, path described by the heel. (The intervals are three frames = 0.093 sec).

the poorest). Further, among the best subjects, the sole showed nearly maximum backward projection (87%) at the end of the extension (spreading) of the legs, and among the poorest the sole was nearly invisible (13%). Thus, the poorest subjects showed considerable slipping during spreading and a relatively long recovery (see Figure 2).

In tethered swimming almost no closing of the legs occurred after extension as in normal breaststroke swimming, and thus, extension seemed to be the most important action. There is considerable backward displacement of the feet, and therefore the paddle wheel principle is primarily used (the swimmer being towed slightly backward at that moment).

Table 1.   Reliability of two repeated measurements on the same subject for some flexibility measurements ($N = 178$)

	Mean 1	Mean 2	SD 1	SD 2	S error 1	S error 2	$r_{1,2}$	t ratio	Two-tail probability
Extension, L[b]	145.5	145.4	7.2	7.6	0.36	0.66	0.900[a]	0.44	0.66
Extension, R[b]	145.8	145.8	6.6	6.9	0.57	0.61	0.900[a]	−0.29	0.77
Flexion, L[b]	80.8	80.2	5.8	6.3	0.51	0.55	0.818[a]	1.42	0.16
Flexion, R[b]	82.1	81.7	5.8	5.9	0.51	0.52	0.784[a]	1.16	0.25
Supination	51.0	50.7	16.5	16.6	0.14	0.14	0.981[a]	1.14	0.26
External rotation	57.2	57.6	13.0	12.4	1.16	1.11	0.965[a]	−1.44	0.15

[a]Significant at 0.01 level of probability.
[b]L, left. R, right.

Table 2.   Comparison of the ±25% poorer swimmers (W) with the better swimmers (B) ($N = 178$)

	Pulling force				Lifting force		Breaststroke, legs alone		Breaststroke total	
	W ($N = 43$)	Bt ($N = 38$)	W (on film) ($N = 12$)	B ($N = 9$)	W ($N = 36$)	Bt^d ($N = 30$)	W ($N = 42$)	Bt^d ($N = 40$)	W ($N = 45$)	Bt^d ($N = 40$)
Pulling force (kg)	7.5	17.4[a]	5.5	19.7[a]	7.4	16.3[a]	6.7	15.5[a]	7.4	15.5[a]
Lifting force (kg)	3.5	7.5[a]	4.0	8.2[a]	2.3	9.1[a]	3.4	7.4[a]	3.8	7.5[a]

Breaststroke, legs alone (sec)	24.9	14.8[a]	24.3	15.4[a]	23.1	14.8[a]	26.9	13.9[a]	24.6	13.9[a]
Breaststroke, total (sec)	14.9	11.5[a]	14.5	11.3[a]	14.4	11.7[a]	15.3	11.8[a]	15.7	11.0[a]
Height (cm)	175.7	178.7[b]	174.1	177.7[b]	176.4	178.5	176.1	178.4	175.6	178.6[b]
Weight (kg)	67.7	73.6[a]	66.5	73.0[a]	69.6	71.6	69.3	69.0	68.4	70.5
Body volume, inspiration (liters)	70.1	73.5	68.5	73.4[a]	70.1	71.7	70.8	72.0		
expiration (liters)	60.5	67.9	66.4	68.7[b]	66.6	67.2	66.7	67.7		
Vital capacity (dl)	54.2	57.1	52.7	57.5	53.7	58.7[b]	54.6	55.8	54.5	55.1
Biacromonial width (cm)	39.1	40.3[b]	39.6	40.2	39.4	39.9	39.2	39.6	38.8	40.1[b]
Bi-iliocristal width (cm)	26.9	26.7	26.7	25.8	27.3	26.5[c]	27.1	26.6	26.6	26.7
Calf girth (cm)	36.2	36.4	35.2	36.5	37.0	36.4	36.9	36.1	36.5	36.4
Surface of sole (cm^2)	190.5	201.7[c]	191.7	197.7[c]	196.6	193.9	193.6	189.8	189.6	190.6
Length of foot (cm)	26.1	27.1[b]	26.7	26.7[b]	26.5	26.8	26.3	26.7	26.1	26.8[b]
Width of foot (cm)	9.9	11.0[b]	9.9	10.1[b]	9.9	10.1	9.9	10.0	10.0	9.8
Extension, L[e] (°)	144.5	146.0	139.4	145.4[b]	144.7	144.9	144.0	147.5[c]	142.8	146.4[b]
Extension, R[e] (°)	145.4	146.4	140.0	145.7[b]	145.6	145.3	144.7	148.1[b]	143.6	146.5[b]
Flexion, L[e] (°)	81.0	82.5	80.0	81.4	80.4	79.0	81.3	79.2[c]	81.9	80.5
Flexion, R[e] (°)	82.4	84.0	81.4	83.4	82.1	80.4	82.6	80.9	82.8	81.5
Supination (°)	54.1	41.1[a]	63.2	39.3[a]	53.2	49.1	54.0	45.3[b]	55.6	43.1[a]
External rotation (°)	55.8	59.5	52.4	59.3[b]	52.6	60.9[b]	54.0	63.0[a]	54.2	62.4[a]

[a]Significant at 0.01 level of probability.

[b]Significant at 0.05 level.

[c]Significant at 0.10 level.

[d]$t = t$ ratio.

[e]L, left. R, right.

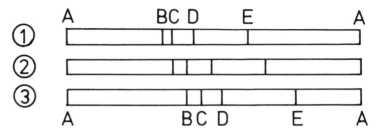

Figure 2. Timing the kick phases in the breaststroke for (*1*) poor swimmers (pulling force <5 kg), (*2*) good swimmers (15-19 kg), and (*3*) the best swimmers (>19 kg). A, B, C, D, and E are defined in Figure 1.

Because long, continued impulses would allow too much backward and forward displacement, small successive impulses seem to be the obvious choice in this test. (The best results were obtained when the swimmers used the alternating impulses of the egg-beater kick). Therefore, it is not surprising that the surface of the sole seemed to be relatively more important in this paddle wheel-like propulsion.

Supination and external rotation increase in importance when swimming speed increases, i.e., when the use of the propeller principle becomes necessary (Counsilman, 1977). The surface of the calf was not important in displacement or in tethered swimming. The velocity of calf girth against the water is probably not high enough and the shape of its surface is not effective.

Cinematographic data of good subjects during the pulling force test showed that they used external rotation, supination, and flexion much more than the poorest subjects. Starting with a simple observation of the movements of the entire group, it was possible (and interesting from a didactic point of view) to link some flexibility data with faulty styles, such as:

1.   The limited number of performers who used a scissors-like kick (14%) showed less external rotation ability (43.5°) than the "normal" kickers (60.7°). They could be more inclined to the crawl kick.

2.   The subjects who swam with both feet extended (28%) had relatively large feet. This swimming style could be explained by the water pressure before the extension of the legs began.

It is clear that cinematographic control of the entire group is necessary to determine which swimmers move correctly and should be investigated for anthropometric and motor characteristics. Further, to obtain more convincing correlations, better swimmers should be tested, and the authors hope that more relevant measurements can be selected from among this population.

SUMMARY

The film data from this study seem particularly useful in safety swimming but not in normal breaststroke swimming. Other areas for applying propulsion principles are seen, and different anthropometric and motor factors seem relevant. As a result the appropriate movement should be filmed.

REFERENCES

Carter, J. E. L. 1966. The somatotype of swimmers. Swimming Tech. 3(3):76–80.

Carter, J. E. L. 1970. The somatotypes of athletes—a review. Human Biol. 42: 535–569.

Clarys, J. P. 1976. Onderzoek naar de hydrodynamische en morfologische aspecten van het menselijk lichaam (Research on the hydrodynamic and morphologic aspects of the human body). Ph.D. thesis, Vrije Universiteit Brussel, Belgium.

Correnti, V., and Zauli, B. 1964. Olimpionici 1960 (Olympiade 1960). Tipolitografia, Marves, Roma.

Counsilman, J. E. 1977. Competitive Swimming Manual. Counsilman Publications, Bloomington, Ind.

Cureton, T. K. 1930. Mechanics and kinesiology of swimming, the crawl flutter kick. Res. Q. 1(4):87–121.

Cureton, T. K. 1951. Physical Fitness of Champion Athletes. University of Illinois Press, Urbana.

De Garay, A. L., Levine, L., and Carter, J. E. L. 1974. Genetic and Anthropological Studies of Olympic Athletes. Academic Press, Inc., New York.

Hebbelinck, M., Carter, L., and De Garay, A. 1975. Body build and somatotype of Olympic swimmers, divers, and water polo players. In: J. P. Clarys and L. Lewillie (eds.), Swimming II, pp. 285–305. University Park Press, Baltimore.

Kohlrausch, W. 1929. Zusammenhänge von Körperform und Leistung. Ergebniss der anthropometrische Messungen an den Athleten der Amsterdammer Olympiade (Relation between body form and performance. Anthropometric measurements within Athletes of the Olympiade in Amsterdam). Arbeitsphysiol. 2:187–198.

Kopf, H. 1957. Über die Abhängigkeit der Leistung im 100-m Freistilschwimmen von Konstitutionsmerkmalen (Relation between the 100 m crawl performance and morphology). Sportmedizin X:279–282.

Kukushkin, G. I. 1963. The pecularities of the physical development of sportsmen of various specializations. Med. Sport 3:701–708.

Maas, G. D. 1974. The Physique of Athletes. Leiden University Press, Leiden.

Martin, R., and Saller, K. 1957. Lehrbuch der Anthropologie (Textbook of Anthropology). Fischer Verlag, Stuttgart.

Persyn, U. 1974. Technisch-hydrodynamische benadering van de bewegende mens in het water (Technical-hydrodynamic approach of human motion in water). Hermes VIII(3-4):5–136.

Persyn, U., De Maeyer, J., and Vervaecke, H. 1975. Investigation of hydrodynamic determinants of competitive swimming strokes. In: J. P. Clarys and L. Lewillie (eds.), Swimming II, pp. 214–222. University Park Press, Baltimore.

Saller, K. 1929. Untersuchungen über Konstitutions- und Rassenformen an Turnern der Deutschen Nordmark. (Research on anthropology within gymnasts of Northern Germany) Z. Konstit. Lehre 14:1–51.

Stroup, F., Harris, A., and McCormick, J. 1967. Anthropometric measurements and swimming performances. Swimming Tech., 4(1):13-18.

Szabö, J., and Szabö, Z. 1969. Anthropometrische und spezifische Gewichtmessungen an ausländischen und hiesigen Teilnehmern des Internationalen Schwimmwettkampfes in Budapest. (Anthropometric and specific weight measurements within competitors of the international swimming event in Budapest). Sportarzt Sportmed. 20:152-157.

Tittel, K., and Wutscherk, H. 1972. Sportanthropometrie. Johann Ambrosius Barth, Leipzig.

Wutscherk, H. 1966. Körperbaumerkmale der leistungsbesten Freistilschwimmern der DDR (unter besonderer Berücksichtigung von Alters und Leistungsgruppen) (Body structure factors of the best crawl swimmers in DDR (from the viewpoint of age and performance groups)). Wissensch. Z. Deutsch. Hochschule Körperkult. Leipzig 8:127-133.

Comparison of Somatotype and Speed in Competitive Swimming at Different Phases of Training

C. G. S. Araújo, R. C. Pavel, and P. S. C. Gomes

Many researchers have investigated somatotypes of athletes and nonathletes, using mainly the anthropometric method of Heath and Carter (1967) (Carter and Phillips, 1969; Carter, 1970; Carter and Rahe, 1975). Perhaps the most important investigations were those concerned with the somatotypes of Olympic athletes who participated in the Mexico City Olympic Games in 1968 (De Garay, Levine, and Carter, 1974).

Research groups in some countries have collected data on reference populations for different sport modalities (Hebbelinck, 1975; Gomes and Araújo, 1977, 1978b; Araújo, 1978b; Araújo, Gomes, and Novaes, 1978; Araújo and Moutinho, 1978), so that it is now possible to suggest the "ideal" somatotypes of each modality that can be used to evaluate "top" athletes.

Analyses of somatotypes can also be used to select subjects best suited for a sport modality. Despite this, only a few studies have dealt with somatotypes from a practical standpoint (Carter, 1976; Araújo, 1978b), and although the relationship between somatotype and lean body mass (Slaughter, Lohman, and Boileau, 1977) was determined in one study, there have been no investigations of somatotypes in relation to speed.

PURPOSE OF THE STUDY

This study was done to analyze the relationship between ratings of somatotype components and sprinting speed in the water of competitive swimmers at four different phases of their training.

METHODS

Competitive swimmers ($N = 16$), eleven males and five females of the Gama Filho Swimming Team, were the subjects for this study. The Heath and Carter anthropometric somatotype method was used to analyze somatotypes. To evaluate somatotypes, the following measurements were obtained: triceps, subscapular, suprailiac and medial calf skinfolds, condylar diameters of the humerus and femur, girths of the upper arm when flexed with muscles contracted, height and weight, and girth of the calf. The measuring instruments included Harpenden skinfold caliper, Mitutoyo vernier caliper, Stanley flexible steel metric tape, stadiometer (Ross et al., 1976), and a calibrated balance. These were used according to previously published methods (Gomes and Araújo, 1978a), which were similar to the procedures described by Carter (1975). All anthropometric measurements were done by the principal author in either the late afternoon or early evening. For more details concerning the methodology of the Heath-Carter anthropometric somatotyping, see De Garay, Levine, and Carter (1974) and Heath and Carter (1967).

For the speed test, the observer stood on the deck of the pool while a swimmer performed three 25-m sprints at maximum speed using the front crawl stroke. A digital stop watch, Cronus 3-D or Hewlett-Packard 55, was used to measure the time required to swim 12.5 m (from 8.75 to 21.25 m during the sprint) to the nearest 0.01 sec. The observer stood at the first mark and then walked toward the second mark; the swimmer's head was used as the reference point (see Figure 1). The swimmers were tested individually and were requested not to breathe. At least 2 min were allowed between each trial for each subject. The best result of the three trials was used for analysis. Differences in reaction time, starting technique, final touch, and respiratory rate did not influence the test results because of nature of the test situation.

The swimmers were evaluated on four distinct occasions, corresponding to different phases of their training. In the first evaluation, in August, they returned to competitive swimming training, so this phase was termed zero phase and corresponded to the beginning of the season. The next evaluation was done in October (phase 1), when the training was approximately 18 km/day of endurance swimming, and the swimmers also participated in three weekly weight training and two flexibility sessions before an afternoon's workout. The third evaluation was conducted 1 week before the Rio de Janeiro age-group swimming championships on November 19, 1977 (phase 2), for which the swimmers were not "tapering off." At this time, however, their training emphasized quality more than quantity. The swimmers reduced their volume of training at this time, so that they were swimming approximately 10 km/day. Finally, the fourth evaluation (phase 3), was intended to coincide with the period when the swimmers were in peak condition. This was just before the Brazilian age-group swimming championships, in which the Gama Filho Swimming Team placed fourth and established some age-group national records. All swimmers were "tapering off" for this official competition.

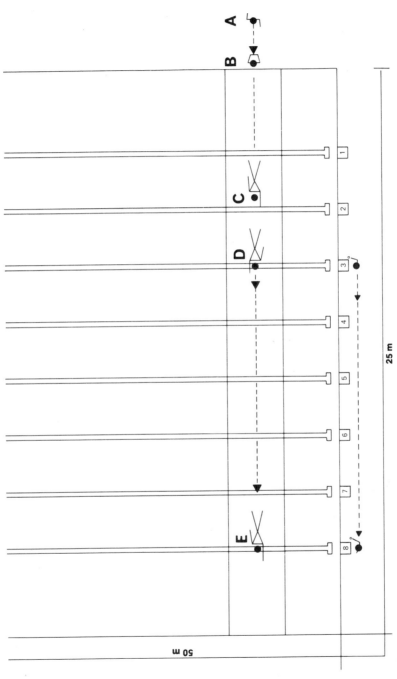

Figure 1. Schematic of the speed test procedure. A, the start position. B, the start. C, position in the water after "takeoff." D, the first mark, the observer presses the start button of his stop watch. E, the second mark, the observer presses the stop button of his stop watch.

Table 1.   Mean heights, weights, and ages of male and female Gama Filho swimmers at four different training phases[a]

	0	1	2	3
Males ($N = 11$)				
height (cm)	174.00	173.93	174.26	175.23
	(1.92)	(1.74)	(1.74)	(1.77)
weight (kg)	63.15	63.46	62.91	63.07
	(2.19)	(2.14)	(2.14)	(1.88)
age (years)	15.40	15.52	15.63	15.81
	(0.37)	(0.37)	(0.37)	(0.37)
Females ($N = 5$)				
height (cm)	158.86	159.16	159.30	159.18
	(4.24)	(4.23)	(4.14)	(4.27)
weight (kg)	53.08	52.82	52.37	52.20
	(4.43)	(4.01)	(4.57)	(4.56)
age (years)	15.22	15.34	15.45	15.63
	(0.58)	(0.58)	(0.58)	(0.58)

[a]Standard errors are in parentheses.

The elapsed time between the measurements for somatotype and speed determinations never exceeded 2 weeks, and most of the time both measurements were done in the same week. Simple linear correlation coefficients were calculated, and a 0.05 level of probability was used for the significance of the relationships.

RESULTS

The height, weight, and age (0.01 year) (Araújo, 1978a) of swimmers are presented in Table 1 for each of the four training phases. The different training phases, 0 to 3, and the mean values for somatotype component ratings and speed test results are shown in Table 2.

The male swimmers decreased in their endomorphic rating toward the end of the season, while the female swimmers, although showing a similar tendency, increased their endomorphic rating in phase 3. The mesomorphy of male and female swimmers attained a peak value at phases 1 and 2, showing a smaller degree of muscular-skeletal development at the start and at the end of the season. Ectomorphy tended to increase toward the "tapering off" period. The speed test results showed an improvement in the velocity from phase 0 to 3 for the males, while the female group had their best performance at the start of the season. Table 3 shows the correlation coefficients obtained between somatotype component ratings and speed test results for each phase and for the composite results (G).

Table 2.   Mean somatotype component ratings and the speed test results for male and female Gama Filho swimmers at four different training phases[a]

	0	1	2	3
Males ($N = 11$)				
endomorphy	2.48	2.32	2.18	2.17
	(0.23)	(0.17)	(0.20)	(0.19)
mesomorphy	4.09	4.28	4.25	3.98
	(0.17)	(0.21)	(0.18)	(0.20)
ectomorphy	3.45	3.40	3.55	3.65
	(0.20)	(0.19)	(0.19)	(0.20)
speed test (sec)	7.53	7.51	7.41	7.24
	(0.11)	(0.12)	(0.11)	(0.10)
Females ($N = 5$)				
endomorphy	3.45	3.47	3.12	3.40
	(0.54)	(0.58)	(0.60)	(0.59)
mesomorphy	3.83	3.79	3.78	3.56
	(0.17)	(0.27)	(0.16)	(0.16)
ectomorphy	2.46	2.54	2.70	2.71
	(0.16)	(0.23)	(0.29)	(0.20)
speed test (sec)	8.10	8.33	8.19	8.24
	(0.18)	(0.24)	(0.15)	(0.18)

[a]Standard errors are in parentheses.

DISCUSSION

The authors believe that it is important to verify the actual importance of tests applied in sport sciences. In a previous article, it was proposed that somatotype seems to be an important factor in swimming performance; however, until now no attempt has been made to test the relationship between swimming time and somatotype. In this study, a simple test applied to one competitive swimming team to evaluate swimming velocity was correlated with the somatotype component ratings obtained during the same period on 16 swimmers.

From the data in Table 1, the time that elapsed between each somatotype evaluation was calculated; it was 0.12, 0.11, and 0.18 year. The differences in the mean height of the female group could be attributed to methodological variations; however, in the male group small growth was observed during the season, mainly between phases 2 and 3. Because the subjects were at an age where measurable growth can occur, these changes during a season could be similar to those described by Shepard et al. (1977) for French Canadian children, 6-12 years old. Another hypothesis concerns possible methodological variations in the height measurements; however, the measurements were done by the same examiner, at the same place, with the same material, and almost at the same time of the day (range, 5–8 p.m.).

The data in Table 2 show that small changes occurred in somatotype components during one season, and these changes probably were related to the type of workout performed in each phase. The endomorphic component seemed to decrease with swimming training as expected. The results for the females were somewhat contradictory, but they may have been caused by a change in the diet of two of the five female swimmers in the middle of the season. The higher values for mesomorphy in midseason for both male or female groups were probably related to the weight training period. These sessions were held three times a week for all swimmers and consisted of 15 isotonic exercises performed as circuit training. The swimmers performed each exercise for 10 sec at their maximum speed, and the loads were adjusted individually as the training sequence progressed. In this kind of work, the ATP-CP is probably the major factor responsible for the muscle metabolism (Margaria et al. 1969; Poortmans, 1976). Ectomorphy increased for all swimmers with training, with generally a small increase in height (male) or a small decrease in weight (female) toward the end of the season.

Speed test results showed a decrease in the time required to swim 12.5 m for male swimmers from phases 0 to 3; in the female group, a similar change was observed; however, the results of phase 0 were faster than other phases. This result could have been caused by the presence of two distance swimmers in the female group.

The most important conclusions of this study were drawn from the correlation coefficients in Table 3. One correlation was significant at the 0.05 level of probability. It occurred in the endomorphy/speed relationship for the male swimmers.

Table 3. Correlation coefficients between somatotype component ratings and speed test results for male and female Gama Filho swimmers at four different phases of training

	0	1	2	3	G
Males (N = 11)					
endo-speed	0.22	0.39	0.21	0.58	0.36[a]
meso-speed	−0.08	0.22	0.32	0.05	0.14
ecto-speed	0.22	0.15	−0.20	−0.16	−0.06
Females (N = 5)					
endo-speed	0.30	0.08	0.07	−0.09	0.06
meso-speed	0.16	0.40	0.15	0.05	0.21
ecto-speed	−0.56	−0.72	−0.23	−0.18	−0.38

[a]Significant at the 0.05 level of probability.

Because the correlations were calculated between time required to cover 12.5 m and the other variables, we can conclude that endomorphy was inversely related to the speed in the water. This seems to be obvious because the adipose tissue does not contribute to work done but increases the cross-sectional area of the body, which increases the swimmer's frontal resistance (Clarys, 1978). Moreover, rarely does a competitive swimmer have a high endomorphy value (Hebbelinck, 1975; Araújo, 1978b), although a channel swimmer did exhibit, in general, a higher value for the first component (Pugh et al. 1960).

Despite the fact that the other correlations were not statistically significant, a tendency toward a positive relationship between mesomorphy and speed was surprising because it means that if a swimmer were strong, he would be slow in the water. Lower values for mesomorphy were found when the swimmers were in the "tapering off" period.

For both male and female swimmers, between phases 1 and 2, an increase in the mesomorphic component was expected because of the weight training sessions performed during this period. As cited previously, the speed test and the weight training program were related to the ATP-CP system, so we might assume that changes in these variables would occur. However, it is difficult to explain from a physiological standpoint why speed would increase 3 months after a weight training program stopped. It would make more sense if there were a concomitant improvement in both variables. Although this study was not designed to analyze the effects of a weight training program on swimming speed, one might suspect that there was a deleterious effect of this type of dry-land program on swimming speed; this was probably related to the mechanical efficiency of swimming.

One other point deserves consideration, and that concerns the differences observed in the growth curves of male and female swimmers, based on the mean age of both groups. One would expect a small amount of growth in the female swimmers, similar to that observed in this study, if the curves proposed by Ross et al. (1976) for young Canadian skaters are applicable. At 15 years of age, Ross reported that the rate of growth was almost 0 for girls, while the boys had a peak rate at the same age. Moreover, the male swimmers in our study showed appreciable growth from phases 2 to 3, which was the same period during which weight training and distance covered in daily training decreased. In stress situations (e.g., disease) it is common for growth to be retarded. Perhaps the retardation of growth observed in this study was the result of the weight training and/or swimming distance overtraining.

There seems to be no adequate explanation for the ectomorphy/speed relationships, mainly because the swimmers were not very endomorphic. Moreover, the swimmer is not required to carry his weight in the water, so that could be the reason that weight was not important. The question is complicated because for the male group, the height increased, while for the female group, the weight decreased. However, it is possible that an increase in a third component corresponds to an increase in swimming speed. A more suitable answer concerns the swimmer's age, which resulted in small growth in the male swimmers, increasing their ectomorphy value coincident with the "tapering off" period. Nevertheless, the results for the females cannot be explained.

CONCLUSION

Although somatotype can be an important factor in swimming performance, it was not related strongly enough to allow predictions of small changes in one variable, such as speed in the water, and endomorphy in male swimmers could be limiting their swimming speed.

REFERENCES

Araújo, C. G. S. 1978a. Cálculo da idade centesimal (Calculation of centesimal age). Caderno Artus Med. Desportiva 1(1):47-49.

Araújo, C. G. S. 1978b. Somatotyping of top swimmers by the Heath-Carter method. In: B. Eriksson and B. Furberg (eds.), Swimming Medicine IV, pp. 188-198. University Park Press, Baltimore.

Araújo, C. G. S., and Moutinho, M. F. C. S. 1978. Somatotipo e composicao corporal de ginastas olimpicos adolescentes (Somatotypes and body composition of adolescent Olympic gymnasts). Caderno Artus Med. Desportiva 1(1):39-42.

Araújo, C. G. S., Gomes, P. S. C., and Novaes, E. V., 1978. O. Somatotipo de judocas Beasileiros de alto nivel (Somatotype of high-level Brazilian judokas). Caderno Artus Med. Desportiva 1(1):21-30.

Carter, J. E. L. 1970. The somatotype of athletes—a review. Human Biol. 42:535-569.

Carter, J. E. L. 1975. The Heath-Carter Somatotype Method, 2nd Ed. San Diego State University, San Diego.

Carter, J. E. L. 1976. The prediction of outstanding athletic ability—The structural perspective International Congress of Physical Activity Sciences, July 11-16, Quebec City.

Carter, J. E. L., and Phillips, W. H. 1969. Structural changes in exercising middle-aged males during a two-year period. J. Appl. Physiol. 27:787-794.

Carter, J. E. L., and Rahe, R. H. 1975. Effects of stressful underwater demolition training on body structure. Med. Sci. Sports 7(4):304-308.

Clarys, J. P. 1978. An experimental investigation of the application of the fundamental hydrodynamics of the human body. In: B. Eriksson and B. Furberg (eds.), Swimming Medicine IV, pp. 386-394. University Park Press, Baltimore.

Clarys, J. P., and Borms, J. 1971. Typologische studie van waterpolospelers en gymnasten (Typological studies of water polo players and gymnasts). Geneeskunde Sport 4:2-8.

De Garay, A. L., Levine, L., and Carter, J. E. L. (eds.) 1974. Genetic and Anthropological Studies of Olympic Athletes. Academic Press Inc., New York.

Gomes, P. S. C., and Araújo, C. G. S. 1977. O somatotipo no athletismo brasileiro (The somatotype in Brazilian track and field athletes). Rev. Brasileira Educ. Fis. Desportos. Submitted for publication.

Gomes, P. S. C., and Araújo, C. G. S. 1978a. Metodologia do somatotipo anthropométirco de Heath-Carter (Methodology of Heath-Carter anthropometric somatotypes). Caderno Artus Med. Desportiva 1(1):11-20.

Gomes, P. S. C., and Araújo, C. G. S. 1978b. O somatotipo do atleta brasileiro de elite (The somatotype of Brazilian top athletes). Rev. Brasileira Educ. Fis. Desportos. 34:59-71.

Heath, B., and Carter, J. E. L. 1967. A modified somatotype method. Am. J. Phys. Anthrop. 27:57-74.

Hebbelinck, M., Carter, J. E. L., and de Garay, A. 1975. Body build and somatotype of Olympic swimmers, divers and water polo players. In: L. Lewillie and J. P. Clarys (eds.), Swimming II, pp. 285-305. University Park Press, Baltimore.

Margaria, R., Oliva, R. D., di Prampero, P. E., and Cerretelli, P. 1969. Energy utilization in intermittent exercise of supramaximal intensity. J. Appl. Physiol. 26(6):752-756.

Poortmans, J. 1976. Adaptations du metabolism a l'effort (Metabolic adaptations to exercise). Can. J. Appl. Sport Sci. 1(2):101-108.

Pugh, L. G. C. E., et al. 1960. A physiological study of channel swimming. Clin. Sci. 19:257-273.

Ross, W. D., Brown, S. R., Faulkner, R. A., Vadja, A., and Savage, M. V. 1976. Monitoring growth in young skaters. Can. J. Appl. Sports Sci. 1(2):163-167.

Shepard, R. J. et al. 1977. The influence of activity environment and season on the growth of working capacity. Med. Sci. Sports 9(1)(Abstr.):53.

Slaughter, M. H., Lohman, T. G., and Boileau, R. A. 1977. Relationship of Heath and Carters' second component to lean body mass and height in college women. Res. 48(4):759-768.

Effects of a Modified Ball on the Mechanics of Selected Water Polo Skills in Novice Children

D. E. Pittuck and D. A. Dainty

Although more and more children are exposed to water polo each year, relatively few of them remain involved in the sport. Because of the unique demands on the player's skill, this sport can be extremely frustrating to the novice. A major source of this frustration seems to be an inability to acquire ball-handling skills using the large, regulation-sized ball. A plausible solution could be to start with a smaller ball. This approach is supported by other researchers (Egstrom, Logan, and Wallis, 1960; Wright, 1969), who investigated learning skills with modified equipment. Egstrom, Logan, and Wallis showed (1960) that subjects who practiced a throwing skill with a light ball were better able to transfer the skill to a heavier ball than those who practiced with the heavier ball. Morris (1976) indicated that, by changing the mechanical efficiency of a movement pattern, such as throwing, a child's total movement capability could be changed. These changes could be positive if improved mechanical efficiency were obtained by modifying the size, weight, texture, or speed of an implement in a throwing skill. Consequently, the hypothesis that children would learn the proper skill mechanics earlier in training using modified equipment was proposed. More specifically, the purpose of this study was to determine the effects of an experimental ball on the mechanics of the drive-in overhand water polo shot in novice children. A subproblem was to determine whether or not the transfer of skill mechanics was facilitated by the modified equipment. To investigate the hypothesis that modified equipment would be beneficial, as suggested by Morris (1976), a biomechanical approach was undertaken.

Study partially funded by a grant from the Ontario Water Polo Association.

PROCEDURES

Twenty-six children (six females and 20 males), 9–13 years old, were divided into two matched groups. One group was trained using an experimental ball (volleyball), and the other used a regulation-sized water polo ball. Each group was trained independently during four 1.5 hr sessions over a 2-week period in the fundamentals of water polo. A certified instructor followed the same training protocol for each group.

At the end of the training period each group was tested for several mechanical parameters that were important in the drive-in overhand shot (Barr, 1964; Lambert and Gaughran, 1968). Two series of trials were filmed for each group using a side-view and overhead-view camera with frame rates of 64 and 48 frames/sec respectively. The cameras were spring-driven, variable-speed Bolex movie cameras, mounted on stationary tripods. In the first series of trials, each group used the equipment originally assigned. During the second series, the opposite ball was used by each group. The experimental task in both series was to dribble the ball as quickly as possible, while maintaining control, to a point 4 m from the goal line; then, on hearing a whistle command, the subject was to pick up the ball and shoot at a target 24 inches in diameter.

The filmed records were then analyzed using a Vanguard motion analyzer to obtain displacement-time data. Because of the low velocities encountered in the children's throwing motion and the visibility of only a few frames (less than 15) of hand-ball contact for each trial, traditional digital smoothing techniques could not be used. Thus, each trial was analyzed three times, and the mean was taken as the true displacement in each instance.

The results from the two groups were then compared with each other and with a third group of skilled junior players of comparable age. The data for this third group were obtained in a previous study by Pittuck (unpublished data). A one-way analysis of variance, with a Scheffé post hoc test for significance, was conducted among the three groups.

For analysis, the data were divided into three phases of the shot: 1) dribbling, 2) ball handling, and 3) shooting. The parameters studied were: 1) dribbling velocity, 2) location of the ball during the dribbling phase, 3) ball-handling time, 4) location of the ball at the moment of contact, 5) ball-handling technique, 6) shooting time, 7) linear displacement of the wrist during the shooting phase, 8) wrist velocity at the moment of release, 9) angle of the elbow at the moment of release, 10) angle of the upper limb at the moment of release, and 11) ball velocity at the moment of release.

RESULTS

Phase I: Dribbling

Both of the novice groups differed significantly from the expert regulation (ER) group in dribbling ability. However, the group means (see Table 1) indicated that the novice experimental (NE) group performed at an average of 96.7% of their maximum dribbling velocity, which had been predetermined. The novice regulation (NR) group performed at 75.8% of their maximum, while the ER group swam at 79.0% of their maximum dribbling velocity.

Subjective observation by the experimenters indicated that the NR group showed a poorer dribbling technique than the other groups. Although 86.3% of this group did not contact the ball during the dribbling phase, 93.8% of the NE group made no contact. The results of phase I are summarized in Table 1.

Phase II: Ball Handling

All subjects of the NE group used the underneath method of picking up the ball. In the NR group, 87.5% preferred the underneath technique. Conversely, 78.6% of the ER subjects used the top-and-roll method. Thus, it was not possible to determine the ball-handling time of the novice subjects because the exact moment of contact was not visible beneath the surface of the water.

Three distinct body areas were used by the subjects in contacting the ball to pick it up: 1) in front and perpendicular to the shooting shoulder, 2) in front and outside the perpendicular line to the shoulder, and 3) inside the perpendicular line to the shooting shoulder. All groups preferred the second location—in front and outside the perpendicular line to the shooting shoulder. The results of phase II are summarized in Table 2.

Phase III: Shooting

All groups had a mean shooting time of 0.22 sec. The mean linear displacement of the wrist was 0.61 m for the NR group and 0.71 m for the NE group (see Table 3). The F value indicated there was a significant difference among the groups. The Scheffé test revealed that the difference was between the NR and ER groups, not between the NE and ER groups. Because there was no difference in shooting time, the difference between the groups must have been in the speed at which the arm was traveling during the shooting phase.

One subject was selected from each group as being representative of the average of his group, and the results are shown in Figures 1 and 2. Figure 1 represents the displacement of the wrist during the shooting phase. Figure 2 illustrates the wrist velocity during phase III.

Table 1. Summary of dribbling parameters (phase I)

Parameter	Expert regulation	Novice regulation	Novice experimental	df	F value
Maximum dribbling velocity (test) (m/sec)	$N = 14$ $\bar{X} = 1.35$ $SD = 0.15$	$N = 12$ $\bar{X} = 0.87$ $SD = 0.12$	$N = 14$ $\bar{X} = 0.86$ $SD = 0.11$	2.37	62.67[a]
Dribbling velocity, phase I (m/sec)	$N = 13$ $\bar{X} = 1.03$ $SD = 0.13$	$N = 12$ $\bar{X} = 0.67$ $SD = 0.15$	$N = 12$ $\bar{X} = 0.86$ $SD = 0.10$	2.34	25.59[a]
Location of ball during phase I	71.43% (no contact) 28.57% (no contact)	86.3% (no contact) 13.7% (contact)	93.75% (no contact) 6.25% (contact)	NA	NA

[a]Significant at the 0.05 level of probability.

Table 2. Summary of ball-handling parameters (phase II)

Parameter	Expert regulation	Novice regulation	Novice experimental	df	F value
Ball-handling time (sec)	$N = 13$ $\bar{X} = 1.14$ $SD = 0.17$	underneath method	underneath method	NA	NA
Ball-handling technique	78.6% (top and roll) 21.4% (underneath)	12.5% (top and roll) 87.5% (underneath)	100% (underneath)	NA	NA
Location of ball	1) 23.08% 2) 46.15% 3) 30.77%	1) 29.2% 2) 41.7% 20.5% N.V.[a] 3) 8.39%	1) 18.75% 2) 75.00% 3) 6.25%	NA	NA

[a]N.V. = not visible (data extracted from film).

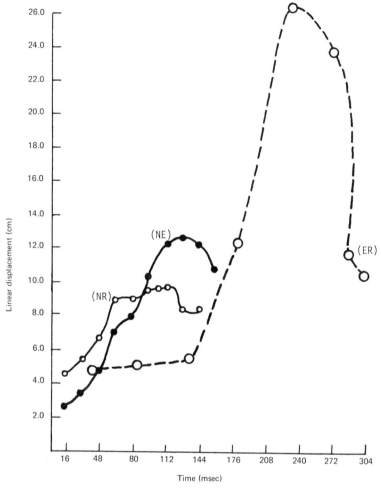

Figure 1. Linear displacement of wrist during phase III.

The patterns of the NE and ER groups are very similar in both figures.

The average wrist release velocity was 5.62 m/sec for the NE group and 4.45 m/sec for the NR group. The ER group had a mean velocity of 8.14 m/sec.

There was a significant difference between both novice groups and the expert group. Although there was no significant difference between the two novice groups, the NE group did have a greater mean wrist release velocity than the NR group. The NE group also exhibited a greater average wrist displacement during phase III (see Table 3). There was a significant difference between the ER group and both novice groups in the

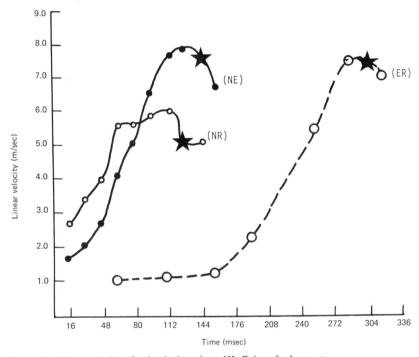

Figure 2. Linear velocity of wrist during phase III. Point of release: ★.

ball velocity at release. The results of phase III are summarized in Table 3.

DISCUSSION

The results of the phase I parameters indicate that under skill test conditions the smaller and lighter ball facilitated higher dribbling velocities in the novice swimmers; the regulation ball prompted a poorer dribbling technique. The smaller ball also facilitated better ball-handling skills. There were fewer unsuccessful shots attributed to ball-handling difficulties in the NE group than in the NR group.

The shooting phase analysis indicated that those subjects who used a lighter and smaller ball could maintain a greater wrist velocity throughout phase III over a greater displacement. Those same subjects also averaged a greater wrist release and ball release velocity than the NR group.

The results of the transfer data illustrate that members of the novice experimental group were more successful with the equipment originally assigned to them and that they also had a higher success rate when they transfered to the regulation ball.

Table 3. Summary of shooting parameters (phase III)

Parameter	Expert regulation	Novice regulation	Novice experimental	df	F value
Shooting time (sec)	$N = 14$ $\overline{X} = 0.22$ SD = 0.04	$N = 11$ $\overline{X} = 0.22$ SD = 0.05	$N = 13$ $\overline{X} = 0.22$ SD = 0.07	NA	NA
Linear Displacement of wrist during phase III (cm)	$N = 13$ $\overline{X} = 82.91$ SD = 11.71	$N = 11$ $\overline{X} = 61.19$ SD = 1.09	$N = 11$ $\overline{X} = 70.54$ SD = 1.46	2.32	6.45[a]
Wrist velocity at moment of release (m/sec)	$N = 14$ $\overline{X} = 8.14$ SD = 1.32	$N = 11$ $\overline{X} = 4.45$ SD = 1.09	$N = 11$ $\overline{X} = 5.62$ SD = 1.46	2.33	26.56[a]
Angle of elbow at release (°)	$N = 14$ $\overline{X} = 141.30$ SD = 12.52	$N = 8$ $\overline{X} = 136.86$ SD = 20.99	$N = 6$ $\overline{X} = 119.18$ SD = 17.87	2.25	3.87[a]
Angle of upper limb at release (°)	$N = 14$ $\overline{X} = 53.52$ SD = 6.27	$N = 8$ $\overline{X} = 52.28$ SD = 9.54	$N = 6$ $\overline{X} = 45.52$ SD = 10.15	2.25	2.08
Ball velocity at moment of release (m/sec)	$N = 13$ $\overline{X} = 12.53$ SD = 1.55	$N = 10$ $\overline{X} = 7.05$ SD = 1.11	N $\overline{X} = 7.575$ SD = 1.038	2.26	57.67[a]

[a]Significant at the 0.05 level of probability.

CONCLUSION

Within the scope and limitation of the study, it was concluded that for novice children, between the ages of 9 and 13 years, the use of a smaller and lighter ball promotes superior dribbling and ball-handling and shooting skills.

REFERENCES

Barr, D., 1964. A Guide to Water Polo. Museum Press Ltd., London, England.

Egstrom, G. G., Logan, G. A., and Wallis, E. L. 1960. Acquisition of throwing skill involving projectiles of varying weights. Res. Q. 31:842.

Lambert, A., and Gaughran, R. 1968. The technique of water polo. Swimming World.

Morris, G. S., 1976. How to Change the Games Children Play. Burgess Publishing Company, Minneapolis.

Wright, E. J., 1969. Effects of light and heavy equipment on acquisition of sport-type skills by young children. Res. Q. 38:705–708.